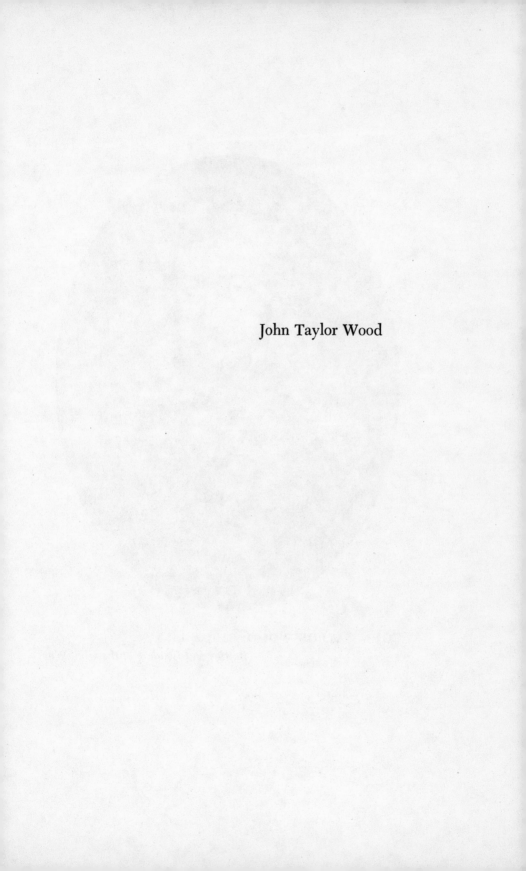

John Taylor Wood

JOHN TAYLOR WOOD, CIRCA 1858
(*Battles and Leaders of the Civil War*)

Royce Gordon
Shingleton

John
Taylor
Wood

Sea Ghost
of the Confederacy

The
University of Georgia
Press
Athens

Copyright © 1979 by the University of Georgia Press
Athens 30602

Set in 11 on 14 point Caledonia type
Printed in the United States of America

Library of Congress Cataloging in Publication Data

Shingleton, Royce.
    John Taylor Wood, Sea Ghost of the Confederacy.
    Bibliography.
    Includes index.
    1. Wood, John Taylor.   2. United States—History
—Civil War, 1861–1865—Naval operations.   3. Ship-
masters—Southern States—Biography.   I. Title.
E467.1.w86s47   973.7′5′0924   78–13934
ISBN 0–8203–0466–2

For Ruth, Royce Jr., and Justin

If any human agency can insure success [of the mission] I think it will be accomplished by Col. Wood.

Robert E. Lee

Contents

Illustrations

Maps
cartography by Richard Walker

Preface

The American Civil War has been called "the most dramatic single event in our history." Popular interest in the conflict continues as more is written and read about the period than any other in the American past. It was by far the nation's bloodiest war. Almost as many Americans died in the Civil War as in all of the country's other wars combined. The North lost 360,022 and the South approximately 258,000, for a total of over 618,000 who died from various causes during the four-year struggle. The momentous event, however, settled more than most wars: industrial capitalism triumphed, slavery was abolished, and most importantly, an answer came to the long-debated issue of whether a state could secede from the Union.

Union victory almost certainly would have been impossible without the contribution of its navy. The number of vessels in the Federal navy rose from only 42 at the beginning of the war to over 670 by December 1864, by which time the Federals had established an effective blockade of all Confederate ports. The number of officers who shifted from the Federal to the Confederate navy at the onset of hostilities has been estimated at up to 332, but prior to siding with the South these officers relinquished their ships, an act they considered honorable and for which they have never been given proper credit. The result, however, was that the South was lacking in ships, and the small Confederate navy was extremely hard pressed throughout the war, confining its activities (except for the use of commerce destroyers) mostly to the inland waters. Although armor, steam power, screw propulsion, shell guns, and rifled pieces were all less than fifty years old, the Confederates were driven by necessity to create even more original methods of sea warfare, including underwater explosives and a primitive submarine. In addition to these novel approaches to war at sea, the men of the southern navy also carried out daring raids against enemy ships, and in these expeditions there was none so able and courageous as the swashbuckler John Taylor Wood.

The writer became interested in Wood's career while working on a biography of Richard Peters (1810–89), a native of Philadelphia who became an influential Atlanta pioneer and outstanding Georgia stockman. During the Civil War, Peters helped organize a blockade-running company that included among its fleet a British-built ship of advanced design named the *Atlanta*. On 18 July 1864 the Confederate navy department commandeered the *Atlanta* at Wilmington, North Carolina, and converted the vessel into a commerce destroyer. Rechristened the C.S.S. *Tallahassee*, the raider, under the command of Wood, steamed out of Wilmington and successfully attacked Union merchant ships along the North Atlantic coast.

The Peters manuscript was temporarily set aside in order to develop two articles about the ship: one article tells of the voyages of the *Atlanta* and the other describes the cruise of the *Tallahassee*. William C. Davis, editor of *Civil War Times Illustrated*, in which one of the articles appeared, mentioned that the Wood family papers are located in the Southern Historical Collection at the University of North Carolina, Chapel Hill. The "Guide to Manuscripts" of the collection revealed that the Wood papers probably contained sufficient information, when added to other key sources, to make a biography of Wood feasible. (Strictly speaking, this is not a biography because it is chiefly an account of Wood's Civil War exploits with a brief summary of his early and later years.)

The idea of further inquiry into Wood's career seemed to merit a visit to the Southern Historical Collection, where Richard A.

Shrader made available to me a small room for the long hours of sifting through papers, a process of tedium mixed with the excitement of discovery. Having been born and reared in eastern North Carolina near Kinston and Wilmington increased my interest in the project after my research made clear that these were sites closely associated with two of Wood's most arduous raids. Then came visits to Emory University's Woodruff Center and other depositories. Information of a more limited nature was gleaned by corresponding with such competent individuals as Harry Schwartz of the Military Archives Division of the National Archives. Finally, the time came for writing, and the advice on style by Jan Snouck-Hurgronje of the Naval Institute Press enhanced the prose. A word of thanks is extended to the Albany Junior College Foundation for a grant awarded in partial subvention of the maps that appear in this book. Every step of the way and in every conceivable way, the process of research and writing was made easier by my wife Ruth. Hence the Wood manuscript took shape, an offshoot of a somewhat longer work in progress.

It is difficult to say why there has been no previous biography of Wood, who was descended from one of America's most illustrious families and who established a brilliant war record. He was well known in his own time for his nighttime boarding-party expeditions against Union commercial vessels and gunboats in waters where the Federals had naval supremacy. Indeed, he was recognized during the war as the South's greatest coastal raider, and his expeditions are an exciting part of Confederate naval history.

Wood is a worthy subject for a biography because of his coastal raids alone (which repeatedly helped raise southern morale), but he is historically significant for other reasons. He wielded considerable influence in the Confederate government, particularly in the navy department, where his voice grew increasingly powerful during the last years of the war. He helped establish merit over seniority as the basis for promotion and assignment of southern naval officers, and his recommendations for improving the de-

fenses of Wilmington lengthened the war by increasing the number of months that southerners could run the blockade. His
wartime career is therefore important as well as exciting, and he
deserves to be remembered.

[1]

The South
Beckons

In the spring of 1865 a lone horseman slowly made his way through the pine forests of south Georgia. He bestrode a lean mount fitted out with saddle and bridle patched with various scraps of leather, and he wore tattered gray trousers that contrasted with his civilian shirt, all of which suggested that the rider was a soldier of a defeated nation returning home from war. Armed only with a small derringer, he relied mainly on his wits for protection against both the uncertainty of the times and an enemy who had labeled him a pirate. Like all fugitives he was alert for possible danger, but as the miles drifted by, his mind turned to thoughts of better days and battles past.

The man on horseback was John Taylor Wood. A remarkable fighter, Wood's Civil War adventures could easily have come from the imagination of a writer of fiction. He participated in naval engagements involving the latest advances in ship construction, motive power, and naval ordnance (including the first battle between ironclads), but another specialty, an old method of sea warfare, was the cutting-out expedition. In a truly dramatic wartime career he seized over forty prizes, ranking second only to Raphael Semmes in the number of vessels captured. Most of Wood's victims fell prey to the dreaded ocean-going commerce destroyer he commanded late in the war, and the remainder he captured by leading boarding parties in a series of midnight raids against Union ships. Moving his boarding cutters overland on wagons by day, the amphibious "Horse Marine" suddenly emerged from an unexpected place at night to board and capture enemy vessels, and the prizes taken in this hazardous work included several armed gunboats. Alarmed Union authorities distributed printed pamphlets warning their commanders against Wood's surprise attacks, but there is no record that he was ever repulsed once he moved alongside an enemy ship.

Wood was also an exceptional leader of men and a commanding personality who was usually found in the mainstream of Civil War activity. A tall, strongly built man, he bore himself erect. His demeanor suggested considerable intellect, and he looked pleasant except when contemplating or confronting the enemy. Immense personal integrity, an easy civility, and ready adaptability enhanced his capacity for leadership. Totally committed to the Confederacy, Wood enjoyed the confidence of the South's highest officials, and although a strict disciplinarian, he was no mere authoritarian who exercised power solely because of influential relatives; rather it was his coolness and quick thinking in hand-to-hand combat that inspired the men he commanded. His planning equaled his execution, with each man in his command individually selected for a specific task, and all of them followed him into battle without question or complaint. Wood is significant because of his considerable influence in the Confederate government, especially the Navy Department, and he is interesting as a result of his many colorful exploits.

A scion of America's political and military leadership, Wood joined the United States navy on 7 April 1847, deviating slightly from family tradition by choosing the navy over the military. The Taylor progenitor in America was James Taylor from Carlise, England, who came to Virginia about 1640, and his descendants, including James Madison, Richard Henry Lee, and John Taylor of Caroline (a Virginia county), overshadowed a distinguished Wood family heritage which also included a notable military tradition. Most outstanding among Wood's recent forebears was his grandfather, Zachary "Old Rough and Ready" Taylor, who quickly rode Mexican War fame to the White House. Wood's father, Major Robert Crooke Wood, a career army surgeon who married

ROBERT CROOKE WOOD, SR.

A loyal Union man, Wood, Sr., served with distinction in the Federal medical service during the war and was later promoted to general.

(Library of Congress)

Taylor's eldest daughter, Anne Mackall Taylor, encouraged the popular general to seek the presidency.

Another army officer, Lieutenant Jefferson Davis, married Taylor's second daughter, Sarah Knox Taylor. A West Point graduate, Davis served in frontier posts in Illinois and Wisconsin and in the Black Hawk War, after which he fell in love with Sarah Taylor, whose father, then Colonel Taylor, was Davis's commanding officer. When Taylor disapproved of the match, Davis resigned his commission in June 1835 and married Sarah at her aunt's home in Kentucky. Family tradition denies that Sarah eloped with Davis; the young couple had her parents' permission when they married at her aunt's, but her parents refused to attend because of an earlier "contest" between the two men when Davis served under Taylor. Joseph Davis, a wealthy older brother, helped Davis establish a plantation, Brierfield, in Mississippi. Tragedy struck when the Davises fell ill with malaria and Sarah died. Although Sarah lived only three months after the marriage, still Davis was Wood's uncle.[1]

Wood was born at an army outpost, Fort Snelling, then Iowa Territory (St. Paul, Minnesota) 13 August 1830 (?), and since his father was from Rhode Island, his mother from Louisiana, and Wood himself made his home in the border state of Maryland, it is difficult to connect him with an individual state or section. His training as a sea officer, although entirely within the United States navy, was a combination of the French method of classroom study and the British preference for training at sea. Wood entered the Annapolis Naval School in June 1847 for a brief preparatory course; then, after serving at the Brazil station on the frigate *Brandywine* and in the Pacific Ocean on the ship-of-the-line *Ohio* during the Mexican War, there followed five more months of instruction at the Naval School in 1850 and a tour of duty suppressing the African slave trade on the sloop-of-war *Germantown* and the brig *Porpoise*.[2] Returning to the renamed Naval Academy 1 October 1852, Wood graduated second in his class on 10 June 1853, and shipped to the Mediterranean aboard the sloop-of-war

Cumberland, a ship he would later help destroy. Back at the Academy as assistant commandant, he was commissioned a lieutenant as of 16 September 1855. During his intervals at Annapolis, Wood met and fell in love with Lola Mackubin, daughter of a prominent Maryland public official, and on 26 November 1856 they were married.[3]

In June 1858, leaving Lola and their first-born, Anne, behind, Wood again went to sea, this time as a gunnery officer on the steam frigate *Wabash,* the flagship of the Mediterranean Squadron. But this voyage was different. The ports of this eighteen months' cruise from New York to Key West and then Gibraltar, Spain, Italy, Greece, Turkey, and the Middle East were already familiar to him from a cruise five years earlier. Much of Wood's spare time was spent writing over a hundred letters to Lola, numbering each in the manner of field dispatches, and filling them with sentiment, description, and local history.[4] In 1859, saddened by the news of the death of their little daughter, and grieving for Lola, so "cruelly tried" during his absence, Wood became extremely weary of sea duty and took a hard look at his future in the navy: "I can't look ahead at my prospects in the navy without being made sick at heart." His future seemed doomed to a life of drudgery. Four years earlier he had stood at the top of the list of lieutenants and the situation had not changed; furthermore there was no probability of advancement for twenty years to come. In the meantime, he would have to sacrifice family and comforts to be promoted at the age of fifty to a commander. (Lieutenant Raphael Semmes also complained of the outdated seniority system, saying the navy was "barnacled with mossbacks.")[5] When the *Wabash* stood into New York in December 1859 Wood thanked his "Heavenly Father we are in at last" and sent for Lola to meet him at the Astor House.

Determined to obtain shore duty, Wood applied for an instructorship at the Naval Academy in January 1860 and, with his father's assistance in Washington, lobbied hard for the position. Wood's anxiety concerning his prospects for duty at the Yard was intensified when the U.S.S. *Merrimac* docked at Jamestown on February 11, bringing more competitors for the position, and he set out immediately for Washington where he and his father forced the issue to a successful conclusion. To his initial assignment of teaching the theory of gunnery were soon added additional courses in seamanship and naval tactics. A lack of texts and models at the Academy at that time led to arduous duties for an instructor, and Wood, in the absence of books on seamanship and naval tactics suited to the needs of the midshipmen, had to do a good deal of compiling and translating. Since he had no police duties, and hence was denied his request for a house in the Yard, Wood took a house in the village—his first home. Then after narrowly escaping summer-cruise duty aboard the school's training ship, Wood considered his new situation ideal.

One reason Wood was anxious to avoid the training cruise was that he had started farming operations at Woodland, a small tract he had recently purchased outside Annapolis. He hired most of the work done and never really made it a home, but often walked to it during evening inspection trips and occasionally worked there laying off fields, burning shells, planting fruit trees, and erecting a barn. To round out his farming enterprise, Wood purchased a few animals and implements, and studied agricultural literature.

Wood relished his new life as farmer-professor, but unmistakable signs of sectional strife were apparent as he settled into his dual role. While visiting the House of Representatives in Washington, he witnessed a disgraceful brawl on the floor of the chamber after one member brandished a pistol. Wood believed "some Oliver Cromwell ought to disperse them." In the more dignified Senate he watched Davis and John J. Crittenden of Kentucky speak on the burning issue of the extension of slavery into the western territories. Wood considered his uncle, whom he referred to as Colonel Davis (and Davis's second wife as Aunt Varina), the most able orator in the Senate.

Davis's ability as a speaker had made him a Democratic leader.

THE WOOD BROTHERS

Shown in the early 1850s, John Taylor Wood (*left*) was a midshipman at Annapolis, and his younger brother, Robert C. Wood, Jr., was a cadet at West Point. After serving as a lieutenant in the 2nd U.S. Cavalry, Robert commanded Wood's Cavalry, C.S.A. with the rank of colonel and rode with John H. Morgan; later Robert commanded Confederate forces in the Central District of Mississippi.

(Southern Historical Collection, University of North Carolina)

After the death of Sarah Taylor Davis, he had spent ten years building up his plantation, often working in the fields alongside his slaves. A successful planter by 1845, he married Varina Howell of Mississippi, and despite a difference of eighteen years in their ages, she followed Davis's political career closely, advising him on appointments and often serving as his personal secretary. She was only twenty years old in 1846 when Davis became colonel of a regiment of Mississippi volunteers in the Mexican War (again Davis served under Zachary Taylor), but she proved a capable manager of their plantation during her husband's absence. At the battle of Buena Vista, Davis distinguished himself, taking a severe wound in the process, and became widely known as "the hero of Buena Vista." After the war Davis began his career in the U.S. Senate, serving from 1847 until his resignation in 1851, was then secretary of war during the administration of Franklin Pierce from 1853 to 1857, after which Mississippi again sent him to the Senate, where Davis championed the South. John J. Crittenden, who would eventually help secure Kentucky for the Union, at the time followed the trend set by former Kentucky Senator Henry Clay ("the Great Compromiser"), and prepared an amendment to the U.S. Constitution calling for the extension of the 36° 30′ Missouri Compromise line to the Pacific Ocean with slavery allowed below the line. Undoubtedly, Crittenden's compromise proposal offered the best hope to avert war.

Richard Taylor of Louisiana, only son of "Old Rough and Ready," was also an uncle of Wood's. This future Confederate general was at the time a delegate to the Democratic Convention in Baltimore and provided Wood access to those proceedings. The party had failed to agree on a candidate in Charleston, South Carolina, in April because delegates from the deep South withdrew from the hall after northern delegates, who backed Stephen A. Douglas of Illinois, refused to support a strong plank calling for federal protection of slavery in the territories. This was the reason why the factions met separately in Baltimore in June. The northern Democrats nominated Douglas, who championed popular sovereignty, i.e., local control of slavery in the territories, while the southern Democrats, with Davis's help, nominated John C. Breckinridge of Kentucky, who became the spokesman for the deep South. Breckinridge, grandson of John Breckinridge of Thomas Jefferson's Cabinet, had served in the Mexican War and had been a congressman. At the time of his nomination, he was vice president under President James Buchanan, and thus president of the Senate. In that capacity he favored the Crittenden Compromise, but he was a strong advocate of states' rights and eventually became a secessionist. To further complicate the election of 1860, a group of conservative elder statesmen calling themselves the Constitutional Union Party met in Baltimore in May and nominated John Bell of Tennessee. This group evidently hoped to throw the election into the House of Representatives where they might control the balance of power.

The Republicans, sensing victory, gathered in Chicago in May. Formed in 1854 to oppose slavery, the Republican Party now produced a broad economic platform and went so far as to affirm slavery where it already existed in the South, but opposed the expansion of slavery. As for their choice of candidate, the Republicans passed over the leading contender, William H. Seward of New York, and nominated a rustic prairie lawyer, Abraham Lincoln. (Both Davis and Lincoln had been born at about the same time in Kentucky, but while the Davises moved to Mississippi, the Lincolns moved to Illinois.) Lincoln had risen to national prominence two years earlier in the famous Lincoln-Douglas debates, yet Lincoln was still obscure enough to have few political enemies within the Republican Party. Along with almost everyone else, Wood was surprised when the Republicans nominated the gaunt rail splitter, and personally supported the southern Democrat Breckinridge, with whom Wood was destined to become closely associated.

During the campaign two of the candidates deviated from the customary practice of issuing written statements of their views. Lincoln refused to write the usual position papers, saying anything he wrote would be misrepresented by southerners. On the other hand, Douglas broke with tradition by embarking on a personal speaking tour instead of leaving that work to lesser party luminaries. He seemed more interested in attacking Breckinridge as a disunionist than in defeating Lincoln. No candidate developed strength on a national scale, which demonstrated the extent of polarization in America. In the November election northerners voted for either Lincoln or Douglas and southerners cast their ballots for Breckinridge or Bell. Lincoln carried every free state (except New Jersey, which he split with Douglas) for 180 electoral votes, which was more than all the other candidates combined. Breckinridge carried the deep south as well as North Carolina, Delaware, and Maryland for 72 electoral votes, the second highest number. The electoral votes of Kentucky, Tennessee, and Virginia went to Bell. In spite of winning 29 percent of the overall popular vote, Douglas carried only the border state of Missouri. Although Lincoln was a minority president with only 40 percent of the popular vote, he and Douglas together had taken 69 percent, and the most significant fact about the election was that an unquestioned majority of Americans, most of them in the more densely populated North, wanted to end the expansion of slavery. This hard fact was further demonstrated to southerners when president-elect Lincoln, by refusing his support, quashed the proposed Crittenden Compromise.

Following Lincoln's election, Wood observed that "news from the South continues to be the theme of all tongues." Quite aware that secessionist sentiment grew stronger after the defeat of Breckinridge, Wood prayed that disunion schemes would be stifled. His prayers went unheeded as southerners began to resign from federal positions. Davis reflected southern bitterness when on 21 January 1861 he delivered an impassioned resignation speech in the Senate. The indecisive response of lame-duck President Buchanan to the growing crisis was to wait for his successor to take office. Meanwhile he avoided a collision of arms, hoping that the policy of nonaggression by the federal government would avert secession

on a large scale. Wood criticized Buchanan for pursuing a "tortuous course, pleasing no one." Unfortunately, there was no prece-
dent for collaboration between the president and president-elect
to effect a smooth transition, which was a serious defect in the
political system.

The sectional crisis caused a breakup of the Naval Academy.
The South Carolina midshipmen led the exodus by resigning as a
group a few weeks after the election. By the following March
midshipmen were leaving in batches of thirty, reducing the total
to less than two hundred. Because there were so few students,
Wood was relieved of his sections in seamanship and tactics,
which left him in charge of only two recitations a week in gunnery. The new situation was not especially welcomed since he was
proud of his progress as an instructor. New administrative duties
carried the privilege of taking up quarters in the Yard, but the
earlier desire to move inside the Yard brought little satisfaction
to Wood under the circumstances since bickering among the staff,
late pay, and lack of supplies contributed to the school's decline.

Events in the South were taking place so rapidly, Wood declared, they could only be seen "in the aggregate."[6] During the
four months from Lincoln's election on November 6 to his inauguration on 4 March 1861, seven states in the deep South seceded
and began the occupation of area Federal military installations.
Representatives of the seceded states met at Montgomery, Alabama, in early February 1861 and formed a southern nation which
they named the Confederate States of America. The delegates at
Montgomery adapted a provisional constitution (which they proclaimed permanent a month later) structured on the one recently
discarded but with a stronger states' rights bent. The delegates
also chose a provisional president and vice-president, and then
served as a provisional legislature until elections in November
1861 would establish the leaders of the permanent government,
who would take office in February 1862. The Montgomery convention elected Davis as president. Although a firm advocate of
southern rights, Davis was a moderate compared to firebrands

such as William L. Yancey of Alabama and Robert B. Rhett of South Carolina. For vice-president the delegates named Alexander H. Stephens of Georgia, who had been an outright anti-secessionist and would act out his part in the new government with little enthusiasm. Apparently the selection of Davis and Stephens was designed to influence southern moderates and conservatives to support the secession movement, especially those in the slave states that had not yet seceded.

The Confederate president assumed his duties in Montgomery, the "cradle of the Confederacy," on 18 February 1861, in spite of poor health. William Howard Russell, London *Times* war correspondent, visited Montgomery shortly after the inauguration and observed that Davis suffered from painful attacks of neuralgia, including a facial tic that caused one eye to water. Otherwise Russell found the president "neat and clean-looking, with hair trimmed, and boots brushed," and was especially impressed, and evidently surprised, that Davis refrained from the universal American custom of chewing tobacco.

> He is like a gentleman—has a slight, light figure, little exceeding middle height, and holds himself erect and straight. He was dressed in a rustic suit of slate-colored stuff, with a black silk handkerchief round his neck; his manner is plain, and rather reserved and drastic; his head is well formed, with a fine full forehead, square and high, covered with innumerable fine lines and wrinkles, features regular, though the cheekbones are too high, and the jaws too hollow to be handsome; the lips are thin, flexible, and curved, the chin square, well defined; the nose very regular, with wide nostrils; and the eyes deep-set, large and full.[7]

Davis was disappointed with his role in the new government, preferring instead to be named military commander of the Confederate forces. The "hero of Buena Vista" and former secretary of war was convinced that he was something of a military genius, a belief that was to handicap him in his relations with several Confederate generals, and probably accounts for the fact that a modern command system was not developed in the South. He was a popular choice for president, although military reverses and the necessity of taking more power into his own hands during the war would result in hostile criticism. Self-confident and with a well-developed habit of command, Davis would continue to work hard for the southern cause in the midst of complaints from generals, civilian officials and the southern populace, and on the whole he made few blunders.

President Davis's choice for secretary of the navy was hard-working Stephen R. Mallory, one of the few Confederate cabinet members to remain to the end. Chosen partly because he was from Florida, Mallory's competency was questioned at first, but he would prove himself forceful and capable as the war progressed. He was a former U.S. senator who had served as chairman of the Naval Affairs Committee, and in that capacity had attempted to bring about advances in marine architecture and ordnance. This progressivism was especially needed by the Confederacy, which had the difficult task of defending thirty-five hundred miles of coastline against enemy attack, challenging the federal blockade of southern ports, and attacking northern commerce on the seas. In view of the lack of material and other resources in the South, Mallory, with the aid of some outstanding naval officers, was to develop a remarkable Confederate sea arm.

As the critical events of March and April unfolded, Wood noted the rending of the national fabric with growing alarm. Lincoln, en route to the northern capital to assume the presidency, made at different points speeches that did nothing to improve his reputation as an enigma. His decision to reserve his announcement of policy until his inaugural address caused his utterances at various towns to appear colorless and trivial. After reading the remarks in the newspapers, Wood termed the orations a series of "most extraordinary speeches which are preventing a settlement." Wood was in Washington on March 4, but did not see Lincoln because fear of assassination caused the president-elect to be heavily guarded by the military, and Wood avoided the capitol building because of the large crowds and excitement. In this atmosphere of apprehension and armed force, the new president, with the unfinished capitol dome in the background symbolizing to many a broken nation, set forth his unalterable opposition to secession. Upon reading Lincoln's inaugural address on the following day, Wood labeled the speech "a declaration of war against the South."

Seeing Lincoln for the first time in a church in Washington on April 7, Wood thought of the U.S. naval provisioning expedition preparing to depart New York for Fort Sumter, located on an island in Charleston harbor where the federal garrison was destined to receive the first shots of the war, and predicted that "old Abe's army afloat will have a rough time of it." The following day Wood learned that Gideon Welles of Connecticut would be Lincoln's secretary of the navy, an appointment made chiefly because Welles was a former Democrat and a New Englander. Wood commented that Welles was "said to be very slow." The northern press was highly critical of Welles during the war, but although the secretary knew little of such things as navigation and ship construction, he was an able administrator and valuable advisor to Lincoln on general policy.

Wood seemed unprepared for the events about to take place at Charleston. Although pro-southern in sentiment, he did not rejoice when Confederate forces under General P. G. T. Beauregard bombarded Fort Sumter into surrender while the ships of the relief expedition, off the entrance to the harbor, made no attempt to enter. On April 13, the day following the initial roar of guns, Wood set down a moving passage in his diary: "War, that terrible calamity, is upon us, and worst of all among ourselves. This news has made me sick at heart."

Indeed, there was no doubt that war had come, and at this juncture four slave states of the upper South, whose leaders had decided that Lincoln's election was not sufficient cause to leave the Union, now joined the secession adventure. This made a total of eleven states in the Confederacy. Four other slave states of the upper South—Kentucky, Missouri, Delaware, and Maryland—remained in the Union, although Missouri and Maryland perhaps would have seceded had not Lincoln employed military force to ensure their loyalty. In these four border states a genuine civil war developed as friends and families chose sides amid bitter acrimony.

The beginning of hostilities between North and South caused Wood to feel uneasy at the Yard as he believed he would soon receive orders giving him an active role in the Union navy. He visited his parents in Washington for a long talk on the distressing situation. His New England father, with thirty-six years' service in the army, was unconditionally for the Union, and his southern mother stood by her husband. But the family was already split; Robert Crooke Wood, Jr., Wood's younger brother, had gone to Montgomery in February where Davis appointed him adjutant-general on General Braxton Bragg's staff.[8] Wood wanted to support the Union but could not take up arms against the South, and thus hoped to remain neutral. His diary entries reflect his misery; he felt he belonged to neither side.

Upon his return to Annapolis, Wood found that there was great excitement and activity in the Yard. He learned that on April 19 the Sixth Massachusetts Regiment, moving through Baltimore en route to Washington, had been mobbed by southern sympathizers as it passed through the city. Baltimore was temporarily closed to traffic, and Annapolis became a crowded thoroughfare; Wood counted sixteen ships in the harbor from Bluff Point and troops landed by the thousands. Property was seized, citizens arrested, and newspapers suppressed as Marylanders suffered the indignity of military occupation under the maladroit hand of General Benjamin F. Butler. Union soldiers en route to Washington marched by Woodland; others seized the Yard and turned it into a depot, barracks, and hospital, stripping the school of its beauty. Soon a railroad and telegraph would be run into the Yard, and a water station set up in front of Wood's house. Commandant of Midshipmen Christopher R. P. Rodgers of New York, Wood's friend and shipmate on the *Wabash*, helped move the remnant of the Academy to Newport, Rhode Island, and attempted to influence south-

ern midshipmen to Union loyalty. Rodgers's brother, George W.
Rodgers, commander of the school ship, U.S.S. *Constitution,* con-
veyed the midshipmen to Newport and saved the ship from capture by secessionists.[9] On April 21, not wishing to move to
Newport, his "blood boiling over with indignation" at the Union
occupation of the state, Wood resigned his commission in the
navy.

Troop depredations, partisan insults, and stealing began, all of
which added to the tense atmosphere. Two days after his resignation from the navy, Wood moved his furniture from his quarters
in the Yard to Strawberry Hill, the nearby Mackubin plantation.
Fearful of arrest for treason, he did not interfere when marauding
soldiers repeatedly visited Strawberry Hill. He seldom went to
Annapolis, and confined his visits mostly to after-dark hours. Un-
rest in the border state made travel difficult. Wood was sometimes
followed by the military, and complained that he was "suspected
everywhere." Local partisans uprooted rail tracks and distrusted
strangers. Twice local citizens questioned Wood about suspected
espionage as he helped repair the railroad during another trip to
Washington. There he found his loyalist father deeply troubled by
the resignation and in a disgruntled frame of mind, but he promised to look into the matter. Then Wood made the uneasy trip
back to Lola and his in-laws at Strawberry Hill. He still hoped to
remain a neutral between his parents and younger brother and
between North and South.

The Maryland legislature, belatedly called into session in Frederick rather than secession-ridden Baltimore by Unionist Governor
Thomas Hicks, also struggled to retain a neutral position and even
to act as mediator between the sections. Early in May it passed a
resolution declaring the military occupation of the state unconsti-
tutional and calling on Lincoln to stop the war and recognize the
independence of the Confederacy. A committee from the legislature even journeyed to Montgomery and returned with a letter
from Davis echoing the Maryland legislature's desire for an end to

hostilities, and inviting the state join the Confederacy. The strategic location of the border state made its control crucial to the Union, and the Lincoln administration kept the Maryland legislature under "close military surveillance," eventually making political prisoners of nineteen of its members.[10]

For weeks there was an ominous silence in Washington concerning his resignation, but Wood considered himself a civilian and regretted leaving the navy only slightly. Then on May 17 he heard from his father that his resignation had been refused. In answer, Wood informed his father that since he did not want to be drawn into the struggle, he could not continue in the navy. This persistence spurred a quick response. Three days later Wood received his dismissal from the navy in spite of his father's efforts to prevent it, effective as of the second of April. Thus, Wood's prejudicial release was given the additional odium of being set prior to the outbreak of hostilities at Fort Sumter (and was not corrected by the Navy Department until 1931).[11] On the day he received his dismissal, Wood recorded in his diary: "In ordinary times this would have disgraced and dishonored me, but now I feel no concern about it except so far as it may affect father." The resignation was handled in a manner characteristic of the Navy Department at that time, and this petty, bureaucratic vindictiveness did nothing toward preserving Wood's neutrality.

Wood's insistence on leaving the navy and his growing southern sentiment completely alienated his father, and the two broke off all contact with each other. In early August he met with his more friendly mother in Baltimore, and she attempted to persuade him to accompany her to the family home in Newport. Wood refused, thinking it unsafe for him, probably because of the relocated Naval Academy. Turning his attention to Woodland, which was his sole means of support now, Wood concentrated on his grain and clover harvests in June and July. Having no suitable house on the farm, he really had no place to live, although he was apparently welcome at Strawberry Hill. He did fix up a room among his workers at the farm in order to spend the night occasionally. Union soldiers visited Woodland, but engaged in no serious depredations.

Wood paced his farm, realizing from the troop buildup both North and South that the war must soon open in earnest. In June he learned that the Confederate capital, at the request of Virginia delegates, was transferred from Montgomery to Richmond. The Old Dominion was an important state and would need a vigorous defense. Richmond, the cultural center of the South, had the added attraction of being sufficiently large to accommodate the government; it was to become the symbol of the Confederacy and its capture a major objective in the war strategy of the North.

By mid-1861 the border states were saved from secession, including Maryland, and Confederate efforts to "liberate" the state during the war were unsuccessful. Attention now turned to the Virginia battle front, where the protection of Richmond by one side and Washington by the other made it the most important theater of war throughout the conflict. The first real battle of the war occurred on July 21 when Union General Irvin McDowell attacked Confederate forces under generals Beauregard and Joseph E. Johnston at First Bull Run (Manassas Junction), named for a small stream located a few miles southwest of Washington. The Federal troops made a gallant effort through most of the day, but when ordered to fall back by McDowell they soon panicked, throwing away their arms and equipment as they ran pell-mell into Washington alongside U.S. congressmen and other spectators. (A paper victory for the South, the clash actually benefited the North by stimulating war production.) When news of the battle reached Wood at the end of July, he welcomed the apparent southern victory. In the wake of Bull Run, Union troops in Maryland increased the arrest of local citizens suspected of disloyalty and imprisoned them in the Yard. It was enough, fumed Wood, "to make the stones cry out."

Since the southern counties of Maryland had more secessionists than the upper tier near Pennsylvania, lower Maryland was in turmoil. Wood purchased a Colt revolver for protection, and decided to move his family from Strawberry Hill. For weeks Wood, Lola, and their small son, Zach, traveled mostly between friends and friendly relatives in Elk Ridge below Baltimore, and on the eastern shore across Chesapeake Bay. During this time Wood became increasingly restless. At the end of August, after a long discussion with Lola about their "affairs and prospects," Wood returned to Woodland. There he cleaned grain, paid bills in Annapolis, packed personal belongings in trunks, and departed. Meeting his wife and son near Baltimore, Wood buried his silver on September 3 and started south with his family.

The Woods reached the Potomac River at a point near George Washington's birthplace, which was located across the river in Westmoreland County. Wood found a small open boat, took in his family and belongings, and embarked under an angry sky that soon erupted into a rage, lashing the water over the gunwales. Wood struggled with the heavily loaded craft in a losing battle until he threw some baggage overboard to prevent the boat from swamping. Finally the soaked refugees landed safely in Westmoreland County on the Virginia side, where they suffered some privations because of the loss of clothing and supplies. But they moved inland and received food and lodging from a number of friendly Virginians as they made their way to Fredericksburg and boarded a train on the Richmond, Petersburg, and Potomac Railroad for Richmond, where Wood's uncle, Jefferson Davis, was president of the Confederacy.[12]

Why did Wood go south? At age thirty-one or thirty-two (he wasn't sure which) and with a family to consider, he deliberated at length before making his decision. First of all, as Wood's diary makes clear, his admiration of Davis was a southern magnet. Another factor in Wood's decision was his strong sense of relation to the Taylors. He signed his name J. Taylor Wood, gave Louisiana as his home state when he entered Confederate service, and when a distant relative named Taylor distinguished himself during the war, Wood's praise was that "he was a credit to the family name."

But it does not follow that Wood fought to preserve slavery, even though the Taylors were slaveholders. President Zachary Taylor, a slaveholder himself, had nonetheless disapproved of the extension of slavery. Further, Wood was disappointed when Maryland failed to secede and left only when it became apparent that the Lincolnites would prevail in the state. He had little property to lose, and anyway he thought that the South would win the war. Wood's naval background and fondness for adventure, which devotion to Lola never entirely suppressed, made extended neutrality on his part improbable. But it was the United States navy, as much as anything else, that made Wood a Rebel.

[2]
Aboard the
C. S. S. *Virginia*

Quiet prevailed on the Virginia front for many months following First Bull Run. To replace McDowell, Lincoln called to Washington General George B. McClellan, one of the most controversial military leaders of the war. One critic wrote: "McClellan was not a real general. McClellan was not even a disciplined, truthful soldier. McClellan was merely an attractive but vain and unstable man, with considerable military knowledge, who sat a horse well and wanted to be President." Yet the general's critics admit that he performed splendidly when organizing and training an army. During the fall and winter, while Johnston's Army of Northern Virginia occupied Bull Run, McClellan held grand reviews to demonstrate progress in forming and equipping the Army of the Potomac, with Lincoln reviewing fifty thousand men to the stirring flourish of drums and bugles, a spectacle on a scale heretofore unknown in the United States. McClellan worked as well on a master plan for an overwhelming offensive calculated to crush the Confederacy. "A trained army of a quarter-million, drilled and organized after European models, with a formidable fleet for support, was what he wanted."[1]

McClellan's plan of attack, reluctantly approved by Lincoln, became known as the Peninsular Campaign. The York and James rivers form a triangular peninsula which extends from its inland base near Richmond to its point where Hampton Roads joins the southern end of Chesapeake Bay. The tip of this topographical triangle was crowned by Fort Monroe, a heavily fortified Union military installation commanded by General John E. Wool, and a naval supply and staging base for the Chesapeake Bay and Atlantic blockading fleets under the command of Admiral Louis M. Goldsborough. Approximately one-fourth of the way up the peninsula northwest of Fort Monroe is Yorktown, situated at the mouth of the York River. This historic town, scene of the dramatic conclusion of the Revolutionary War, was now held by another group of Rebels who had set up a defense line southward from Yorktown across the peninsula to the James River.

Lincoln preferred a direct march on Richmond in order to keep the Federal army between the Confederates and Washington, but McClellan decided to embark down the Potomac with a combined land and naval force to Fort Monroe, and then approach the southern capital along the peninsula, using the York River as a supply line. As the months passed, Lincoln, increasingly under pressure from the northern public and Congress for an advance, began to recognize in McClellan a serious fault—the general had a case of "the slows." McClellan, for his part, found Lincoln's persistent urgings for an offensive and other advice on military affairs "perfectly sickening."[2]

Across Hampton Roads from Fort Monroe was Confederate-held Norfolk and nearby Portsmouth with its Gosport Navy Yard. Both cities had been hurriedly evacuated by the Federals on 19 April 1861, without sufficient reason, and both were linked to the interior by rail—the Norfolk and Petersburg Railroad connected the naval center to Richmond, and the Seaboard and Roanoke Railroad stretched to Weldon, North Carolina. The Gosport Navy Yard was enclosed by a high brick fence and could have been defended by its garrison of eighteen hundred Union marines and sailors supported by several large ships in the adjoining Elizabeth River, yet it was abandoned to two local volunteer companies. The evacuation by the Federals was a tremendous windfall for the Confederates. Among the spoils were 1198 heavy cannon which the Confederates used to fortify Norfolk and the batteries on the Potomac, Rappahannock, York, and James rivers in Virginia, as well as those at Roanoke Island, Wilmington, Charleston,

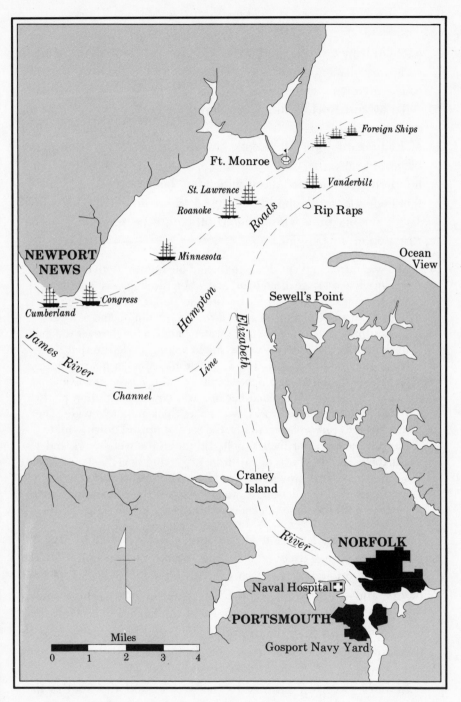

Hampton Roads and vicinity

Mobile, New Orleans, and Vicksburg. As for the Federal effort to recapture the important naval complex, McClellan was "satisfied to leave Norfolk to be turned by his advance on the peninsula."

To defend Norfolk, the Confederates needed an ironclad at the earliest possible date. In June 1861 Mallory approved the plans of Lieutenant John M. Brooke, an accomplished naval ordnance officer, to raise the U.S.S. *Merrimac*, a steam frigate of thirty-five hundred tons and forty guns which had been burned and sunk by the Federals, and rebuild the vessel as an ironclad. This would save valuable time which would otherwise be spent in the construction of new engines.

> She was raised and cut down to the old birth-deck. Both ends for seventy feet were covered over, and when the ship was in fighting trim were just awash. On the midship section, 170 feet in length, was built at an angle of [35] degrees a roof of pitch-pine and oak [22] inches thick, extending from the water-line to a height over the gun-deck of 7 feet. Both ends of the shield were rounded so that the pivot-guns could be used as bow and stern chasers or quartering. Over the gun-deck was a light grating, making a promenade about twenty feet wide. The wood backing was covered with iron plates, rolled at the Tredegar works, two inches thick and eight wide. The first tier was put on horizontally, the second up and down,—all to the thickness of four inches, bolted through the wood-work and clinched. The prow was of cast-iron, projecting [2½] feet, and badly secured, as events proved. The rudder and propellar were entirely unprotected. The pilot-house was forward of the smoke-stack, and covered with the same thickness of iron as the sides.[3]

Thus the exposed portion of the ship was protected by twenty-two inches of wood covered by four inches of iron plate. Unlike the plated shield, the pilothouse was cast solid. She had no boat davits, and shutters only at her four quarter ports. The ironclad was built specifically for the defense of the harbor at Norfolk, and was unsuited for high winds and heavy seas; the experiment with the submerged ends was a feature of naval architecture that was not retained.[4]

Mallory gave top priority to the project and the South's first ironclad was built during the following fall and winter at the Gosport Navy Yard, with naval constructor John L. Porter superintending the construction of the hull and Brooke in charge of the armor and guns. Most of the necessary materials were on hand in the yard except the plate which was shipped in from the Tredegar Iron Works in Richmond. Built at an estimated cost of $110,000, mostly for labor, the armored vessel was a bargain. Confederates rechristened the converted ship the C.S.S. *Virginia*.

Wood noted with keen interest this new type of fighting ship under preparation at Gosport Navy Yard. He knew that although the world's maritime powers had already experimented with partly armored vessels, very few naval experts were convinced of their utility, and no ironclad had been "tried by the test of battle, if we except a few floating batteries, thinly clad, used in the Crimean War." Wood was eager for service in the experimental *Virginia* because testing the South's first ironclad in battle would be exciting duty; besides, in rendering this unusual service to the navy, he could bring into use his gunnery experience.

Davis had appointed Wood a lieutenant in the Confederate navy effective 4 October 1861. Wood had first entered the service of the state of Virginia, and his Confederate commission of 7 December 1861 was made retroactive to the earlier date. Like many other southern naval officers, Wood found that duty afloat was difficult to obtain because the South had few ships. After settling Lola and Zach away from the center of war in Richmond to the relative quiet of Petersburg, he reported for duty to Captain Frederick Chatard, a native Marylander, at the Aquia Creek Landing batteries on the Virginia side of the Potomac River below Washington. The Confederates stationed at these batteries learned the range of different points on the river, and the resulting accurate fire disrupted Union shipping during the first year of the war.[5]

Considering Wood's influence in Richmond, it is not surprising that in January 1862 the Navy Department assigned him to the *Virginia*, which was still under construction at Portsmouth. His first duty was to collect and train a crew of enlisted men for the converted vessel. This was no easy task. The Confederacy had an abundance of naval brass, but almost all of the nation's seamen before the war had been northerners, and when the war began most southern men entered the army. Wood discovered sailors in Norfolk who had recently escaped from Confederate gunboats in the sounds of North Carolina as the area was captured by the Federals, but he found it necessary also to ask for volunteers from the military. He visited army commands in Yorktown, Richmond, and Petersburg, where local officers called their troops into formation and Wood explained what he wanted. He then inspected and selected from the volunteers a total of three hundred men, some of whom were from southern seaports and had some experience with ships or boats, but for the most part soldiers made up the crew of the *Virginia*.

During his recruitment travels, Wood learned that army commanders were reluctant to cooperate with the navy. He was forced to visit Yorktown a second time, after which General J. Bankhead Magruder sent to Norfolk a group of misfits that included only two of the men chosen by Wood. As a result, Wood complained to Commodore Franklin Buchanan, commander of the navy's Bureau of Orders and Detail, that the men sent by Magruder were "a very different class of men from those I selected." Wood's complaint immediately went to the Cabinet level. Mallory wrote to Secretary of War Judah P. Benjamin: "I suggest for your consideration better cooperation from officers in the army so that we get for seamen the men we designate and who desire to enter naval service." Although the navy continued to experience a shortage of seamen (3,674 men in November 1864),[6] from the time he recruited the men for the *Virginia* Wood had no further difficulty obtaining first-rate crews for special service.

Whipping the crew into shape proved as difficult as finding seamen. Construction delays caused by the limited resources of the Tredegar foundry resulted in the vessel's being crowded with workmen until the time of sailing, which allowed the crew no op-

MONITOR VS. VIRGINIA

The famous sketch shows the heavy indentations in the armor of the *Virginia* near Wood's aft pivot.

(*Battles and Leaders of the Civil War*)

portunity to practice behind the guns of the *Virginia* herself until actual battle. Instead, Wood trained the men at the guns of the old frigate *United States,* holding drills every day for two weeks. The crew members were strangers to each other and unfamiliar with the unique design of the armored ship. The two decks inside the ironclad, particularly the berth deck located below the gun deck, were damp and unhealthy. The ill-ventilated interior retained the heat or cold transmitted by the armor, and the humid decks were constantly filled with gasses from the furnaces. Over twenty per-cent of the crew was continuously on the sick list, but recovered immediately in the Norfolk Naval Hospital. In spite of these unde-sirable conditions aboard ship, by the time the vessel cast off for the first time Wood had drilled the crew into what he described as a "gallant and trusty body of men."

Amid considerable commotion and a throng of spectators, many of whom believed the ironclad would soon be "an enormous metal-lic burial-case" for her crew, the *Virginia* was launched beneath a clear sky at noon on March 8, and, escorted by two small gun-boats, the *Raleigh* and the *Beaufort,* bearing one gun each, steamed down the unusually smooth and glassy Elizabeth River for what was expected to be a trial cruise. Hardly a revolution of her engines had been made when the ship's mechanical defects immediately became apparent. She was slow, with a speed not ex-ceeding five knots. The dual-engine power plant, original equip-ment in the *Merrimac,* had earlier been condemned as "radically defective," and the burning and sinking of the ship when the Federals evacuated Norfolk did nothing to improve them. "A more ill-contrived or unreliable pair of engines could only have been found in some vessels of the United States navy," moaned Wood. Her rudder response was so sluggish that it took thirty to forty minutes and an "inland sea" to turn the long armored monster around, while at the same time the ironclad's great draft of twenty-one feet forward and twenty-two feet aft restricted her to the deeper channels in Hampton Roads. All in all the *Virginia* was "as unmanageable as a water-logged vessel."

A stellar list of ship's officers was headed by sixty-year-old Buchanan, who had been transferred from the Bureau of Orders and Detail to this highly desirable sea duty. Mallory had appointed him flag officer of the James River naval defenses rather than simply the ship's captain, and in this way Buchanan commanded the *Virginia* without possible interference from a senior officer. He had a distinguished record dating from 1815 which included a major role in founding the United States Naval Academy, and Wood, who usually preferred younger officers, agreed that Buchanan deserved the command. Confederate troops at the batteries on Craney Island cheered the *Virginia* as she chugged by on her way to the mouth of the Elizabeth River. As the ironclad steamed out of the river on a high tide, the men on board could see arrayed along the opposite shore a long line of enemy ships, the best of the Union fleet. Near strongly fortified Newport News across the channel the U.S.S. *Cumberland*, with thirty guns, and the U.S.S. *Congress*, with fifty guns, rode lazily at anchor on the calm waters.

Buchanan decided to attack without delay. He considered the *Cumberland*, which he mistakenly believed had several new long-range guns, the only threat to the *Virginia*. The ironclad carried ten guns—one six-inch rifle and three nine-inch smoothbores along each side and a seven-inch rifle at each end—and her escort, including the James River Squadron which joined the battle in progress, had seventeen guns for a total of twenty-seven guns against at least a hundred Federal guns at a given location. Buchanan mustered the crew, gave a brief speech about duty in battle and the protection of the state for which the *Virginia* was named, and pointed to the enemy fleet: "Those ships must be taken, and you shall not complain that I do not take you close enough. Go to your guns." Wood was in charge of the after pivot, a seven-inch Brooke rifle (a type that had three-inch steel bands shrunk around the breech for reinforcement), which, along with the bow pivot, was the first designed by Brooke. Each pivot could be fired from one of three ports. Well suited for this duty by training and experience, Wood's gunnery expertise was a source of pride to him, as evidenced by his comment after target practice aboard the *Wabash* off Italy before the war: "My division struck [the target] six times. . . . I can almost knock a man over at the distance of a mile."[7]

As the Confederates approached the enemy ships, they could see the Saturday wash drying in the rigging and boats hanging low on the davits. The *Virginia* was not expected. When it came within three-fourths of a mile, however, great activity was seen aboard the *Cumberland* and the *Congress* as the ships were put into fighting trim. Then the two Union ships opened with their heavy guns, and Union shore batteries and the Confederate gunboats joined to form a general engagement. Once within easy range, the *Virginia* responded with her forward pivot, killing and wounding the crew of the *Cumberland's* after gun. Steering directly for the *Cumberland*, Buchanan decided to use the ironclad's wedge-shaped, 1500-pound prow, located 2 feet under water and projecting 2½ feet from the stem. The *Virginia* rammed through the timbers placed around the *Cumberland's* bow for protection against mines, and struck the starboard side of the vessel at a right angle. The Confederates rocked the victim by firing their forward pivot as well on impact, all of which caused the tall masts of the enemy ship to sway wildly. The effect of the blow, barely perceptible on board the *Virginia*, could be seen as the ironclad, with considerable difficulty, backed away. A hole large enough, according to Wood, "to drive in a horse and cart" was opened in the side of the wooden vessel on which he had served before the war. The *Cumberland* listed and filled rapidly, her defiant crew firing until, with colors flying, she went down with a roar and settled on the bottom fifty feet below, her pennant still visible at the peak above the waves.

The battle created grand theater. A few citizens of Norfolk and Portsmouth prayed in nearby churches, but thousands watched from the surrounding shores; a few excited observers used spyglasses and gave to bystanders detailed commentary on the flaming action. To the amazement of the many Confederate civilians

and soldiers who had rushed to the shore in the vicinity of Ragged
Island to view the outdoor drama, the intense cannonade could
not be heard. They were close to the action but a strong March
wind was blowing directly from them toward Newport News.
These spectators could hardly believe their senses as they watched
in awe the constant flash of the guns and the clouds of smoke, but
"not a single report was audible."

In the next scene the *Virginia* turned to engage the *Congress,*
and for the first time Wood could use his after pivot. He quickly
fired three shots which caused extensive damage and alarm
aboard the *Congress,* whose commander, Lieutenant Joseph B.
Smith, had believed the *Virginia,* in her sweeping turn, was retreating. Wood's first shot dismounted the frigate's starboard stern
thirty-two pounder and broke off the muzzle; the second killed
and wounded several crewmen, including cooks and ship's boys
who were passing powder from the after magazine; the third apparently dismounted the only other stern gun aboard. At this point
the Confederate gunboats of the James River Squadron, the *Patrick Henry* (twelve guns), the *Jamestown* (two guns), and the
Teaser (one gun), moved out of the James and joined the *Virginia*
in the assault on the *Congress,* which had intentionally grounded
to escape being rammed. The decks of the *Congress* were soon
"reeking with slaughter," and blood ran through her scuppers onto
the deck of her tug. The ship's commander, Smith, was among
those killed; thereafter, a white flag appeared on her mast.

An unfortunate development added to the carnage. Buchanan
came up on the deck of the *Virginia* and sent the *Beaufort* under
Commander William H. Parker over to take the surrender and
allow the crew to land. Then, probably because she was grounded
within range of Union shore batteries, Parker was to burn the *Congress.* When the *Beaufort* pulled alongside the frigate, Lieutenant
Austin Pendergrast, who had taken command upon the death of
Smith, went on board and surrendered his ship. Suddenly, Union
shore batteries and small arms began pouring a tremendous fire
upon both the *Congress,* still flying the white flag, and the *Beau-*

fort. Having no control over the shore batteries, Pendergrast requested permission to bring down his wounded, then took the opportunity to jump overboard and escape to shore. With men on both ships falling, Parker hauled off with some thirty prisoners to the *Virginia,* where Buchanan, incensed by the Federal attack on the white flag, ordered hot shot into the *Congress* to set her ablaze. While directing the operation, he was severely wounded in the hip by a Minié ball from shore and Lieutenant Catesby Jones assumed command of the *Virginia.* The *Congress* was destined to be burned, indeed was already burning in places, and the Federal shore batteries merely caused additional havoc. Particularly wasteful was sending the Union wounded down with the ship.[8]

The next target of the *Virginia* was the U.S.S. *Minnesota,* which along with the U.S.S. *Roanoke* and the U.S.S. *St. Lawrence,* had started from the direction of Fort Monroe in an attempt to join the action. The *Roanoke* and the *St. Lawrence* grounded almost immediately, and their guns roared out at the intruder mostly in token protest, but the *Minnesota* steamed halfway between Fort Monroe and Newport News before she grounded in a position to be engaged.

> Just at that moment the scene was one of unsurpassed magnificence. The bright afternoon sun shone upon the glancing waters. The fortifications of Newport News were seen swarming with soldiers, now idle spectators of a conflict far beyond the range of their batteries, and the flames were just bursting from the abandoned *Congress.* The stranded *Minnesota* seemed a huge monster at bay, surrounded by the *Virginia* and the gun-boats. The entire horizon was lighted up by the continual flashes of the artillery of these combatants, the broadsides of the *Roanoke* and *St. Lawrence* and the Sewell's Point batteries; clouds of white smoke rose in spiral columns to the skies, illumined by the evening sunlight, while land and water seemed to tremble under the thunders of the cannonade.[9]

The situation for the *Minnesota* was desperate, but the *Virginia* was unable to reach her prey because of an ebb tide, and after ex-

changing shots with her adversary, retired through the approaching darkness to Sewell's Point. There she anchored, leaving the
damaged Union vessel safe for the night.

Wood was eager to inspect the exterior of the ironclad. He found
ninety-eight indentations made by solid shot that had glanced off
without damaging the iron plate, but the muzzles had been shot
off two guns; the prow, with "inconceivable stupidity" made of
cast iron, had been damaged while ramming the *Cumberland;* one
anchor, the smokestack, and all railings and stanchions had been
carried away. The flag staff, hit repeatedly, had been replaced by
a boarding pike. It was nearly midnight before the men took their
first meal since eight o'clock that morning, then as the magazine
of the burning *Congress* exploded and scattered fragments over
the darkened waters, the tired crew of the *Virginia,* grimy from
powder residue, settled to sleep by their guns, ready to resume
the battle the next day.

Daybreak on Sunday revealed the *Minnesota* still grounded.
After Buchanan and the other wounded were landed at Sewell's
Point for transfer to the Norfolk Naval Hospital, the *Virginia*
weighed anchor and, greeted by a rising sun, steamed toward the
prey. Soon the surprised Confederates observed a strange little
craft standing near the wooden vessel. Was it a water tank or ammunition ship used to supply the *Minnesota?* Wood recognized it
at once as the U.S.S. *Monitor.* Unlike the broadside ironclad *Virginia,* the *Monitor* was a turret ironclad. She boasted two eleven-
inch guns which were fired from a large rotary turret located
amidship, its revolving mechanism powered by a small steam engine. The ship's complement of 58 officers and men was a much
smaller crew than the 260 effectives on board the *Virginia.* The
Monitor had been towed from New York and arrived during the
night. Confederate authorities had known of her construction and
she had been expected in Hampton Roads, but not at such an inopportune time. This "tin can on a shingle," or "cheese box," now
stood in the way of Confederate plans to destroy the *Minnesota.*
"She appeared but a pigmy compared with the lofty frigate which

she guarded, but in her size was one great element of her success," explained Wood.

The *Virginia,* "like the roof of a very big barn belching forth smoke as from a chimney fire," moved to the attack. The Confederates first directed their fire at the *Minnesota,* causing a small fire to break out on board the wooden ship, and creating great consternation by blowing up one of her tugs. But the *Monitor* steamed between the *Virginia* and her intended victim and the conflict became an epic struggle between the two ironclads. Wood later recalled: "In this battle old things passed away, and the experience of a thousand years of battle and breeze was forgotten."[10]

The two ironclads circled each other in a grueling four-hour duel that would have sunk any other vessels afloat. The entire battle was at close range, from half a mile to a few yards. The *Monitor,* drawing only twelve feet, was much more maneuverable than the *Virginia,* which grounded at least once. On the other hand, the revolving turret of the *Monitor* could not be accurately controlled, and her guns were fired "on the fly" as the turret started on its revolving journey in search of the *Virginia.* At one point, the *Monitor* attempted to cripple the Virginia's unprotected propeller by running into it, but narrowly missed. Next, Jones attempted to ram the *Monitor.* For nearly an hour the Confederates maneuvered for a favorable position, but with no smokestack to create a draft, the *Virginia* had little motive power. The ship was "as unwieldy as Noah's ark," complained Wood. When at last the run was made, the disabled ram and slow speed allowed only an ineffectual glancing blow.

Then, with the two vessels almost touching each other, the big guns in the *Monitor's* turret rang out twice, both shots hitting abreast of Wood's pivot about halfway up the shield. The impact forced the side in two or three inches, drawing giant splinters from the casemate wall, and hurling Wood and his crew to the deck. Wood, bleeding at the nose and ears from the concussion, stared at the damaged wall. He realized better than anyone else on board that "another shot at the same place would have penetrated."

When Jones saw that the *Virginia*'s guns only dented the *Monitor*'s turret, he ordered his gun commanders to concentrate their fire on her pilothouse. The vessels wore around until the *Virginia*'s stern was only ten yards from the *Monitor*'s pilothouse. Wood quickly barked out the necessary orders to his gun crew: "Run out tackle handsomely! Steady! Stand clear!" A lightning flash erupted from the muzzle of the powerful Brooke rifle and a heavy shell seared the air to strike against the front of the *Monitor*'s pilothouse, directly in the observation slit. The explosion cracked the iron and partly lifted the top. The commander of the *Monitor*, Lieutenant John L. Worden, was standing immediately behind the eye hole. The blow partly stunned the commander and filled his eyes with powder, temporarily blinding him. The sightless Worden incorrectly believed that the pilothouse was severely damaged and the steering gear impaired, so he ordered the *Monitor* to "sheer off" from the action and sent for his executive officer, Lieutenant S. Dana Greene. As Greene made his way from the turret where he had been directing the fire from the *Monitor*'s guns, he found Worden standing at the foot of the ladder that led to the pilothouse.

> He was a ghastly sight, with his eyes closed and the blood apparently rushing from every pore in the upper part of his face. He told me that he was seriously wounded, and directed me to take command. I assisted in leading him to a sofa in his cabin, where he was tenderly cared for . . . and then I assumed command. Blind and suffering as he was, Worden's fortitude never forsook him; he frequently asked from his bed of pain of the progress of affairs.[11]

The *Monitor* retired briefly, and Wood hoped his shot had disabled the enemy vessel, but "the revolution again of her turret and the heavy blows of her eleven-inch shot on our sides soon undeceived us."

Wood now had an idea that foreshadowed his special place in

the war. As a last hope to defeat the *Monitor,* he called for volunteers to form a boarding party which he intended to lead to the enemy deck. The response was enthusiastic, and Wood organized the group into special forces, each with a specific task. Some collected sledge hammers and spikes to wedge the *Monitor's* turret. Others were ready to fling oakum-ball grenades down the pipes and cover all openings with canvas to cut off visibility and air. A third gang gathered heavy ropes and chains to bind the *Monitor* to the *Virginia* for towing to Norfolk. A few men carried pistols, boarding pikes, and cutlasses in the event of hand-to-hand combat. The Confederates intended to win this battle with brains, seamanship, heroism, and the "juster cause."

When all was ready, the *Virginia* made a run for the *Monitor.* The boarding party watched from the ports, each man "burning for the signal to swarm aboard the foe." The blood was "fairly tumbling through our veins" recalled one crew member as the hoarse bark of the boatswain called "boarders away." At that moment, however, the *Monitor* frustrated the scheme by standing away and steaming to shallow water. One excited boarder was almost through the port and had to be pulled back inside the *Virginia.* Wood was disappointed, and with good reason, since the would-be boarders might well have succeeded.

By this time it was early afternoon, and with the *Monitor* temporarily retired, Jones called the officers of the *Virginia* together for consultation. He hoped to renew the attack on the *Minnesota,* but the pilots noted that the tide was falling and leaks were forcing the ironclad even lower in the water, and to have run aground during an ebb tide probably would have meant disaster. Wood suggested that there was enough water to steam to Fort Monroe and "clean up the Yankee ships there or run them out to sea," but all the other officers advised withdrawing, and at two o'clock Jones ordered a course for Norfolk. Wood's proposal to Jones serves well to illustrate his character as a sea devil and his attitude toward the Union. He fought for southern independence with as much determination as anyone in the Confederate navy, including the man generally considered the service's supreme Yankee-hater, Raphael Semmes. As the *Virginia* moved from the channel, Wood's stern gun roared out repeatedly at the *Monitor*, and she returned the fire.

Both sides claimed victory on the grounds that the other ship had left the scene of battle, and at Norfolk the following day there was a victory prayer on board the *Virginia*. Wood believed that the *Monitor* had been handled well, but was of the opinion that her eleven-inch guns could have been used to greater effect by firing at the *Virginia*'s water line, which would have dealt a fatal blow to the unprotected part of the vessel; or had the *Monitor*'s battery concentrated on one place on her shield, or used larger charges, the sides of the *Virginia* would have been pierced. In the 2 days of fighting, the Confederates suffered damage to 2 gunboats and lost some 2 dozen killed and wounded, mostly during the first day when a shot from the *Minnesota* exploded the boiler of the *Patrick Henry*. The Union lost 4 ships; 3 more, including the *Minnesota* which was finally floated free, had been damaged; over 30 sailors were captured; and at least 250 men were killed and wounded.[12] Essentially, in spite of a great victory against wooden ships the first day, the Confederates had been temporarily repulsed on the second, and local commanders would no longer decide the outcome still to be determined in the coming weeks.

Wood barely had time to wire Lola that he was safe, when Buchanan sent for him to come to the naval hospital. The commodore congratulated Wood for handling the stern pivot "admirably," thanked him for his valuable suggestions during the action, and concluded that his "zeal and industry in drilling the crew contributed materially to our success."[13] Buchanan then dictated a short dispatch to Mallory, and directed Wood to take the note and flag of the *Congress* to Richmond, where he was to render a verbal report of the battle and condition of the *Virginia*.

Boarding the next train of the Norfolk and Petersburg Railroad for the Confederate capital, Wood soon learned that he was something of a hero. News of the first day of battle had preceded him,

causing people to gather at stations along the line to applaud and
coax from him a first-hand account of the action. At Suffolk,
Wakefield, Waverly, and Petersburg, Wood found himself "warm-
ly received." Time after time he repeated to attentive crowds an
account of the engagement. Recent southern reverses in eastern
North Carolina and western Tennessee had caused dread "at every
throb of the electric wire," but suddenly all was changed. Wood
noticed an unmistakable lift in morale at every station along the
way.

Indeed, the unexpected success of the little Confederate navy
caused news of the battle to be enthusiastically received throughout the South, and too much came to be expected of the *Virginia:*
she would raise the blockade, lay northern coastal cities under
contribution, and level Washington. Northern fears of the *Virginia*
equaled southern expectations judging from Secretary of War
Edwin M. Stanton's famous remark at the special Cabinet meeting
called by Lincoln. "Not unlikely, we shall have a shell or cannon-
ball from one of her guns in the White House before we leave this
room." The *Virginia* taught the Federal government that it must
be more liberal in naval expenditures and the name *monitor* was
to become generic.[14]

The naval battle resulted in a Cabinet meeting in the South as
well as in the North. As soon as Wood reached Richmond, he reported to Mallory and the two walked over to Davis's office. The
president greeted Wood heartily and then called in several other
Cabinet members, including Benjamin, who a few days later became secretary of state. In a long session that lasted late into the
night, Wood gave his report of the two-day ordeal at Hampton
Roads, and the changes and repairs needed by the *Virginia*. In
realistic fashion, he said the *Monitor* was equal to the *Virginia*
and that he could not predict the result of a return engagement.
Davis's keen interest, unusual in naval matters, reflected the significance of the battle. He asked a number of questions concerning the capabilities of the *Virginia*, and urged early completion of
the repairs and alterations.[15] News of the battle came at an oppor-

tune time for Mallory. Davis had been installed as president of the permanent government in a brief ceremony on February 22, but Mallory had been criticized for lack of new ship construction, and a victory by the *Virginia* had been needed to assure his confirmation by the Senate.

The next day Wood entrained for the return trip to Norfolk as spring began to send forth its green leaves and first blossoms. Upon arrival he visited the naval hospital with bittersweet news for Buchanan. Because of his wound, the commodore would be retired from command of the *Virginia*, but he would be promoted to admiral. As Buchanan's successor, Wood strongly favored a hopeful Jones, who as executive officer had fitted out the ship and then commanded her with distinction during the second day of battle. Both Wood and Jones were disappointed in Mallory's choice of Commodore Josiah Tattnall. Wood respected Tattnall, but considered the choice reminiscent of the old navy's stagnation system.[16]

By the time Tattnall took command on March 29, repairs and improvements on the *Virginia* were almost completed. A new and heavier ram was attached to the bow, the damaged armor plates were replaced, and wrought-iron shutters were fitted over the broadside and end gun ports. To improve the vulnerable water line area, two-inch iron plate was added to a depth of four feet below the original shield. With an additional hundred tons of ballast added to her fantails, evidently to protect the propeller, the *Virginia's* draft was increased to twenty-three feet. In a new encounter with the *Monitor*, Wood would be firing steel-pointed solid shot for greater penetrating power. The changes improved the *Virginia's* attacking and resisting capabilities, but decreased the ironclad's mobility and reduced her speed to four knots.

On April 2 McClellan at long last arrived at Fort Monroe with the vanguard of his army, and two days later the cautious general began a month-long siege of Yorktown. During these weeks a huge Union force of 112,000 was transported from Washington to the peninsula, but Lincoln, in one of the most controversial acts of the war, withheld General Irvin McDowell's corps of 40,000 men for the defense of Washington, thus depriving McClellan of much of his intended strength of over 150,000 on the peninsula.[17] To defend the York River base of McClellan's Peninsular Campaign and the Potomac River approach to Washington against attack by the Virginia, Welles restricted the Monitor's movements. At the same time Secretary Mallory directed Tattnall not to approach the powerful Federal forts, because the Virginia's destruction would expose the James River and Richmond. Wood reluctantly agreed with Mallory's decision to restrict the movements of the Virginia, but still expected to continue the battle in the channel.

Soon after daylight on April 11 the Virginia, followed by the James River Squadron, stood down the Elizabeth River. At Wood's suggestion Tattnall mustered the crew for a prayer, after which Wood's "courage and spirits rose at once." He also believed prayer inspired the men, and might even reduce cursing aboard the Virginia, where Wood was "shocked hourly with oaths."[18] As they rounded Sewell's Point, the expectant Confederates could see newly arrived wooden ships anchored off Fort Monroe, among them the powerful side-wheeler U.S.S. Vanderbilt. The shed-like form of the Virginia moved closer, but all Union ships remained immobile, protected by Federal batteries at Fort Monroe and on an island near the entrance to Hampton Roads known as the Rip Raps. For a while nothing happened. Then, as the Federal navy watched, the small Confederate steamer Jamestown captured three Union merchant vessels off Hampton—two of them loaded with supplies for McClellan's army—and towed the prizes, their American flags hoisted upside down, around the aquatic arena. Foreign observers anchored nearby looked upon the spectacle with amusement. But the Monitor could not be coaxed out, and the Virginia, after exchanging a few shots with Union shore batteries, returned toward night to buoy off Craney Island. Wood did not consider the day a total loss since the men on the French and English warships had witnessed the ignominious conduct of the Federals. The English crew of H.M.S. Rinaldo, commanded by

Captain Sir William Hewett, had even raised an enthusiastic cheer for the Confederates.[19]

A few days later the *Virginia* moved out again, this time accompanied by four small gunboats equipped to grapple and tow the *Monitor*. The gunboat crews were organized to carry out Wood's earlier boarding plan, but the *Monitor* would not venture beyond the range of her protective shore batteries. Again the *Virginia* exchanged a few shots with the forts, after which the vessel's cranky engines broke down, forcing her into the Norfolk dry dock for repairs.[20]

Repeated efforts to coax the *Monitor* into the Roads failed, and events on land decided the final outcome of the world's first battle between ironclads. Southern troops evacuated Yorktown the night of May 3, but the long Union siege gave Johnston ample time to concentrate his troops between McClellan and Richmond, and Confederate General James Longstreet's rearguard defense at the battle of Williamsburg on May 5 frustrated the Union general's plan to attack the main Confederate force. At McClellan's request, Goldsborough sent seven gunboats into the York River to support the Union army, while the remainder of the fleet, including the *Monitor*, remained in the Roads to watch the *Virginia*. McClellan then moved along the line of the York River toward Richmond, the spring rains slowing the movement of both armies.

The Union advance up the peninsula rendered the Confederate position in Norfolk untenable, so Mallory ordered ships and essential supplies and equipment to Richmond and Charlotte and everything else destroyed. The city was to be abandoned. The *Virginia* cruised between the city and Sewell's Point, convoying the gunboats of the James River Squadron to the James for the ascent toward Richmond. Wood watched the preparations in Gosport Navy Yard for firing the buildings and blowing up the dry docks. Calling the situation "melancholy," Wood prophesied that "the Confederacy in our day will never have another such yard."[21]

Lincoln, realizing the Confederates were losing their hold on Norfolk, visited Fort Monroe on May 6 and urged an attack on the city from the north, during which time a few Union vessels could stand into the James. Accordingly, two days later the *Monitor* and other Federal ships steamed out and began shelling Sewell's Point in preparation for the landing, and a newly arrived ironclad, the U.S.S. *Galena,* along with two gunboats, the *Aroostook* and the *Port Royal,* began their ascent of the river. The shelling brought the *Virginia* out of the Elizabeth River, and the Federals evidently intended to ram her, but retired near their forts when the *Virginia* approached. The details of this particular standoff are debated more than usual by the opposing forces. There is little question that some of the Union's wooden ships, whose bows had been reinforced with heavy timbers for ramming, were bolder than previously, but Wood maintained that they all kept a respectable distance from the *Virginia:* "A single vessel defied and kept at bay a score of their most powerful vessels. . . . It was the most cowardly exhibition I have ever seen."[22] After cruising for several hours in the Roads, the Confederate ironclad came to buoy for the night off Sewell's Point.

At sunrise on May 9 the men on the *Virginia* were amazed to find that no flag flew over their shore batteries at Sewell's Point. A boat was sent ashore and the works were found abandoned. Then Tattnall dispatched a scouting party to Norfolk which returned late in the afternoon to report Norfolk's being evacuated and the Gosport Navy Yard on fire. Without warning, Confederate troops had abandoned their heroic ironclad.

When the Confederate commander at Norfolk, General Benjamin Huger, ordered southern forces from the coastal batteries he was almost overrun by Union troops before he had an opportunity to destroy the Yard. The Federals had learned late on May 8 that Huger was preparing to evacuate, and Lincoln, hoping to capture the naval center intact, ordered an immediate advance. Troops under Wool soon embarked from Fort Monroe and landed unopposed at Ocean View, located across the sand spit from Willoughby's Bay where shallow water prevented interference by the *Virginia.* But as the Union soldiers entered the deserted entrenchments, two unnamed generals entered into a dispute concerning rank, which caused a delay that gave Huger time to fire the Yard. Lincoln, angered by the costly and unnecessary delay, "with vehement action threw his tall hat on the floor, and uttering strongly his disapproval and disappointment," sent word for Wool to push "rapidly forward." Wool, soon to be relieved of command, marched his men to Norfolk on May 10 and occupied the city.[23]

[3]

The Naval Battle of Drewry's Bluff

The precipitate Confederate withdrawal from Norfolk, at least a week ahead of schedule and without notifying the men on the *Virginia*, left the ironclad in enemy territory and without a land base. Prior to the evacuation Mallory had directed that a council of army and navy officers be formed to decide the disposition of the *Virginia*. The council had vetoed Tattnall's suggestion that he attempt to run by the Federal forts and ships to attack McClellan's base of operations at Yorktown, or lift the blockade of southern ports, because such efforts would likely result in the loss of the ship.[1] The *Virginia*'s unreliable engines would have precluded a sustained voyage anyway, according to Wood, who believed they could not be depended on "for six hours at a time." Thus it was already understood that the ironclad would have to remain on the inland side of Fort Monroe to protect Richmond, and now after the evacuation of Norfolk there was no choice but to ascend the James River.

Tattnall decided to lighten the ship and stand up the James to some point below Richmond where the *Virginia* could be put back in fighting trim for the defense of the Confederate capital. The ship's pilots repeatedly said that with an eighteen-foot draft the *Virginia* could make the trip, so on the evening of May 10 Tattnall ordered everything overboard except powder and shot in order to reduce the draft by five feet. Time was an important factor because the batteries at Newport News would have to be passed before daylight. The crew jumped to the task, throwing out the ballast from the fantails and below, and all spare stores. By midnight the vessel had been lightened three feet; then with part of the hull vulnerable near the water line, the pilots suddenly became apprehensive, saying it was useless to lighten further because with the prevailing westerly wind the tide would not be sufficient to ascend the James even as far as the site of the early settlement at Jamestown. "This extraordinary conduct of the pilots rendered some other plan immediately necessary," fumed Wood.

The ironclad's weight could not be restored because letting in water would extinguish the furnace fires and flood the magazines. Tattnall was now in a very difficult position. In this new emergency it was suggested that the vessel be abandoned intact to the Federals, then "after they had indulged in a sufficient amount of exultation, that John Taylor Wood (our young Nelson) should slip out late some afternoon and sink her with the *Torpedo* or *Teaser*." This shock tactic, probably a tongue-in-cheek proposal, implied that Wood could accomplish with a one-gun tug what the Federal fleet had failed to do. On the other hand, the suggestion could have been a serious call for Wood to lead a nighttime boarding party. In any event, the idea was discarded because the Confederates could not "for a single moment" allow the enemy flag over the *Virginia*.[2]

Tattnall opted to save his crew by destroying the *Virginia*. He ran her ashore at Craney Island, and the men landed with their small arms and two days' provisions. Having only two boats, the operation took three hours. Then at 3:00 A.M. on May 11 Wood and Jones packed inflammable cotton and other combustibles fore and aft, and set the powder trains. They were the last to disembark from the historic vessel, pulling for the shore as flames from the *Virginia* leaped into the dawn. Two hours later she blew up as fire reached the thirty-six thousand pounds of powder in her magazines, shaking forests and buildings for miles. The crew heard the explosion as they marched the twenty-two miles to Suffolk, where they boarded a Norfolk and Petersburg railroad train for Richmond. The destruction of the *Virginia* left the water route to Richmond wide open, and enemy vessels raced into the James during the "pyrotechnic display" to join their consorts already up-stream. Wood believed the moral was that "all officers, as far as possible, should learn to do their own piloting."

A tremendous outpouring of criticism descended on Tattnall, chiefly because southerners had come to expect so much from their pioneer ironclad. To deal with this widespread indignation, Tattnall put his unblemished reputation of fifty years' service to the test by demanding a court of inquiry, and, when the result was critical of him, a court martial, which acquitted him and praised his judgment. Tattnall's ordeal before his peers was certainly not cursory, and the judgment must remain that he had acted in a professional manner typical of most Confederate naval commanders. Wood agreed with Tattnall's decision because the *Virginia,* with hull exposed, was *hors de combat;* battle would have meant the destruction or capture of ship and crew.[3] As it was, not only was the enemy denied the use of the ship but Wood and his shipmates escaped, and within thirty-six hours were on the upper peninsula preparing for their final meeting with the *Monitor.*

The upper half of the peninsula is divided lengthwise by the Chickahominy River, a sluggish stream that rises fifteen miles north of Richmond and runs eastward forty miles, then turns sharply southward and eases into the James. North of the Chicka-hominy, on the Pamunkey River, a tributary of the York, was White House Landing, the home of Colonel W. H. F. Lee. South of the Chickahominy was Drewry's Bluff on the James, eight miles from Richmond and the location of the nearest high bank below the city. Farther downstream was Harrison's Landing, site of Berkeley Mansion, the birthplace of William Henry Harrison, and also Westover Mansion, whose owner William Byrd founded Rich-mond in 1737 at the head of navigation on the James, some ninety miles by water from the sea. As the crow flies, Harrison's Landing was approximately twenty miles below Richmond.

The Confederate army had retreated to a position between the Pamunkey and Chickahominy rivers, where Johnston, under the

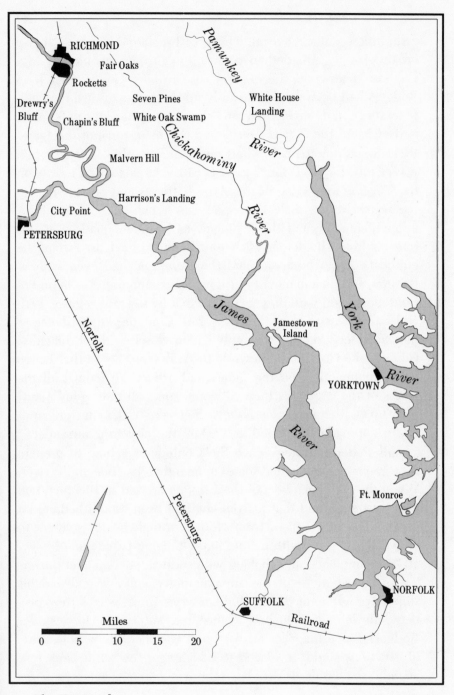

RICHMOND

Fair Oaks

Rocketts

Drewry's
Bluff

Seven Pines

White House
Landing

Chapin's Bluff

White Oak Swamp

Pamunkey

Chickahominy

River

Malvern Hill

Harrison's Landing

City Point

River

PETERSBURG

James

River

Jamestown
Island

York

Norfolk

YORKTOWN

River

River

Petersburg

Ft. Monroe

Miles

0   5   10   15   20

SUFFOLK

Railroad

NORFOLK

The Peninsula

assumption that some local defense of Richmond had been set up on the James, intended to contest the further advance of Mc-Clellan. Meanwhile, the Federal flotilla under Commander John Rodgers had been moving steadily up the James toward the Confederate capital, having met only slight resistance by Confederate batteries and the *Patrick Henry* and the *Jamestown* of the James River Squadron at Rock Wharf and Hardin's Bluff. The situation was critical for the Confederates because, having relied mostly on the *Virginia* for river defense, shore batteries and obstructions in the water were grossly inadequate for repelling a water attack upon Richmond, and the light gunboats of the squadron at this time could hardly defend Richmond against ironclads. Two of the gunboats, the *Nansemond* and the *Hampton*, had been built at Norfolk, and, in a manner typical of the extemporaneous nature of Confederate shipbuilding, were powered by sawmill engines. Federal policy was to clear the river of all Confederate resistance as they advanced in order to supply Union vessels without difficulty. Commodore Goldsborough wrote to Welles on May 12 that Union naval commanders on the James had orders "to reduce all the works of the enemy as they go along, spike all their guns, [and] blow up all their magazines." Only then were the Union commanders to approach Richmond and "shell the city to a surrender."[4]

This Federal strategy gave the Confederates time to prepare for a major engagement at some commanding position on the river. When the crew members of the *Virginia* arrived in Richmond on May 12 they found that martial law had been established, and a great influx of refugees from Norfolk mingled with soldiers to crowd the streets "with a continually moving panorama of war," all "greeting, cheering, choking with sudden emotion, and quivering in anticipation" of the approaching enemy.[5] Wood and his shipmates left immediately for Drewry's Bluff, where they prepared to defend Richmond against the waterborne force under Rodgers. Since the river at that point was less than a mile wide, obstructions could be placed to advantage; the south bank rose acutely two hundred feet above the water so that shore batteries could fire down upon the enemy, while the Federals would find it difficult to elevate their gun muzzles high enough to fire on the cliff top. Building onto earthworks begun by the army, the men of the *Virginia*, aided by crews from the gunboats that had escaped up the river before Norfolk was abandoned, worked feverishly in rain and mud for two days mounting five guns from the gunboats, three 32- and two 64-pound shell guns. All trees that might obstruct the line of fire were cut away, and the hill protected with a layer of logs down the cliff to prevent caving by enemy shells. The steamer *Jamestown* and some smaller vessels were sunk in the channel and secured by chains to strengthen existing obstructions of piles filled with logs, stone, and rubbish. Although high water caused by the heavy rain reduced the effectiveness of these obstacles, the only sure passage for the Federals was a narrow channel below the guns on the bluff.

Late in the afternoon of May 14 Wood learned that the enemy flotilla had reached a point only a few miles below Drewry's Bluff. He wanted to have a look. Gathering a small band of sharpshooters armed with Enfield rifles, he crossed the river to the north bank and moved downstream a short distance to Chapin's Bluff. From the bluff Wood could see the enemy ships proceeding cautiously, with men in small boats carefully examining each bank and piece of driftwood for mines. A concerted attack by Wood was out of the question, but he could not resist ordering a volley into the vessels at long range. The enemy responded by lobbing a few shells in Wood's direction. Soon it was dusk and Wood concealed his men on the bank of the river. This same day Johnston learned, too late to be of much help, that the *Virginia* had been destroyed and enemy gunboats on the James were approaching Richmond.

Since the Federals had passed the Confederate defenses on the lower James River with little difficulty, they were becoming more confident that they would soon be shelling Richmond. At 7:30 A.M. on Thursday, May 15, the familiar shape of the *Monitor*, accompanied by two other ironclads, the *Galena* and the *Naugatuck*, and followed by the two wooden gunboats, the *Aroostook* and the

Port Royal, steamed into view. As the three ironclads approached to within six or seven hundred yards of Drewry's Bluff (called Fort Darling by northerners), the Union seamen were surprised to see the colors from the *Virginia* floating defiantly in the breeze above the bluff—a strong indication that the pending battle would be anything but another routine reduction of Confederate river defenses. Undaunted, Commander Rodgers maneuvered his flagship *Galena* to her buoy with astonishing precision and deliberation, obviously quite accustomed to the procedure, and from the impressed Confederates on shore he drew praise in future accounts of the battle. Wood himself observed that the ship was "handled very skillfully."

Confederate seamen at the shore batteries and a group of marine sharpshooters on the same side of the river opened fire on the Federal ironclads. The light armor of the *Galena* had yet to be seriously tested by severe fire, but the northern public had confidence in her, and Rodgers had "resolved to give the matter a fair trial." The *Monitor* steamed closer to the bluff, but could not elevate her guns sufficiently from that position, and returned to take a station beside the *Galena.* There she blasted away, her iron cover impervious to Confederate fire. The Parrott rifle of the *Naugatuck* burst after sending up sixteen shells and she retired, but the other guns on ship and shore roared for nearly three hours.

On the opposite bank, Wood had increased his force by rallying some of the Confederates in the vicinity of Chapin's Bluff. Many of these southern defenders, expecting Union troops to disembark for a land assault, were retreating up the river. Two batteries of Confederate artillery, fearing a Federal landing, withdrew without firing a shot, although Wood promised to scout downstream and warn them immediately should the enemy land troops. However, a regiment of "riflemen" (either sharpshooters or regular infantry) agreed to remain, and Wood stationed the men with his sharpshooters. This regiment was perhaps one sent by Johnston during the day of the battle to aid in the defense of Drewry's Bluff. After distributing his combined force along a high ridge, Wood gave orders for each man to select his position and maintain an intense fire on the enemy vessels, concentrating particularly on the wooden ships the *Aroostook* and the *Port Royal,* which according to usual Federal practice remained some distance behind the ironclads when neutralizing Confederate shore battteries. Several times Wood's men drove the ships' crews from their guns, but at other times the enemy replied with cannon and small arms in an effort to silence the constant fusillade from the river bank. As a result, the wooden vessels could not cooperate in shelling Drewry's Bluff.

Soon after 11:00 A.M., the badly battered *Galena* began to withdraw. She had fired 283 shot and shell, and according to Rodgers, retired only because of low ammunition, but further exposure to Confederate fire probably would have sent the vessel to the bottom. She had been hit twenty-eight times, and proved especially vulnerable at the water line, where her armor was repeatedly penetrated. The Federal retreat was a result of underestimating the river defenses and overestimating the "shot proof" armor of the *Galena.* Most of the Union losses of thirteen killed and fourteen wounded were her crew members. The Confederates lost seven killed and nine wounded and had two guns dismounted. As the Federal ships took the current toward their base at City Point for repairs, Wood and his sharpshooters followed and harassed them for over a mile. At one point Wood was quite close to the retreating *Monitor.* Aware that the vessel's new commander was Lieutenant William N. Jeffers, like Wood a former Annapolis instructor, Wood called out to an officer in her pilothouse: "Tell Capt. Jeffers that is not the way to Richmond."

The Federals had missed two opportunities to take Richmond the easy way. Given a less cautious attitude, they could have moved ships quickly up the James in two or three days and passed Drewry's Bluff on May 13, when Confederate shore batteries, river obstructions, and gunboats could offer only slight resistance. By May 15 it was too late without land support, which suggests the second missed opportunity, as explained by Wood:

Had Commander Rodgers been supported by a few brigades, landed at City Point or above on the south side, Richmond would have been evacuated. The *Virginia's* crew alone barred his way to Richmond; otherwise the obstructions would not have prevented his steaming up to the city, which would have been as much at his mercy as was New Orleans before the fleet of Farragut.[6]

McClellan still had time for a land assault along the south bank of the James. Confederate defenses at Drewry's Bluff constituted the only obstacle to direct passage up the James to Richmond, which a small Union land force could have reduced. But McClellan thought only in terms of a mass offensive. In spite of the inclement weather, his advanced divisions had moved to within fifteen miles of Richmond during the day of the battle at Drewry's Bluff and established a supply depot at White House on the Pamunkey. Goldsborough visited White House with Rodgers's report of the battle, and offered the support of the flotilla if McClellan would attack Drewry's Bluff. McClellan, according to Goldsborough, replied that "he would prefer to defer his answer until he got his army on the other side of the Chickahominy." Even when considering a large-scale attack, there was a crucial period of two or three days when McClellan had the choice of striking directly eastward from the White House or along the line of the James. "The army was admirably placed for adopting either," McClellan commented, "and my decision was to take that of the James, operating on either bank as might prove advisable, but always preferring the southern."

The opportunity to attack via the James soon slipped through McClellan's hands. On May 18 Secretary of War Stanton telegraphed McClellan that McDowell's corps would be released after all and would advance from Fredericksburg. McClellan was directed to extend his right wing to the north of Richmond in order to establish communication with McDowell and supply him from the depot at White House. The Army of the Potomac would now be divided by the Chickahominy and much time lost building bridges across the stream, whereas if he could have crossed to the

James his army would be united and the Confederates could neither turn its flank nor interrupt its new line of supply on the James. Ironically, orders from Washington, while promising the long-desired support of McDowell, came at such a time as to impose the less desirable line of operations on McClellan. "Herein lay the failure of the campaign," complained the hesitant general.

Although little noticed at the time, the naval encounter at Drewry's Bluff was a significant battle of the war. Compared to the battles of the great opposing armies, this battle between a few hundred sailors seemed a relatively minor engagement as evidenced by the scant attention it received in the Richmond newspapers. One paper of the day did point out that the people of Richmond could be thankful that it was the *Virginia's* crew who worked the guns at the bluff, "and not Yahoos, ignorant of discipline, and command, and military business." Wood termed the action "one of the boldest and best-conducted operations of the war." The clash proved the effectiveness of even hastily constructed shore batteries protecting river obstructions against a waterborne force operating in a narrow channel, and Richmond thereafter was considered an inland town to be taken by army troops, not river craft.[7] (Two years later when General U. S. Grant was moving against Richmond near Cold Harbor, Butler landed at Bermuda Hundred above City Point and moved up the south bank of the James with forty thousand troops, but was repelled 13–16 May 1864 by an army of thirty thousand under Beauregard. Thus the second battle of Drewry's Bluff was a major land battle.)

The naval battle of Drewry's Bluff was not properly appreciated in Richmond because of other overwhelming events. First came news that New Orleans, probably the greatest southern city and of strategic importance because of its river and ocean commerce, had fallen on April 29 to a combined Union water and land force. Then the nearness of McClellan's army created great confusion and fright in Richmond. The alarmed citizenry believed the government would be forced to evacuate the city. The Confederate archives were shipped to Columbia, South Carolina, and the public treasure was kept on cars ready for removal to a place of safety. The city reverberated to "the tramp of rusty battalions, the short imperious stroke of the alarm-bell, the clash of passing bands, [and] the gallop of eager horsemen." Johnston, anticipating the possibility that McClellan might change his base to the James, withdrew to the south bank of the Chickahominy soon after the Drewry's Bluff affair in order to be in a position to oppose McClellan's approach from either the White House or the James. The Confederate general centered his forces, numbering 85,000, near Seven Pines, which allowed McClellan to advance with about 100,000 to within seven miles of the Confederate capital.[8]

The Confederate high command, namely Davis and his military advisor, General Robert E. Lee, had recently made one of their best decisions of the war. In order to occupy McDowell and prevent him from joining McClellan, General Thomas J. "Stonewall" Jackson, Confederate commander in the Shenandoah Valley, was reinforced to 17,000 men and ordered on an incursion northward in an apparent threat to Washington by way of Harper's Ferry. The brilliant Jackson drove through two Federal armies on his way northward during May, causing Lincoln to rush forces, including McDowell's corps of 40,000, to the Valley. Jackson, keeping the Federals "mystified as to his movements," then slipped back toward Richmond, leaving McDowell's men fatigued and far from McClellan.[9]

As McClellan's army drew near the gates of Richmond, a massive Confederate laboring force, made up of soldiers from the ranks and slaves impressed from surrounding counties, built entrenchments in front of the city. After Wood moved his family from Petersburg to Greensboro, North Carolina, he joined the general effort by helping to strengthen the defenses at Drewry's Bluff. The work was similar to that of a Construction Battalion (seabee) of a later day. Dressed in a "new flannel shirt, country trousers and untouched shoes," his hair cut short, and "ready for work of any kind," he directed a large road-building crew. Occasionally, Wood scouted downstream to learn whether the enemy intended to attack the bluff. On May 28 he reported that Goldsborough was increasing his force at City Point and predicted: "If he comes near us, we will drive him off."[10] The test never came as subsequent events during the Peninsular Campaign made Federal ships offensively useless on the James River.

McClellan approached the Chickahominy east of Richmond, where the narrow stream was fringed with a dense growth of trees and low marshlands that varied in width from one-half to one mile. A single rainstorm caused the volume of water in the Chickahominy and bottomlands to vary greatly, rendering the stream impassable without long bridges, and McClellan found that the Confederates had destroyed all the bridges except the one at Mechanicsville on his right, where Confederate batteries on high bluffs across the river held a commanding position. An attack there without McDowell's corps was out of the question. Hence McClellan's first task was to divide his army, moving part of it across the swampy Chickahominy to the south side and keeping part of it on the north bank in a position to link with McDowell. The first bridges he constructed were swept away by floods, necessitating more solid structures with log approaches, a difficult task carried out by Union soldiers working in water and often under fire.

On Friday, May 30, rain fell in torrents all day and into the night, inundating the entire front along the Chickahominy. Johnston, aware that McClellan's army was divided by the Chickahominy and that the destruction of the bridges was again threatened, struck the next day in a savage assault seven miles east of Richmond at Fair Oaks (Seven Pines). The battle was a major engagement of the war, involving three Union corps totaling 50,000 men and four Confederate divisions totaling 39,000 troops. The Confederate advance was hampered by muddy woods and thickets, and in many places knee-deep water, but 350 Union prisoners were taken, along with 10 pieces of artillery, 6700 muskets and rifles, medical, commissary, quartermaster, and ordnance stores, and 5 flags. Toward nightfall Johnston gave the order for his men to maintain their positions and to resume the attack the following morning. Then at half-past seven a musket ball ripped into Johnston's shoulder, followed by a shell fragment in the chest which unhorsed him. The redoubtable curmudgeon was borne from the field as darkness settled in to end the first day of battle.

The women of Richmond quietly began to receive the wounded, and soon the city was "one vast hospital."

> Night brought a lull in the cannonading. People lay down dressed upon beds, but not to sleep, while the weary soldiers slept upon their arms. Early next morning the whole town was on the street. Ambulances, litters, carts, every vehicle that the city could produce, went and came with a gastly burden; those who could walk limped painfully home, in some cases so black with gunpowder they passed unrecognized. Women with pallid faces flitted bareheaded through the streets searching for their dead or wounded.[11]

Wood visited the overflowing hospitals in Richmond and was initiated into the aftermath of large-scale warfare. The wounded were everywhere, filling the streets and the "dreary rooms" of the hotels. Some lay on pew cushions sewn together, others on bare boards with a haversack or army blanket for a pillow. Obviously moved, Wood lamented: "What a Sabbath this had been. Why all this bloodshed? Why all this suffering?" Then with awesome reality his thoughts turned to his personal role in the war: "What a terrible responsibility rests upon those of us who made it."[12] Wood was indeed becoming an important Confederate leader, with influence out of all proportion to his relatively low rank, and he developed an unshakable separatist faith.

All the while President Davis, tall and erect, was a familiar figure on the streets. He could be seen early in the morning walking with a "dignified and soldierly bearing" through the Capitol square from his residence to his office. At dusk Davis rode out to visit the military headquarters near the city, and during the battle was under enemy fire. "He was clad always in Confederate gray cloth, and wore a soft felt hat with wide brim. Afoot, his step was brisk and firm; in the saddle he rode admirably."

To replace the severely wounded Johnston, Davis chose Robert E. Lee, who at the time was a War Department staff officer serving as advisor to the president. Son of "Light Horse Harry" Lee and a distant kinsman of Wood, he married Mary Custis, daughter of Washington's adopted son. A graduate of West Point who served with distinction on the staff of General Winfield Scott during the Mexican War, Lee then served as superintendent of West Point, and on the eve of the war was in Texas policing the border area against Indians. He was home on leave when he captured the abolitionist John Brown at Harper's Ferry. Although an anti-secessionist, he found little attraction in a Union held together by force, and refused an offer to be successor to the aging Scott. A military engineer (as was McClellan), Lee had served in South Carolina and Georgia early in the war constructing coastal fortifications. He was a splendid figure of a man with a ruddy face, brown eyes, and dark wavy hair that was beginning to show streaks of gray. His great dignity, like that of his hero, Washington, repelled familiarity. As a field commander he would display flashes of brilliant strategy, and since he realized the weaker side must take chances, he was daring.

The South's greatest general assumed command of the Army of Northern Virginia under difficult circumstances. The enemy host still lay astride the Chickahominy, with two divisions only four miles from the Confederate capital. Rain continued for three weeks following the battle of Fair Oaks, while McClellan continued to call for reinforcements, improve his bridges, and wait for "favorable conditions of earth and sky" so that the ground would allow passage of artillery prior to attacking Richmond. At the same time, Lee's battle plan was taking shape. After his cavalry general, J. E. B. Stuart, encircled McClellan's army and reported on enemy troop positions, Lee massed his army in preparation for a devastating strike on the isolated one-third of McClellan's army on the north side of the river, after which he would crush the

larger portion on the south side. The element of risk in Lee's plan
was that McClellan might discover there was only a small Confederate force left to defend Richmond.

McClellan, however, was now thinking of evacuating his army
from the marshes of the Chickahominy. Finally despairing of the
aid of McDowell's corps, he decided to alter his base of operations
from White House on the Pamunkey to Harrison's Landing on the
James, then act on his earlier inclination to advance on Richmond
along the James with a combined land and water force. On June
29 he established communication with Rodgers, whose James
River Flotilla had been increased by the arrival of several gunboats
—the *Susquehanna*, the *Decotah*, the *Mahaska*, the *Jacob Bell*, the
Southfield, the *Maratanza*, the *Stepping Stones*, the *Delaware*, and
the *Satellite*. McClellan's decision to change his base probably
saved his army, as Lee was prepared to deal with a retreat to the
York.

On June 26 Lee and Jackson moved against McClellan's right
on the north side of the Chickahominy at Mechanicsville, touching
off a series of bloody encounters known as the Seven Days, which
is the name given McClellan's march across the peninsula to Harrison's Landing. The battle of Gaines's Mill occurred on June 27,
Savage Station on June 29, and on June 30 Frayser's Farm. The
final battle took place on July 1 near Harrison's Landing at Malvern Hill, "one of the most terrible battles of the war," where the
Federal army, assisted by Rodgers's gunboats, dealt the attacking
Confederates a bloody repulse. Dashing the final few miles to Harrison's Landing, the Federals destroyed a key bridge, chopped
down trees to block the road, and threw sheaves of wheat into the
muddy clay ruts to support the wheels of hundreds of supply wagons. Total Union losses in the Peninsular Campaign were 15,849,
compared to 19,749 for the Confederates, but McClellan's objective of taking Richmond remained unfulfilled.

From Drewry's Bluff, Wood could hear the distant roar of guns
during the Seven Days, and as the sounds of battle faded early in
July, he wondered what would happen next. He realized it was a

mistake to consider the enemy completely demoralized. McClellan had gunboats and transports which would protect him from capture, and could even strike again up the river, although the James had been increasingly mined by Lieutenant Hunter Davidson, and ten guns had been mounted at Chapin's Bluff where Wood kept his sharpshooters. But each passing day, as Wood knew, made another attack unlikely. He was optimistic that southern independence would be obtained by total victory on the battlefield or through English mediation. The latter was preferable to Wood because without foreign intervention a war of extinction might occur, which he termed "alien to our religion and boast of civilization."[13]

Ensconced at Harrison's Landing, McClellan was still only some twenty-five miles from Richmond by water, but bitter recriminations between McClellan and Lincoln caused a change of plans. Lincoln visited Harrison's Landing on July 9 and was "grievously disappointed" with the lack of success. To him "change of base" spelled "retreat," and he was unimpressed when McClellan pointed out that the army was "safe." Furthermore, England might recognize the Confederacy, the northern public was discontent, and the Republicans might lose strength in the coming Congressional election. Finally, the high-handed general sorely tried Lincoln's patience by writing the "Harrison's Landing letter," a sweeping reproof of the president's national policy. Lincoln replaced McClellan with General John Pope and ordered the withdrawal of the Army of the Potomac from Harrison's Landing for a new operation along the overland route from Washington to Richmond.

Lee anticipated the new Federal strategy and moved his army to the new location, sending Jackson northward through Thoroughfare Gap in the Bull Run Mountains. Jackson flanked the right wing of the Federal army and reached the rear, where he struck Pope's line of communication, causing the unwitting general to draw close to Washington. When news of these developments reached Wood at Drewry's Bluff, he contrasted Jackson and Pope by saying they represented the difference between Rebels and Yankees: "The first is just, truthful and Christian; the latter cruel, a liar and notorious profligate." Jackson soon slipped back into position near Lee, after which the brilliant Confederate duo smashed Pope on August 29–30 at Second Bull Run—a major battle that served as a postscript to Union efforts against Richmond in the Peninsular Campaign.[14]

The rapport that Lee enjoyed with Davis was clearly lacking between McClellan and Lincoln. Had Lincoln not held out to McClellan the hope of reinforcement by McDowell's corps, McClellan probably would have moved earlier to the James, which the destruction of the *Virginia* on May 11 made possible, and where in combination with Rodgers he was invincible. Whether McClellan could have taken Richmond via the James is open to question, but had he gained the capital with naval support, it is doubtful if Lee could have turned the city into a Union "death trap." There is little question that for McClellan the key to Richmond was along the line of the James, and as matters turned out, his best hope had been at Drewry's Bluff.

[4]
Beginning of the Midnight Raids

Arise! though the stars have a rugged glare,
And the moon has a wrath-blurred crown—
Brothers! a blessing is ambushed there
In the cliffs of the Father's frown.

From "The Battle Cry of the South" by James R. Randall

The Union disbanded its James River Flotilla on 31 August 1862 and assigned most of the ships elsewhere. This left the upper river in undisputed control of the Confederates, and duty at Drewry's Bluff became routine, which prompted Wood to seek other assignments. He was encouraged by a new law that offered promotion as a result of distinguished service in battle, thereby enhancing professionalism at the expense of the politicians. Promoted to first lieutenant 29 September 1862, chiefly as a result of his service on the *Virginia*, Wood considered battle essential for morale within, and public support of, the naval program. Although convinced that unless there was reward for fighting the navy would lapse into inertia, he also began to contemplate a more drastic overhaul of the command system. Too many "old infirm drones" were retarding the service at a time when the Navy Department was struggling to secure and develop advanced weapons and techniques to counter the naval supremacy held by the Union. Wood, then, was attracted to undertakings which helped ensure that the southern navy would be "kicked into vitality." [1]

New Confederate ironclads were regarded as part of the answer to Union naval supremacy, but their slow construction offered lit-

tle opportunity for service afloat, and Wood's thoughts turned
more and more to an older method of naval combat—the cutting-
out expedition. The idea was not new to him; he had even been
thinking of it before he advocated boarding the *Monitor*. Earlier
in the war, when stationed at Aquia Creek, he had observed opportunities for striking at Federal gunboats and merchant vessels
on the Potomac River by boarding them from small boats in the
tradition of Stephen Decatur's famous 1804 night attack in Tripoli
Harbor. Probably influenced by Decatur's raid, Wood now proposed to Mallory the construction of a few craft of whaleboat design capable of carrying up to fifteen or twenty men, with space
for arms and equipment, and a week's supplies. Mallory liked the
drama of raids, and with his approval the boats were built at the
Rocketts Navy Yard, located on the north bank of the James River
just below Richmond. Wood also had supports and braces fitted to
army wagons in order to transport the boats overland. The amphibious nature of the strike force would provide the increased
mobility necessary for surprise and escape.

Wood's proposal was less expensive and somewhat different in
nature from that of Matthew F. Maury, approved 23 December
1861 in spite of Mallory's opposition, which allotted 2 million dollars for a fleet of small wooden steamboats with a single heavy gun
on each, i.e., a kind of patrol boat. But with the advent of ironclad
ships which could destroy the small craft with impunity, construction of the miniature fleet was stopped and the money diverted to
ironclads. Maury's scheme was also complicated by a feud with
Mallory dating from 1855, when Mallory's retiring board requested
the already famous oceanographer to step down.[2]

Detached from the James River Squadron for special duty with
verbal orders from Mallory, Wood set about organizing his "navy
on wheels" for a raid. At 8:00 A.M. on October 1 he slipped out of
Richmond undetected and headed northward for the Potomac.
His special services force consisted of fifteen or twenty carefully
chosen men equipped with two or three boats and an ambulance.
Wood was leading a naval "commando" mission, although that

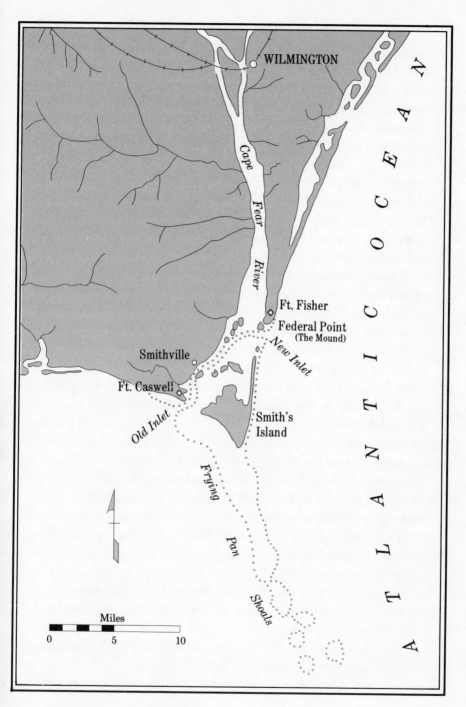

WILMINGTON

Cape

Fear

River

Ft. Fisher
Federal Point
(The Mound)

New Inlet

Smithville

Ft. Caswell

Old Inlet

Smith's
Island

Frying

Pan

Shoals

A T L A N T I C   O C E A N

Miles

0   5   10

Approaches to Wilmington

word was not a part of the Civil War soldier's or sailor's vocabu-
lary. The detachments that Wood took on his expeditions came
from the James River Squadron and had no special designation;
they were described simply as "picked men."[3]

Wood's first raid had an inauspicious beginning. Bad roads
caused one of the wagons to turn bottom side up during the first
day, and Wood chafed at the delay. At dark, he was in Essex
County, actually a good day's travel, but he had expected to be
across the Rappahannock River, and was beginning to think that
Lola had been right in urging him not to undertake the raid. But
he did not turn back. Pushing on into Westmoreland County and
approaching the Potomac, Wood sent part of his force to scout the
shoreline for enemy ships at anchor, and the men fanned out over
a thirty-mile stretch. Wood did not hear from them for days. "Our
trip so far," he commented, "has been but a chapter of accidents."

The prey proved elusive, and for several days Wood stalked the
banks of the Potomac, sleeping and eating in the homes of acquaintances, in public buildings, and in camp. He passed the place
where he and Lola and Zach had made the storm-tossed passage
into Virginia from Maryland the year before, and wrote Lola that
"everyone remembers our crossing." On October 6 he was in the
village of Oak Grove, and from there he sent a few of his men who
had become sick back to Richmond in the ambulance. Next, he
continued into King George County and assembled the men of his
command. No one had spotted a likely target, and he was reluctantly considering abandoning the raid when the United States
transport schooner *Frances Elmore,* loaded with hay, anchored for
the night off Pope's Creek on the Maryland side of the Potomac.
She was soon to be Wood's first prize of the war.

After dark on October 7 Wood ordered the boarding cutters
launched and mustered his men for a final briefing, distribution of
arms, and a sustaining prayer. By midnight all was in readiness.
Taking his place in the leading boat, Wood gave out the standard
commands: "Up oars—shove off—let fall—give way." The last men
to enter the boats were the bowmen, carefully selected by Wood

for their dependability, who jumped in after shoving off and took up their oars without orders. As the boats moved silently across the water, Wood gave directional commands in a lowered voice: "Back your starboard oars—give way your port oars." Approaching the *Frances Elmore* it was "in bows—way enough," at which the bowmen "tossed" oars and rose to their feet. Resting their heels against the thwarts, these hearties threw their grappling hooks as the boats rushed the final yards and slammed into the side of the ship. The rebound created a gap which the bowmen closed by pulling on the ropes attached to the grappling hooks. The boats were fast to the schooner.

Wood, with determination inherited from "Old Rough and Ready," led his men onto the deck of the ship. The night raiders quickly overpowered the bewildered crew of the transport vessel: Captain J. Smith, a mate, and five hands. After the Confederates stripped the schooner of valuables, Wood ordered the vessel fired. He then returned with his prisoners to the boats as the flames leaped upward against the October night. A few minutes later, watchmen aboard the U.S.S. *Yankee* of the Potomac Flotilla saw the burning ship, but upon arrival at the scene the crew of the *Yankee* found the transport's stern and masts already consumed by the flames. The "partisan rangers" were not to be seen; they had already reached the Virginia shore with their prisoners. Wood, his spirits rising, loaded his boats on the wagons and returned to Richmond, where the prisoners were incarcerated in the large brick tobacco factory called Libby Prison.[4]

Encouraged by the success of his first night attack, Wood organized another raid within a week. Lieutenant Sidney Lee, second in command, and a crew of eighteen from the *Patrick Henry* along with three boats made up the strike force. This time Wood moved eastward from Richmond to Matthews County. Adjoining the Chesapeake, Matthews County became a favorite base of operations for junior naval officers who, following Wood's example, raided the enemy's line of communication between Fort Monroe and the North—burning lighthouses, cutting the underwater U.S.

telegraph cable across the Bay, and capturing Union vessels. John Yates Beall operated from Matthews County until captured, but Beall, who intended to become the "Mosby of the Chesapeake," was essentially a privateer in spite of an acting master's commission granted by Mallory.[5] The people of this area of Chesapeake Bay, already accustomed to partisan sniping and blockade running, graciously opened their homes to Wood, but he usually slept on the ground or in a boat since he spent most of the time traveling or scouting. After establishing a base camp in the woods between Matthews Courthouse and New Point Comfort, Wood impressed a local pilot, Peter Smith, into the raiding party, and began the nocturnal hunt for potential victims along the edge of the Bay. By October 24, a week after leaving Richmond, he was again becoming discouraged by the lack of enemy ships at night anchor. "You were probably right, I shouldn't have come," he wrote Lola, "but I once get anything in my head, I can't get it out."

Wood continued the search with bulldog tenacity. For a number of nights during stormy weather, he led his men several miles out onto the rain-swept Bay without finding a vessel. Then, on the night of October 28, after rowing twelve miles toward the northeast, Wood sighted a ship anchored off Gwyn's Island some twenty miles from the mouth of the Rappahannock River. She was the 1400-ton *Alleganian*, a Union merchant ship loaded with guano en route from Baltimore to London, which had anchored against a headwind produced by the storm. Wood ordered his three boats forward, with himself, Lieutenant Lee, and the pilot, Smith, as boat commanders. It was almost midnight when Seaman James L. Jackson, on watch aboard the *Alleganian*, dutifully challenged the silent forms fast closing on the ship. The noncommittal answer, "Arabs," drifted back to him across the swells. Before Jackson could rouse the ship's crew, Wood had gained the deck, sword in hand, followed by his raiders armed with cutlasses and French revolvers. Wood sought out the astonished master, Captain James G. Bastow, and informed him that the *Alleganian* was a prize of the Confederacy and her 25-man crew were prisoners. There was no resistance.

The pilot, Smith, on Wood's orders, bound the hands of the prisoners behind them. Then for the next two hours the raiders stripped the captured ship, taking instruments, tea, coffee, and men's clothing. When his raiding party was ready to depart, Wood released some of the prisoners, perhaps as a cover for the raid. They were unbound, given their baggage, passed over the side into the *Alleganian*'s boats, and set adrift. Retained as prisoners were Captain Bastow, First Mate William Williams, and Pilot Joseph Pate. These unfortunates were undoubtedly kept bound because Wood was of the opinion that the "infamous" character of northerners was improved by the occasional practice of handcuffing Federal officers who had been taken prisoner. This was done by Davis's order, in retaliation for the Union's entertaining the notion that southern privateers ought to be hanged. Next, the prize was fired from below as the raiders manned their boats and stood five miles up the Bay, where Wood took the lead from Smith and headed west-southwest, guided to land by a signal fire built by one of his men on shore. Upon landing, Wood loaded the boats on the wagons and sent the main body to the base camp, while he and two or three men remained behind to make sure they were not followed before rejoining the party for breakfast. The raiders then returned to Richmond, arriving on October 31 with their captured instruments, stores, colors, and prisoners.

The raid had occurred within a few miles of enemy gunboats. At 2:30 A.M., shortly after Wood fired the *Alleganian*, watchmen on the U.S.S. *T. A. Ward* and the U.S.S. *Crusader* spotted the flames, and the two gunboats stood to the burning vessel. The *Crusader* arrived first and her crew went on board the *Alleganian* to put out the fire. They were soon followed by the crew of the *Ward*, but by the time the fire was extinguished shortly after daylight, she had burned to within six feet of the water's edge. Salvage operations were begun, although most of the ship and cargo, valued at $200,000, were lost.

When the crew members of the *Alleganian* were picked up by Union gunboats, the men's circumstances, whether planned by Wood or not, appeared extremely suspicious: they had their baggage with them and their officers were missing. The rescued seamen were taken to the Washington Navy Yard under suspicion of mutiny. Welles immediately ordered Commodore Andrew A. Harwood, commander of the Potomac Flotilla, to investigate the burning. After questioning the men, Harwood reported on November 5 that there had been no mutiny, only negligence by the ship's master, Captain Bastow. This account was confirmed a few days later after a Union gunboat crew arrested Wood's pilot, Peter Smith, at his home on the York River, put him in double irons, and informed him he would be treated as a pirate or civilian engaged in partisan warfare. A shaken Smith was taken aboard the U.S.S. *Brandywine* off Yorktown where, doing his best under the circumstances, he convinced his captors to treat him as a prisoner of war by saying that Wood had chosen him for pilot because he was one of the best on the Bay, but that he served the raiders against his will, and that Wood had refused his frequent requests prior to the raid to allow him to return home. As a result of Smith's statement, Welles learned that Wood had burned both the *Frances Elmore* and the *Alleganian*. Calling Wood's raids a "feasible plan," and expecting more of the same, Welles alerted not only the gunboats of the Potomac Flotilla but also the ships of the North Atlantic Blockading Squadron.

Wood had made his first two raids between 1 and 31 October 1862, a period of exactly one month, during which he had established a reputation as a Confederate raider. As he had expected, successful raids helped build public support for the Navy Department and did much to end the criticism of Mallory. One newspaper, the *Richmond Examiner*, had called Mallory "ignorant of nautical matters," pronounced the Navy Department full of "inefficiency and effeminacy," and criticized the entire navy as "almost nominal as to existence" and a "mockery." Wood himself was at first privately critical of Mallory. When the Confederate Congress investigated Mallory's competence, Wood mused, "I am afraid his skin is so thick that he will rub through it all. For some reason the President upholds him." But when Mallory approved of Wood's raids, this criticism ended, and on the very day that Wood captured the *Alleganian,* the *Examiner* was calling for more raids on Union ships.[6]

Pleased with the results of his first two expeditions, Wood looked forward to another raid in Virginia waters, but first he wanted the Federals to become complacent again. He was assigned to the ironclad *Richmond,* a vessel under construction as a result of contributions raised by Virginia women to replace the *Virginia,* but since there was scant activtiy on the James River, Wood noted with anticipation an opportunity for a different assignment. He had earlier served as an unofficial observer for the president while on the *Virginia,* and when Colonel Joseph R. Davis, nephew of the president, resigned from Davis's staff to take command of a brigade of Mississippi troops in the Army of Northern Virginia, one nephew replaced another. At the end of 1861 Davis had been authorized by the Confederate Congress to assign military rank to navy men, and perhaps the president should have used this dual appointment power more often, considering the excess of naval officers. On 26 January 1863 he appointed Wood his aide with the rank of Colonel of Cavalry in the army, and on 10 February 1863 the appointment was confirmed by the Senate. One of the few men who held dual rank, Wood served as liaison officer between the navy and army, and inspected coastal defense sites and ironclad construction. During the remainder of the war, Wood signed his reports with either his naval or military rank, according to the nature of the assignment. The new rank also helped in future raids, since Wood sometimes utilized army units for support duty.[7]

As aide to the president, Wood now had an opportunity to inspect the naval installations commanded by mossbacks and suggest improvements. This was important and appealing duty, so much so that Wood declined a request by Lieutenant William H. Murdaugh to join the Confederate raid on Lake Erie.[8] Hence the day Wood's appointment was confirmed, he began an extensive tour of southern sea and river installations. The president wanted a complete report made directly to him, and Wood promptly departed Richmond on February 10 by train. In the major southern ports of the South, Wood called on local commanders and turned a trained eye on vessels afloat, assessing personnel, armament, and powers of offense and defense, the character and estimated time of completion of vessels under construction, machine works, the methods adopted to obstruct channels and rivers, blockade-running statistics, and naval defenses, especially the location and nature of guns bearing on shipping. This sweeping inspection trip lacked the drama and publicity of nighttime cutting-out expeditions, but Wood was shortly to render his most important service to the Confederacy.

The first port Wood visited was Wilmington, and it was there that his influence was most valuable. He found weak defensive works. The only existing obstruction in the Cape Fear River was two miles below the city. It consisted of timbers made into a raft and moored with anchors, and had been swept partially out of place by the current. This surface barrier Wood termed "a very unreliable and imperfect work." Vessels had been sunk at the mouth of the river, but because of the shifting nature of the river bottom they had soon disappeared. Wood urged rows of cribs filled with stone or piles be driven in bunches of four, spaced across the river sufficiently far apart to allow vent to the current, and reaching just below the low-water mark. In addition, he advised the river be mined as quickly as possible, using the few available on the site but not yet placed. Most of the shore batteries covering the water approaches, in Wood's judgment, were well situated and constructed, but most of the guns (over one hundred of them), consisting of 24- and 32-pounders, were too small. Of the two major defensive installations, both needed improvement. Some betterments were underway on Fort Caswell, where the masonry was being covered with sand as far as possible, and two faces of the fort were being fortified with inclined timbers cov-

ered with sandbags and railroad iron. Wood advised that Fort
Fisher, a weak masonry work, receive a metal shield, after which
it could repel any waterborne attack. Then Wood made his most
important recommendation: "The great want, the absolute necessity of the place, if it is to be held against a naval attack, is heavy
guns, larger caliber." He especially wanted more ten- and eleven-
inch guns.

Wood continued to the other ports, making suggestions for defense. He was annoyed that nearly all the heavy guns at Charleston were on Fort Sumter, which he considered the weak point of
the area, instead of distributed around the harbor. In the event
of a Federal attack on Charleston, Wood suggested a counter-
thrust at Union-held Port Royal. Such an assault would be spear-
headed by ironclads from Charleston and Savannah. A student of
Civil War ironclads, William N. Still, called Wood's suggestion
"first-rate strategy" because Port Royal, a chief Union naval refueling and provisioning station, was only some twenty-five miles
from Savannah and could be reached by Confederate ironclads,
and its loss would have damaged the effectiveness of the east
coast blockade. Late in the war Davis urged Beauregard to adopt
the plan, to no avail.

Ironclads, the South's great hope for raising the blockade, were
under construction at several places. Yet most of them would be
ineffective as offensive weapons. They were "wanting in power, 3
or 4 knots will not do, as rams some of them are harmless." Wood
was critical of any armor less than five inches and preferred as a
battery two seven-inch and two nine-inch guns. He thought
Brooke's banded smoothbores which allowed heavy charges were
fine for very short range, but lacked punch at long range. The
Virginia II of the James River Squadron met most of Wood's speci-
fications and was the most powerful at any time in Confederate
service. She had six inches of armor on the sides and eight inches
on each end, and carried two six-inch and two eight-inch Brooke
rifles. While ironclads of various sizes were slowly being built in
port cities and on riverbanks in the South, Mallory sought to have

them built abroad, and had they not been delayed as well, they would have offered fair prospects for lifting the blockade. Meanwhile, little more could be done to spur domestic construction, which continued to be retarded for lack of men, materials, and frequent calls upon workers to meet the threat of attack.

Conditions at most of the ports confirmed what Wood already knew; there was too much naval inertia caused by mossbacks. He wanted younger, more active men in positions of authority. The navy "must be doing something," he complained, and as a result of his "interesting and instructive" tour, there occurred considerable ferment in naval circles. Several major command changes took place in March, and one of those affected was Tattnall in Savannah, who was relieved of sea duty although he retained command of the naval station. Then on May 1 Congress established a provisional navy. Wood strongly favored the new navy for at least the duration of the war, because in effect it would be an alternate navy not bound by the seniority system, giving greater flexibility in choices of command. Enlisted men were assigned to the new navy, and Davis could appoint, with Senate consent, the officers he wanted from civilian life or the regular navy. Thus without interfering with the rank of the officers in the regular navy, younger and more active men could be put in the provisional navy with increased rank. Wood was now "one of the most influential officers in the Confederate navy," and his efficiency as naval aide explains Davis's scant relation with the Navy Department.

In keeping with Wood's suggestions regarding Wilmington, the Confederates mounted heavy guns at Fort Fisher during May, and the Federals aboard blockaders offshore could see quite clearly that they were of large caliber.[9] This defensive strengthening of the port of Wilmington combined with its natural advantages caused it to be the last active southern port, its river entrance dominated by Fort Fisher until the massive Federal amphibious operation in January 1865. (Two other seaports remained in Confederate hands for some time after they were effectively blockaded. The harbor defenses at Charleston successfully resisted all assaults, although Sumter's guns, as Wood had predicted, were silenced. Mobile fell 5 August 1864. The ability of the Confederacy to hold its last few forts as long as it did was "one of the surprising features of the war.")[10] That Lee's troops did not stay in the field after Wilmington was finally closed is probably not coincidental. Southern hopes were bound up in access to the sea—without it they could not continue the war—and it is ironic that Wood himself would later hasten the Union assault that closed this single remaining lifeline of the Confederacy. Nonetheless, Wood's recommendations for the defense of Wilmington constituted by far his most significant, if less colorful, contribution to the southern war effort.

[5]

The Chesapeake Expedition

His inspection duty completed, and finding routine staff duty dull, Wood began in July 1863 to organize his third mission in Virginia waters. Unlike the two previous raids, in which he had captured only merchant vessels, Wood hoped this time to board Federal gunboats on Chesapeake Bay. These Union vessels were making a stringent effort to suppress partisan warfare in eastern Virginia, often cruising far up the rivers to capture locals suspected of either blockade running across the Chesapeake or sniping at Federal ships from the river banks. In gathering his strike force, Wood, aware that it was increasingly difficult to prevent reports of troop movements out of Richmond from reaching the enemy, attempted to insure secrecy by organizing directly under Davis. Wood and Davis did not mention the raid to the other members of the president's staff, and bypassed the Navy Department as often as possible. Wood's note to Lieutenant Frank L. Hoge was typical: "Come up and see me this evening. I have something important to communicate."[1]

Careful planning was important, especially in selecting men who would climb aboard an enemy gunboat and subdue her crew with blazing revolvers and slashing cutlasses. There could be no hesitation when first recognized by the Federals or in the action on deck. Retreat at these critical times could be fatal because the intended victim might then run down the raiders, or bring her big guns to bear on the small boats. Each man selected was also capable of carrying out a specific task aboard ship—that of engineer, fireman, gunner—constituting in the aggregate a full crew with the training necessary for operating a fighting ship. Because of the hazardous nature of the duty, Wood's raiders were a volunteer outfit.

Wood slowly gathered the men, equipment, and supplies for the raid. On August 12, satisfied that all was ready, he moved his special force out of Richmond along the Mechanicsville Road. The destination and objective of the raid were unknown to the seventy-one men and eleven officers, mostly from the *Virginia II* of the James River Squadron. They were well armed and had four boarding cutters. Long after the raiders had disappeared down the road, one member of the crew, late in reporting because he had been on leave in Richmond, urged onward a jolting horse to catch up with the party. He finally managed to do it after a pursuit of three days. This mysterious figure, who accompanied Wood on this and successive raids, was a navy man who wrote accounts of the expeditions as a correspondent for the *Richmond Dispatch*, and is a subject for interesting speculation. Apparently a physician, he called himself simply "Bohemian."[2]

Within a few days, Wood reached the Piankatank River, one of the smaller streams of eastern Virginia, which he selected as a base camp in order to avoid the enemy. In spite of all his precautions regarding the covert operation, a spy reported the expedition to the Federals. Already at the urging of Welles, Commodore Andrew A. Harwood, commander of the Potomac Flotilla, had sent general instructions in pamphlet form to the flotilla's gunboat commanders warning against Wood's attacks, and at this point Harwood issued a full alert with orders that all ships must stay within supporting distance of each other. Thus unknown to Wood, the enemy knew he was coming to attack them. When Wood later reported the breach of security to Davis, the president complained: "I have despaired in the present condition of Richmond to keep secret any movement which is to be made from or through this place."[3]

On the night of August 16 Wood bivouacked on the rolling ground near Turk's Ferry, twenty-five miles up the Piankatank from its mouth at Chesapeake Bay. After the boats were launched in a small creek that flowed into the river, he reconnoitered while his men rested on the grass and cooked over low fires, their camp hidden from view by the surrounding hills. From local activists Wood learned that the gunboats usually positioned at the mouth of the Piankatank had recently been seen on station. When he returned to camp, Wood informed his men for the first time that the objective of the raid was to board and capture a blockader. Excitement mounted as the departure routine began. Wood mustered his command to inspect arms and distribute ammunition. Since the usual practice of rallying around a flag was not suited to a cutting-out exercise, each of Wood's men wore a white armband around the left arm to distinguish comrades in the night battle on the enemy's deck. After Wood said a prayer, the spirited men entered the boarding cutters.

The raiders pulled for the mouth of the Piankatank, making no sound but a soft rippling of water around the bows of the boats. As they neared the entrance to the Bay, Wood saw a light, then he made out two gunboats in the darkness, and finally he heard the sounds of machines in motion. In anticipation of his coming, the ship's commanders had their vessels underway—the best possible defense against boarders. Forced to abandon the hunt for the night, Wood's men rowed some five miles up the river and entered Slum's Creek for concealment. Thoroughly exhausted, officers and men fell on the ground for a few hours' sleep.

Wood had chosen an inopportune time to camp on that particular site, as events the next morning proved. Soon after daylight a gunboat of the North Atlantic Squadron, the U.S.S. *General Putnam,* which was in the area on an incursion against local blockade runners, chugged directly for Wood's camp. Acting Master William J. Hotchkiss, commander of the steamer, had learned of some suspicious-looking craft in the creek and was determined to destroy them. When Hotchkiss anchored near Wood's bivouac and manned five boats, Wood correctly assumed the ship was in pursuit of him, so he quickly formed his plan of

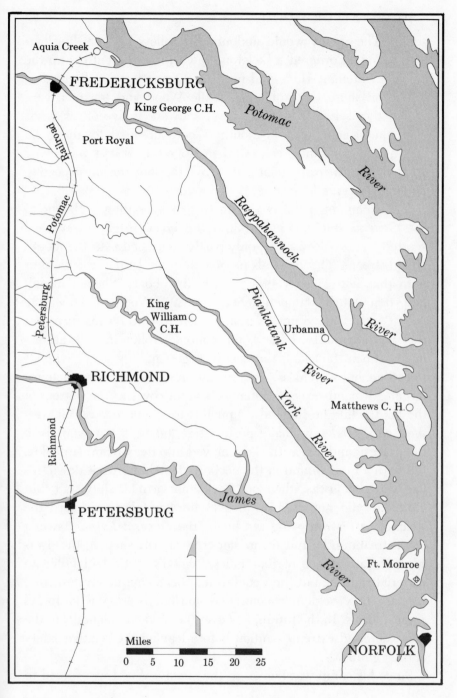

Virginia waters

action. The enemy would undoubtedly follow his boarding cutters, so Wood ordered a skeleton crew to row the cutters up the
creek. Lieutenant Hoge and most of the party were directed to
follow on shore for protection, while Wood and ten men concealed themselves in some undergrowth about five or six yards
from the stream near its mouth. Wood intended to allow the
enemy to pass up the creek and then Hoge was to stalk the enemy
on their return to its mouth, thereby trapping the unsuspecting
Federals in a crossfire.

The enemy, eighty strong, with Hotchkiss leading in the gig of
the *General Putnam*, pulled into the creek. Right away they
spotted one of Wood's men only partly concealed near the mouth
of the stream. The Federals immediately fired upon the careless
individual with rifles, yelling from boat to boat: "Shoot him—kill
him—don't let the damned Rebel get away!" Wood still hoped the
enemy would move upstream and tried to restrain his men, but
they were bound to respond, and poured a volley into the attacking boatmen. Shocked, the enemy began pulling away without
reloading, but Hotchkiss's boat ran aground and became a helpless
target. All hands except Hotchkiss sought cover in the bottom of
the boat, while he shouted commands for them to push off with
their oars. His crew finally pushed free, taking a few wounds in
the process, and just as the boat moved into the stream, Hotchkiss
fell with a fatal wound in the neck. As Hotchkiss went down, his
flag was shot away, then put back upon a makeshift staff, but
Hotchkiss did not rise. He died as he was taken on board the
steamer. After retrieving the boats, the *General Putnam* swung
downstream under full steam, her crew angrily shelling the river-
bank for a distance of four miles.[4] Wood's tactic had failed to
materialize fully, but the Federals had been completely surprised
because they seldom encountered spirited resistance in forays
against locals. In the future, however, Federal commanders in the
area exercised extreme caution before leaving the relative safety
of their gunboats.

Since his camp was known to the enemy, Wood was forced to

alter his base of operations. That afternoon the raiders pulled up the Piankatank to their original point of embarkation at Turk's Ferry and by dark had loaded the boats on the wagons. Wood then moved overland to the Rappahannock, arriving August 19, and launched the boats in Meachum's Creek ten miles upstream from the Chesapeake. The mouth of the river, three to four miles wide, was the station for three Potomac Flotilla gunboats—Wood's new targets.

Mustering his command in late afternoon, Wood started down the creek and pulled out into the river at sunset. As the summer night settled over the Rappahannock, the line of dark boats loaded with armed men glided along under bright stars and a crescent moon, while the cries of birds and insects filled the evening. Upon reaching the mouth of the river late in the night, Wood learned from friendly pickets on the bank that the blockaders were three miles out on the Bay. He called up the other boats alongside his, gave a final briefing and a prayer, and ordered his command onward across the heavier waters of the Chesapeake. But after a careful search, Wood found nothing to attack, and he broke off the hunt in time to return to Meachum's Creek by dawn. There he hid his boats and bivouacked for the day. The same routine was followed the next night, but again there was no sign of the enemy.

On August 21 Wood rested his men while he rendezvoused with Colonel Thomas L. Rosser, commander of the Fifth Virginia Cavalry. Rosser, whose men were mostly from surrounding counties and knew every road and trail in them, had received secret orders to place his regiment at Wood's disposal, and after two days of hard riding from his camp at Fredericksburg, reined in at Saluda, the county seat of Middlesex County. As the two cavalry colonels conferred against the background of a blazing sunset, Wood confirmed Rosser's tentative destination of nearby Urbanna on the Rappahannock, thus providing a port guarded against enemy attack where the raiders could bring any captured prizes. Assured that this part of his plan was taken care of, Wood returned to his bivouac at Meachum's Creek.

The weather was changing rapidly on Saturday night, August 22, as Wood's men again pulled down the Rappahannock to the Chesapeake. The stars began to dim, the moon grew red over the trees, the pines cast foreboding shadows on the water, and the air became still and sultry. Black clouds rose in the sky and produced frequent flashes of lightning as gusts of wind agitated the waters. When the Confederates reached the Bay, the northerly storm broke into full fury, tossing the cutters like children's toys upon the waves.

Suddenly, as the raiders moved along Stingray Point off the lower end of Middlesex County, a flash of lightning revealed two enemy gunboats just off the bows, one-fourth mile from land and some two hundred yards apart, their dark hulls rising in the turbulent waters. Wood called up the other boats and outlined the plan of attack, shouting to be heard above the noisy storm. The gunboats were so close together that it would be necessary to board both simultaneously, and Wood assigned two cutters to each gunboat, with instructions to board at both the port and starboard bow of each intended victim. Carrying the forward sections of the ships first would prevent the crews of the blockaders from slipping the anchor chains and getting underway. Wood, in the second cutter, took command of the cutters numbered one and two, and assigned boats three and four to Hoge. Armbands were checked, Wood said a prayer, and all was in readiness for the advance.

The four cutters moved forward at midnight. Maintaining a line position until within hailing distance, the raiders then separated into pairs of two abreast for the final approach. Wood headed for the port bow of his target and sent the first cutter to the other side. When within fifty yards of the gunboat, Wood heard the challenge of watchman Nelson Frazier, a former slave, singing out above the roar of the storm: "Boat ahoy!" Wood answered, quite truthfully: "Second Cutters." At this, the raiders entered a short period of extreme tension. "Bohemian," in the first cutter, described the feeling and the scene:

It was a moment of anxiety—almost of misgiving. If the Yankees were aware of our approach, destruction was certain. There was no retreat now—death lay in the silent guns ahead and in the mad waters around. The waves had increased, and the sea was fast lashing itself into a fury. Long black lines started from the horizon, ran towards us like some huge leviathan, for a moment raised us in the air, then rolled away in the dusky distance. The sentinel's hail was the signal to give way, and every man put his whole strength to the oars. Our boat nearly sprang out of the water at every stroke, and shot over the waves with the velocity of an arrow. In a few seconds the dark hull rose before us, the boat struck its sides, there were a few shots; and, as quick as thought, twenty of us were climbing over the nettings upon her decks.[5]

The raiders were alongside before Frazier realized the danger, but as the assailants climbed into the anti-boarding netting, a ship's officer ran through the gangway shouting "boarders!" Wood, who insisted on the deadly honor of being the first on board, cut his way through the netting and reached the deck ahead of his men, while Lieutenant William E. Hudgins, in charge of the first cutter, led the way on the starboard side.

Once the Confederates were on board, the tension was released in battle at close quarters. Wood was dispersing his men across the ship as the sleeping crew members were roused from their hammocks. Master at Arms William Bingman, when wakened, was able to distribute only three pistols. One crewman, trying to grab a boarding pike, was hit in the head by a cutlass, and another was killed by a bullet. The most able defense of the vessel was made by Acting Ensign Rudolph Sommers, the executive officer, who engaged the boarders although he was unarmed, and received one bullet and two cutlass wounds. On the other hand, the captain of the gunboat, Acting Master John F. D. Robinson, wanted nothing to do with these midnight raiders who had boarded his ship during a storm. When a crewman ran to his cabin and reported the boarders, Robinson said simply: "Drive them off." He then turned into his cabin and closed the door. When Wood learned that Robinson was in the captain's cabin, he had the Union commander brought to the quarterdeck and ordered him to yell out to his crew that he surrendered the ship. Observing a French revolver pointed at his head and his crew engaged in a desperate hand-to-hand struggle, a shaken Robinson, standing in his underclothes, shouted: "For God's sake, don't shoot. I surrender." Robinson's words caused all resistance to cease, and Wood was the ship's new commander.

The fight had lasted less than ten minutes. The gunboat crew suffered five wounded and two killed; Wood had no casualties. Resistance had been feeble chiefly because of the surprise element, and because no officer had organized the crew to repel boarders. Sommers had set a courageous example by his personal action, but the desired effect was certainly lost upon the engineer, Isaac Johnson, who, after observing Sommers taking multiple wounds, had remained inactive. As a result, there had been no effort to get the gunboat underway.

Once the deck was secured, Wood turned his attention toward the other gunboat. Peering through the darkness, he looked for the prearranged signal from Hoge that the deck was won. Instead, the sounds of sharp firing could be heard above the howl of the wind and crash of sea and storm. Wood immediately sent off a boat to brave the broken waters between the vessels and carry assistance to the Confederates on the other deck.

Hoge had run into determined resistance. When his two cutters approached the other blockader, lookout John Hand immediately awakened the crew, and the men grabbed cutlasses and side arms as they came up the hatch. The ship's commander, Acting Ensign Henry Walters, unlike Robinson, jumped from his hammock on the quarterdeck and ran forward, shouting for someone to slip the cable. A crewman with hammer and chisel, attempting to obey, was shot down before he could drive out the pin. Walters was cut on the hand and shot twice; the second ball, which entered his stomach and came out his hip, sent him reeling onto the pilot-house steps. As he sank to the deck, Walters, unaware the other gunboat had been captured, managed to give a futile blow on the signal whistle. Of the Confederate leaders, Hoge, first on deck, was wounded by a shot through his neck and went down beside the watertank. Midshipman H. S. Cooke received two bullets in the side, but after the bleeding was checked, he assumed command for the severely wounded Hoge. Several members of the crew fought hard, but soon the firing became desultory as members of the crew were captured one by one. Three boarders were wounded; Walters and eight Federal crewmen were wounded, and two were dead. Wood's reinforcements arrived just as the fight ended.

Among the crew members of the two prizes were several Confederate deserters and runaway slaves, who had all the more reason to fear capture, and resistance seems to have been based as much on each crewman's personal situation as on his duty. The two gunboat commanders, Robinson and Walters, later faced a court of inquiry set up by Welles. The court found that Robinson, the ranking officer, had ordered the anchorage in spite of specific warning against raiders. He had taken the insufficient precautions of having the vessels come to bouy within hailing distance of each other by whistle, and erecting anti-boarding nettings. The court concluded that at first hailing, the gunboats should have slipped their cables and gotten underway. Thus the captures resulted from "negligence and incapacity," and Robinson had shown cowardice. When Welles dismissed both commanders from the service, Walters, rather understandably, considered his discharge unfair.[6]

As soon as Wood learned that both gunboats had been captured, he ordered the two vessels be made ready to get underway. Appropriate officers took possession of the engine rooms, pilothouses, quarterdecks, and other parts of the ships, while the prisoners and wounded were taken below. Wood's men also tied the boarding cutters fast astern for towing, coiled unused rope, built up steam, and prepared the guns for action.

While the Confederate crews made the ships taut, Wood had a chance to take a cursory look at his prizes. He had boarded and captured the U.S.S. *Satellite*, a wooden sidewheel steamer of 217 tons, carrying a 32-pound smoothbore, a 12-pound howitzer, and a 40-man crew. The *Satellite's* successful career since joining the Potomac Flotilla included the capture of five ships. The other gunboat, the U.S.S. *Reliance*, a smaller screw steamer of 90 tons and a crew of 40, carried a 32-pound Parrott and a 24-pound howitzer. (The U.S.S. *Currituck*, a 198-ton screw steamer mounting five guns, also assigned to the station, was away at the time on a refueling run.) Wood gave command of the C.S.S. *Reliance* to Hudgins, next in command after the wounded Hoge. With the first gray of daylight, Wood moved out in the C.S.S. *Satellite*, followed by Hudgins in the *Reliance*. The two gunboats stood well up the calmer waters of the Rappahannock, and about sunrise, after a voyage of three hours, dropped anchor off Urbanna, the friendly village protected by Rosser's cavalry.[7]

At Urbanna, Wood directed Midshipman Matthew P. Goodwyn to take charge of moving the wounded, Union and Confederate, from both ships and collecting them in one place for treatment. They were taken to a local residence, "Roseguild," where, in the absence of a qualified Union medical officer from either ship, "Bohemian" and the women of the village cared for them until the arrival of a local physician. As for the prisoners, Wood delivered them—the Confederate deserters and runaway slaves shackled in irons—to Rosser for cavalry escort to Libby Prison.

Wood was determined to continue the raid, although there was only a small quantity of coal aboard the prizes. He divided the several hours' supply between the two gunboats, and took on board three officers and thirty sharpshooters from Rosser's cavalry. A usual complement for a fighting ship, the sharpshooters were especially welcomed by Wood since he had only enough men to man the ships, and he might engage enemy gunboats. At 8:00 P.M. on August 23 the balky engines of the *Reliance* built sufficient steam to move off, and Wood stood down the Rappahannock, expecting to encounter the gunboat *Currituck*. Once underway, Hudgins in the *Reliance* could make only two knots because of

escaping steam pressure. This malfunction was perhaps the work
of the ship's former engineer, who had sabotaged the engines
when he first realized she had been captured. In any event, since
the *Reliance* was unable to live up to her name, Wood sent her
back to Urbanna and continued down the river in the *Satellite*,
but when he reached the mouth there was no sign of the *Currituck*.

Another storm was threatening as Wood stood out onto the Bay
at 11:00 P.M., steaming boldly through the swells in search of
other prey. An increasingly strong wind from the southeast rolled
up the waters of the Bay until the *Satellite* "creaked and groaned
in every seam, and ran heavily against the sea, as if trying to com-
mit suicide." Wood set a course for the eastern shore, and soon
made out a few small white sails barely visible against the darkness, but he wanted to see what else was afloat in those waters. By
1:00 A.M. on Monday, August 24, the pitching sea treated the
Satellite so roughly that the dismounted cavalrymen on board
wore faces of varying shades of pale green. The swirling waters
rendered boarding by positioning the ship alongside a victim impossible, and the boarding cutters would certainly have swamped.
Still Wood continued to hunt for another hour before reluctantly
ordering a course for the Rappahannock. Off Stingray Point Wood
signaled, thinking the *Currituck* might be on station, but no response lighted the howling darkness, and the *Satellite* continued
into the river during the cool morning hours. Wood brought the
gunboat to buoy five miles upstream at Gray's Point, where the
exhausted crew and seasick sharpshooters dropped to the deck
and slept.

The wind and sea remained high throughout the day as Wood
watched and waited. When at dusk three sails appeared in the
Bay, he ran out of the river flying the U.S. flag and steamed for
the largest. After a two-hour chase, the *Satellite* overhauled the
Union commercial vessel off Gwyn's Island near the mouth of
the Piankatank. She was the schooner *Golden Rod*. Wood hailed
the surprised victim: "What is your cargo and where bound?" The

response fell pleasantly on Wood's ears: "From Baltimore to Maine laden with coal." Wood's reply was much less welcomed to the seven-man crew aboard the schooner: "You are my prisoners and the vessel a prize of the Southern Confederacy." Standing up the Bay with his large prize filled with precious fuel in tow, Wood next seized the two small schooners which had anchored near the mouth of the Rappahannock. They were the *Coquette*, fifty tons, and the *Two Brothers*, forty-seven tons, both anchor sweepers from Old Point for Philadelphia, each with a four-man crew and a total of 43,000 pounds of anchors and chains. Wood set a course for Urbanna, his three unwilling catches dangling at the end of their tow lines as if aware of their fate.

The capture of the commercial vessels had taken most of the night, and it was Tuesday, August 25, when Wood again dropped anchor off Urbanna. He remained long enough to pull the *Satellite* alongside the *Golden Rod* to take on coal. "Bohemian" visited the wounded with a few luxuries taken from the prizes, and the mystery doctor found Hoge happily on the mend. Meanwhile, the three sailing vessels were prepared for burning, and Wood instructed Hudgins to fire them should the enemy appear before the *Satellite* returned from another cruise. Wood sent Davis and Mallory a brief progress report on the raid, and the president forwarded the news to Lola with the comment: "I hope we shall soon see him and he will give a fuller account to us of his adventures."[8]

Impatient to be under steam again, Wood was in port only a few hours before lifting anchor for the mouth of the river, where he anchored two miles upstream and sent off a boat to question pickets on shore regarding the *Currituck*. He learned she had returned to station, communicated with the shore, and stood under full steam in the direction of Fort Monroe. Wood had missed the ship. As the day wore on, the sea seemed higher than ever, white caps were frequent, and the paced melancholy of the breakers could be heard aboard the *Satellite*. Late in the afternoon, as Wood scanned the Bay, he was not surprised to spot in the distance smoke rising from the smokestacks of three large gunboats

making their way across the heavy seas toward his position. Greatly outgunned, Wood could not make a stand. He could steam onto
the Bay before their arrival, which he preferred to do, but the sea
was too rough for the engines of the *Satellite,* and his reason prevailed over his boldness. Reluctantly, he ordered a course for
Urbanna.

Wood arrived at the river port ahead of a violent storm and
anchored close to the *Reliance,* which was coaling alongside the
Golden Rod. The weather put an end to any further moves by
pursuer and pursued for the night. At dawn the river continued
to run rough under a clearing sky. Wood was active at first light
making preparations to steam upriver to Port Royal where the big
gunboats of the enemy could not follow. The *Golden Rod* drew
eleven feet of water, too much for easy navigation in the upstream
reaches, and since her cargo of coal had been much reduced by
coaling the gunboats, Wood stripped and fired the large schooner
on the spot, the flames of the vessel sending out a circle of heat in
the early morning chill. Rosser's cavalrymen were sent ashore,
where a few of the troops escorted the prisoners from the three
schooners to Richmond, while the others rode back to their camp
at Fredericksburg. Wood allowed the enemy wounded, including
the officers Walters and Sommers, to remain at Urbanna to be
taken by the Union forces gathering at the mouth of the river.

With the *Coquette* and the *Two Brothers* in tow, the *Satellite*
and the *Reliance* stood upstream, the engines of the *Reliance*
apparently working better, and the two pulled against a strong
ebb tide and headwind. But soon the wind died and the sun appeared. As the weather moderated, Wood hoisted a Confederate
flag on the *Satellite,* and from some old bunting the men of the
Reliance, not to be outdone, fashioned a small flag of the new
pattern, with white field and battle-flag union (the "National Flag"
adopted by the Confederate Congress on 1 May 1863). The little
Confederate fleet, a novelty on the waters, caused quite a sensa-
tion en route. Some people on shore cheered, but others, more
suspicious, thought there must be some Yankee obliquity astir.

The upper Rappahannock was beautiful in summer. The river narrowed between high hills that sloped gradually to the water. Cultivated fields and splendid houses on both sides dotted a natural setting of woodland, and toward the end of the day, as if to honor the view, a peaceful twilight contrasted with the generally stormy weather of the past few days.

Coming to Port Royal, where the Forty-seventh and Forty-eighth Alabama regiments were protecting a foraging train of wagons, the little armada was hailed from shore and warned not to approach too closely until identified. Wood sent in a boat to make known the character of his ships and soon heard welcoming shouts. Early the next morning, Thursday, August 27, Wood went ashore. A group of women in Port Royal wanted to visit the gunboats, and Wood, accustomed to this tradition from long naval experience, consented. Before long news reached him that Union troops were reported at King George Courthouse, fifteen miles away, and could be expected to attack as soon as they learned of his arrival with the prizes. Hence Wood decided to strip and scuttle the vessels. Everything of value was taken, including engines, three guns (one was lost overboard), and well over $26,000 in anchors and chains. At one point during the two-day operation, the enemy shelled the position from the opposite bank without injury, and the Confederates replied with the guns taken from the gunboats. The captured equipment was moved by wagon to Milford Station on the Richmond to Fredericksburg railroad. Wood wired Lola that he would soon be with her, then scuttled all four vessels, loaded his cutters, and returned to Richmond.[9]

Wood's Rappahannock expedition shocked the North and embarrassed the Potomac Flotilla. Months after the raid, Federal naval commanders believed Wood was hiding in the creeks below the Piankatank, ready to strike again. Commodore Harwood of the Potomac Flotilla warned Admiral S. P. Lee, commander of the North Atlantic Squadron, to "watch for Wood." Harwood was aware of Wood's mobility and knew it would require an experienced officer to ferret out the Confederate sea fox. When Lieutenant Edward Hooker of the U.S.S. *Freeborn*, who confirmed the destruction of the captured vessels, volunteered to search for Wood, Harwood consented, but only after permission was received directly from Welles. Hooker demonstrated for two months; several times he saw cavalry units on the river banks and thought they were cover for Wood. On one occasion he became convinced that Wood had returned to Slum's Creek off the Piankatank and wanted to "look up that creek," but Harwood pointed out that Hotchkiss was "killed from ambush" there. "Sound discretion" was necessary when looking for Wood. Harwood advised him to get reliable information on the location and strength of the enemy, then "proceed prudently and well prepared." Small wonder that while Hooker found much that was suspicious on the Piankatank, he did not "deem it prudent to send my boats out of the range of my guns."[10]

Although Wood's raids could not win the war or arrest the overwhelming increase in Union gunboats, the raids certainly justified the detailing of seamen for a few weeks from the mostly inactive James River Squadron. In one raid on waters controlled by the enemy, he had captured and destroyed two gunboats and three commercial vessels, seized valuable equipment for the Confederate navy, carried off some ninety prisoners, and had not lost a man in the process. The raid also boosted Confederate naval morale during a year of southern military reverses that foretold the outcome of the war. After 1863, the key to success against the northern giant seemed to lie in bringing more supplies into the Confederacy, which could be done in two ways: capturing enemy supplies and raising the blockade. It was to this problem of dwindling southern subsistence that Wood next turned his attention.

[6]

Raid in
North Carolina
Waters

As the autumn of 1863 deepened, Wood, who had quietly resumed his duties as aide, often took a late-afternoon horseback ride with Davis. If either man realized it was also the autumn of the Confederacy, the fact was not revealed in their conversation. The President and his nephew rode through the falling leaves of Richmond discussing the future course of the war, particularly the role of the navy. They agreed that the rivers and sounds of eastern North Carolina should be recaptured from the Federals because control of these waters gave the enemy a much more effective blockade of the entire state than was possible by patrolling off the outer banks, and provided a base for the important blockade of Wilmington. Furthermore, Union control of the eastern seaboard threatened the Wilmington to Weldon Railroad, a key line connecting Richmond with Wilmington and from there the South and outside world. Wood and Davis were also aware that retaking eastern North Carolina would provide the Confederacy with enormous supplies, and reduce the strong Unionist sentiment in the Tarheel state. By December, when Davis promoted him to the rank of commander in the navy, effective August 23, for "gallant and meritorious conduct" in the Chesapeake expedition, Wood was already considering another raid.

Early in January 1864 as the first snow of the winter quietly covered Richmond, Wood departed for eastern North Carolina to carry out "verbal instructions" and report back to the president. Confederate ironclad rams were under construction near Halifax on the Roanoke River, in preparation for action against Union-held Plymouth; at Tarboro on the Tar River for action against Little Washington; and at Kinston on the Neuse River for action against New Bern. Wood undoubtedly inspected the ironclads under construction, and began developing plans for a joint expedition into eastern North Carolina by land and sea, in which, due to delays in the building of the ironclads, he would employ his "navy on wheels" in the water phase of the attack. Wood believed that the long period of routine patrol duty had made Union forces in eastern North Carolina careless, and a Confederate surprise attack would not only regain territory, but at the same time result in the capture of enemy gunboats to form the forefront of new Confederate forces afloat in the sounds of North Carolina. (The importance of capturing the Union gunboats on the Neuse had already been demonstrated. An earlier attack on Fort Anderson, an earthwork on the Neuse, by General J. Johnston Pettigrew on 14 March 1863 ended in failure when two Union gunboats opened on the Confederate batteries, driving Pettigrew from the field while covering the landing of Union reinforcements.)[1]

Shortly after Wood returned to Richmond, he visited Lee's headquarters to discuss the use of troops for the land assault in connection with the waterborne raid. Lee realized the potential for more supplies and equipment for his army should the South regain control of eastern North Carolina. He vowed that had he not been needed in Virginia that winter for the very purpose of keeping his men fed and clothed, he would take personal command of the attack; instead, he selected General George E. Pickett as army commander. Lee regretted the ironclads were not completed because without them, although the expedition might prove successful, continued control of the waters would be less certain. Yet captured gunboats might suffice until the rams were completed, which Lee urged finished as soon as possible. Lee wished

Wood "all success," and commended him to the care of "Divine Providence." Then the general added reassuringly, "I have endeavored to anticipate everything."[2]

During the last two weeks of January, Wood organized the naval portion of the expedition. The Navy Department sent telegrams to officers in Richmond, Wilmington, and Charleston to detail handpicked crews, fully armed, equipped, and provisioned, to report to Wood for special service. From the James River Squadron came a select group of men and officers under the command of Lieutenant Benjamin P. Loyall, who was serving as commandant of midshipmen on the Confederate naval schoolship *Patrick Henry,* and who became Wood's second in command. The men were armed with rifles, cutlasses, and as far as possible, revolvers, and provided with forty rounds of ammunition. They also had rations for several days, cooking utensils, and a few axes. Well-clothed and shod against the winter cold, they each wore a pea-jacket and carried a blanket, but had no spare uniform as they would travel light. There were ten boats from the Richmond area, and Wood had learned from experience to order a strip of canvas tacked around inside the gunwales to provide a protective cover for arms and equipment.

For the sake of secrecy, Wood avoided loading his boats in Richmond. At 9:00 A.M. on January 28 he sent the contingent, with Loyall in command, down the James River for Petersburg. The next morning Wood met the party in Petersburg, and instead of using wagons, loaded the boats on railroad cars. Working before the local residents were awake, his men placed the boats on the cars rightside up on their keels and lashed them into position. Then the men took their places in the boats and in this way made the two-day trip to Kinston, the point of rendezvous with the units from Charleston and Wilmington. Along the line, the midshipmen waved their hats to the astonished natives, and at several stations exacted promises from local girls that a kiss could be claimed for each enemy flag captured. Arriving in Kinston during the dark hours of Sunday morning the thirty-first,

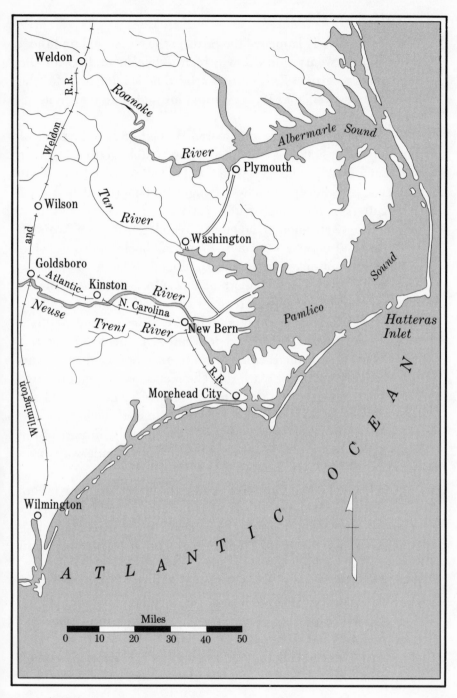

Eastern North Carolina

Wood immediately launched the boats in the Neuse and sent them to an island twenty miles downstream while he waited for the other units to arrive. Kinston was a bustling staging area for the land forces as well, and Wood wanted his raiders to remain as inconspicuous as possible.

In Wilmington, Lieutenant George W. Gift gathered a force of 125 men and 10 officers, but was having trouble getting together the equipment specified by Wood. Gift finally secured two boats and two very heavy launches. Longer and more flat-bottomed than cutters, each launch had a capacity of 45 men, and each mounted a twelve-pound howitzer. Wood wanted the boats to have oars and necessary fittings—grappling hooks and ropes—but ordered Gift not to lose time since the Richmond unit would carry extra parts. It was more important to load the boats on railroad cars and proceed to Goldsboro, rendezvous with Lieutenant Philip Porcher with a detachment of men from Charleston, and continue to Kinston. When Gift arrived in Kinston at noon on Sunday, many hours behind the Richmond contingent, he found an anxious Wood pacing the depot platform. The men soon dragged the two small boats down to the river, but the heavy launches could not be easily moved, so Wood directed Gift to unload them as soon as possible, while Wood, eager to start, moved out with part of the force to join the others. He now had twelve boats underway down the Neuse.[3]

Wood pulled down the Neuse until after sunset, stepping ashore at the bivouac on the small island as his men were finishing their evening meal. He assembled the raiders, 150 or more, including 25 marines under Captain Thomas S. Wilson, for a briefing. Until this time the seamen had been told neither the object nor destination of their mission, but from the name of the commander they knew it would be "nervous work" since he had a reputation for boarding and capturing enemy vessels. Speaking in distinct and terse terms, Wood gave orders dividing the boats into two divisions, one under Loyall and the other under himself, with explicit instructions to each boat's crew. The destination, he said, was New

Bern, a town located on a point of land where the Neuse and Trent rivers met near Pamlico Sound. For nearly two years the Federals had occupied New Bern; they had cut down trees two miles around the town to give a clear view for their artillery fire, and had built fortifications over a twenty-mile area. To strengthen further their position and guard against a surprise attack, three or four gunboats were anchored off the dock at New Bern or cruised the Neuse and Trent rivers. Wood pointed out that their mission was to capture any of the enemy gunboats found at buoy while Pickett's land forces attacked the town. The naval raid would occur that night, after rowing some forty more miles down the Neuse to New Bern.

Wood's men now knew the expedition would involve hand-to-hand fighting, and that they would either capture the enemy or be destroyed. Picked for their vigor and determination, they considered the plan a grand scheme, and would have cheered had not Wood called for strict silence. According to one member of the party, the plan was received by the older men "with looks of admiration" and by "rapture" on the part of the young midshipmen. In his traditional prayer Wood offered up "the most touching appeal to the Almighty," asking God to judge between his men and the enemy.[4] Then each man put on his white armband, and Wood gave "Sumter" as the password. All in readiness, the men manned the boats and pulled silently on the oars.

Descending the Neuse was somewhat like traveling through a series of giant watery hourglasses cut lengthwise and laid end to end. The stream was first narrow and deep, then broadened markedly, forming a succession of little lakes. The two black lines of boats moved down the river with no sound but the steady dip of the oars and whispers of the men discussing their chances of surviving the audacious assault, the latter interrupted occasionally by wild ducks rising at their approach, a startled muskrat jumping from the wet banks to the depths, or the sudden screech of an owl. Gnarled cypress trunks and huge junipers lined the low banks and formed a part of the unbroken forest wall on either side, while the water oaks almost locked their large branches over the stream. Occasionally a fallen log impeded progress, or a boat would run aground, causing those astern to crash into it, the boats of the entire line piling into each other. Behind schedule because of the delay in starting and the intricacy of the river, Wood kept the cold and weary men at the oars hour after hour.

By 3:00 A.M. Wood noticed the river was wider and ran through low marshland. An hour later, after passing two Union picket points unchallenged, the raiders pulled out onto the broad waters at New Bern, taking the familiar salt air as they ran toward the lights of the town in double columns. The night was dark and foggy with light rain. Surprisingly, no ship could be found. Wood searched hard, even up to and around the wharves of the town. He could hear strange voices, probably from the sentries on the dock, but he looked in vain for the prey. With daybreak near, he returned three or four miles up the Neuse and entered Bachelor's Creek, where he camped on a small island covered with tall grass, reeds, and shrubs. He ordered the boats dragged into cover and set up pickets. It was hard for the men to let down from the pitch of excitement and expectation, but they soon fell exhausted to the ground.

At first light the seamen were jolted awake by the discovery that some distance away, but in plain sight of the bivouac, was a tall crow's nest occupied by a Federal lookout on picket duty. Loyall wrote that "I assure you it gave us a creepy, uneasy, feeling to think that our whole movement and intention might be discovered." Then he continued:

And here let me remark that this very situation determines and exemplified what I judge to be a man of war—a leader who does not allow his plans to be upset by what he thinks the enemy is going to do. He must be always combative and not calculating chances. Wood paid no attention to doubts and surmises, but had his eye fixed upon boarding and capturing [enemy ships] and doing his part in the fall of New Bern.[5]

Shortly after sunrise Wood heard sharp firing on the right, and while his men took cold rations, he communicated with Pickett.

The Confederate ground forces had begun a three-pronged assault on New Bern. Plans called for Pickett to march out of Kinston at 1:00 A.M. on February 1 and launch a frontal attack on the town with two brigades of infantry. Meanwhile, General Seth M. Barton, with twelve companies of cavalry and twelve guns, had crossed the Trent the day before to carry out a crucial phase of the attack. Barton was to prevent Federal reinforcements by cutting the Atlantic and North Carolina Railroad to Morehead City, then storm across the railroad bridge into the town from the rear. At the same time Colonel James Dearing, with a regiment each of infantry and cavalry and two guns, crossed the Neuse to threaten Fort Anderson and prevent reinforcements from reaching New Bern over the road from Little Washington. The three ground units were to attack simultaneously Monday morning in a well-conceived plan that showed definite promise. Pickett's entire command consisted of about 4,500 men and fourteen guns. Wood's naval force consisted of over 250 men, two launches with howitzers, and twelve boats. To help assure Confederate success at New Bern, Lee had also ordered a detachment from Wilmington to create a diversion by attacking the Federals in the vicinity of Morehead City.

Pickett opened the attack in good order. One of his brigade commanders, Robert F. Hoke, a North Carolina brigadier general, slammed into the Federals, who made a determined stand near Bachelor's Creek.[6] Although the enemy burned the bridge, Hoke crossed after daylight and pressed hard toward New Bern. It was this firing that Wood's men heard, and as it came nearer and then faded during the day, the raiders knew the Federals were in full retreat. Finally came the report of the guns of the fortifications as the Confederates neared the town. Three large forts and two parks of field artillery effectively protected New Bern from a frontal assault, and Pickett listened anxiously for the sounds of Barton's guns on the rear of the town, which he expected any moment, but the day wore away and there was no news from Barton.

By late afternoon Pickett stood under a tree in full view of New Bern and its fortifications. He was staring towards the Trent. His staff lay on the ground around him, waiting. The general nervously twirled his sword knot around his hand and bit his fingernails. Up rode Hoke. Dismounting, he reported a Federal advance of cavalry, infantry, and artillery to feel the Confederate strength on the right. "They must be driven back," said Pickett, "Can you do it?" "Yes," replied Hoke in obvious satisfaction, "with my own brigade." He jumped into the saddle and rode away, and half an hour later the thunder of heavy artillery near the town revealed that he had succeeded. But the sun went down with the frontal advance stalemated, and still no news from Barton. Pickett, more perplexed than ever, turned from the field. The day's fighting was over for the Confederate land forces.[7]

Back in Kinston, Gift borrowed two mules to drag his launches from the railroad cars to the river. He then mounted the howitzers, ordered the eighty-two men Wood had left with him into the boats, and pulled away amid the cheers of a group of young women on shore. With forty rowers bending to their oars in each large boat, the launches moved downstream at six or seven miles an hour. At 3:00 A.M. Gift landed to rest his men, and was roused by the initial firing at Bachelor's Creek, which he estimated to be five miles away. Thinking that Wood had gone into action without him, Gift immediately set off for Swift Creek, the point of rendezvous with Wood, but Wood was below Swift Creek. Day had been fast breaking when Wood returned up the Neuse, and he apparently had not wanted to risk losing the element of surprise by being sighted by the Federals, who, when he first arrived at Bachelor's Creek, had not retired into their works at New Bern. This would account for the failure to meet Gift at Swift Creek. At 11:00 A.M. Gift learned from some Confederate army officers who came through his camp that Wood had not yet attacked. Gift then sent a courier to Pickett's headquarters and was informed that Wood's position was only two miles down the river. Late in the afternoon 'there was much less risk that Gift's movement would be sighted by the Federals, so Gift cast off again and landed his launches on Wood's island bivouac at sunset, relieved that his arrival was in time for the action.[8]

Following Barton's mysterious lack of cooperation, the water offensive became not only a key element but the deciding factor in the Confederate effort to retake New Bern, and fate, which often meddles in history, entered the game. During the day, Lieutenant G. W. Graves, senior naval officer at New Bern, stationed the Federal gunboats to aid in the defense of the town. He ordered the U.S.S. *Underwriter* and the U.S.S. *Commodore Hull,* both anchored below the town on the eve of returning to patrol duty at Hatteras, to take up positions on the Neuse to command the plain in front of the town. The *Underwriter* was on station by 9:00 A.M. with all her guns trained on the land approach, but the *Hull* grounded and could not be hauled free during the day. The third and remaining gunboat in the neighborhood was Graves's flagship, the U.S.S. *Lockwood.* Hearing from the Union army commander at New Bern, General Innis N. Palmer, that the Confederates were setting up a battery at Brice's Creek, Graves steamed up the Trent as far as possible and anchored for the night.[9]

Shortly before dark, Wood ordered his swiftest boat manned, and with Loyall embarked to scout the estuary for prey. After pulling two miles along the bank of the river, both Wood and Loyall spotted an enemy ship and said in unison: "There she is." With his field glasses to his eyes, Wood studied the gunboat carefully, calculating her size, structure, crew, and guns, in every available detail. She was a steamer anchored close to the right flank of fortifications. Her guards, consisting of a wooden rail with rope nettings from rail to deck, were low, making her relatively easy to board. On their return to camp, Wood informed Loyall that between midnight and 4:00 A.M. they would attack. The vessel was the *Underwriter.*

A few hours later, at 11:00 P.M., Wood mustered his men at the Bachelor's Creek bivouac. His force, together for the first time, was more than necessary for an attack on one gunboat, but Wood hoped that another vessel would be close by when he arrived. Briefing his raiders in his usual businesslike manner, Wood said the target was about one hundred yards from Battery Number Two, and somewhat further from Fort Stevenson. Double columns would be maintained on the approach, with the boats moving directly for the lights of the gunboat. His division would strike the ship forward and Loyall's would hit aft. Gift's two launches would follow with reserves and stand by for towing if necessary. Wood dispersed the marines among the boats to provide sharpshooter fire on the final approach. Oarsmen wore pistols and cutlasses in belts to be drawn for close combat, and the young men chose friends whom they wanted to fight by their side. Then Wood gave the order to man the cutters and launches, and one young man, as he stepped into his boat, looked up at the sky, which was quickly becoming overcast, and remarked: "I wonder, boys, how many of us will be up in those stars by tomorrow morning." The words attracted the attention of the old hands, and they looked to see who had spoken. It was Midshipman Palmer Saunders, a handsome and promising officer of the James River Squadron.

Silently, the raiders pulled down the Neuse and drew near the target, guided at first by the victim's lights, and when heavy mist set in, the ship's bell became their beacon. Rain began to fall as Wood called the boats together for a prayer. Midshipman J. Thomas Scharf recalled this reverent pause before battle: "It was a strange and ghostly sight, the men resting on their oars with heads uncovered, the commander also bareheaded, standing erect in the stern of his boat; the black waters rippling beneath; the dark overhanging clouds pouring down sheets of rain, and in the blackness beyond an unseen bell tolling as if from some phantom cathedral." Wood heard four peals—2:00 A.M.—as he ordered the boats forward with rifles and grappling hooks ready. The raiders approached as planned, with the boarding cutters leading in twin columns and Gift's launches in the rear. Indeed, Wood directed his little fleet with as much ceremony as if the boats were modern battleships.

As the Confederate seamen passed under the guns of the Federal shore defenses, the *Underwriter's* hull suddenly loomed through the darkness only three hundred yards ahead. Wood rode the fast-receding tide to the ship, adjusting his final approach to catch the swirl made by the gunboat, while the splash of the tide against the prospective victim helped drown the sound of the oars. Five bells rang out, quickly followed by the watchman's nervous shout on board the steamer: "Boat ahoy! Boat ahoy!" Wood did not answer, but continued a measured advance, gaining a few precious seconds. Next came the sound of the rattle being sprung on board to alert the crew, followed by dim outlines of hurrying figures. The ship would have to be boarded with the crew armed and at quarters.

Further caution was useless, and Wood jumped to his feet, shouting "Give way! Lay me on board!" Loyall repeated the call to the second division: "Give way boys, give way strong!" The oarsmen, under terrible suspense and with their backs to the fire, pulled with full strength, sending the boats forward at top speed. The Federals were up in good season, and opened on the raiders with a destructive rifle fire, the red blasts outlining men's heads and shoulders above the long black side of the gunboat. Wood's marines, three or four in each boat, stood and returned the fire, swaying on their feet with the motion of the boats. The coxswain in Wood's boat, a brawny Virginian standing with the tiller between his knees and a pistol in each hand as he urged the men on, fell dead on the oarsmen with a ball in his forehead. Wood's rudder-free boat then swerved from its bow position and struck amidship, and the few seconds lost allowed Loyall, whose division hit aft of the pilothouse, to be first on board. The oarsmen were anxious for the climb as the bowmen, with the flashes of small arms in their faces and the smell of burning powder in the air, threw the grappling hooks. The two leading boats under Wood

and Loyall received the hottest fire. "Bohemian," bleeding pro-
fusely from a cut on his forehead inflicted by a flying splinter,
could hardly comprehend the action, but thought at the time that
hardly half the raiders would survive. "Mr. Wood, especially, I
looked every moment to see fall. Standing upright in his boat, he
gave the orders as cooly as he had done an hour before the enemy
was in sight."

Gift, seventy-five yards behind, slowed his launches to avoid
ramming the cutters. As he approached the gunboat, Gift heard
chains clanging and believed she was attempting to get underway,
so he called to Midshipman Scharf to open with the howitzer in
an attempt to damage the machinery of the *Underwriter*. Scharf
sent off one shot from the bow of Gift's launch, which struck the
pilothouse but was ineffectual, having done "no good or harm."
Before Scharf could reload, the boarding cutters had been made
fast to the ship and were swinging alongside with the tide. Unknown to the raiders, the steamer, for several reasons (including
the probability that she was aground), could not have moved off
upon such short notice.

The Federals near the ship's armory, located under the hurri-
cane deck, did not have to reload their small arms; instead they
blasted away as fast as they could with the loaded guns handed
to them. The firing never ceased as Loyall and Engineer Emmet F.
Gill scrambled over the side of the gunboat and tumbled onto the
after deck, followed closely by Wood amidship. These officers led
their men into a "blazing sheet of flame." Gill was shot in four
places and killed. Loyall, rendered nearsighted by the loss of his
glasses, immediately fell flat on the deck, while four of his crew,
on his heels, took six or seven balls apiece and dropped on top of
him. "It seemed the very jaws of death," Loyall said later. Wood,
sword in hand, battled his way to the quarterdeck as more squirrel-
like raiders scrambled over the side of the gunboat. The report of
firearms and rattle of cutlasses made a deafening din, increased by
the frenzied cackling of hens in a coop on deck. The boarders had
to force the fighting, and as each came up, he selected and then

with a wild yell rushed his man, and amid the clash and flash of hand-to-hand combat could be heard impassioned voices: "Take that, you Yankee scoundrel!" and "Take that, you damned Rebel!" Surgeon Daniel B. Conrad came over the side and found the deck slippery from rain and blood. Moving among the wounded, Conrad came upon Midshipman Saunders, his head cut open by "some giant of the forecastle." Wood, "in a stentorian voice," gave orders and encouraged his men as fighting became general across the deck. A few minutes later the raiders merged amidship and forced the ship's crew down the companionways and into the ward room, steerage, and coal bunkers, after which Wood shouted "She's ours! She's ours!" to stop the fighting.

The *Underwriter*, a side-wheel steamer with 800-horsepower engines, was 186 feet long and 35 feet across the beam. At 325 tons she was one of the largest gunboats on the sounds of North Carolina. Commissioned in New York in September 1861, she had fired the first shot at Roanoke Island (where Loyall had been captured). The ship mounted two 8-inch shell guns, one 30-pound rifle, and one 12-pound howitzer, and had a crew, according to her watch bill, of 12 officers and 72 men. Her commander, Acting Master Jacob Westervelt, was not seen on deck during the engagement, and his officers accused him of cowardice.

When the fighting ceased, Wood ordered the *Underwriter* underway as a Confederate cruiser, with his men taking up duties he had previously assigned them. Since she was the largest gunboat at New Bern, he would have temporary command of the waters. But there were problems. The engineers reported that steam was low and the fires were banked, and it would be hours before sufficient steam was built. Wood ordered Gift to try to tow her away with the launches, but this proved impossible because the ship had been heavily moored fore and aft so that her guns covered the land approach along the Neuse road, and Loyall, who had been sent to slip the chains, estimated it would also take hours to free the chains from the buoys. Wood's dilemma suddenly worsened when a terrific explosion rocked the ship. It was soon learned that gunners at Fort Stevenson had fired a shell through the vessel's upper works. The Union soldiers on shore had been aroused by the action aboard ship and, learning from escaped crewmen that she had been captured, began to pour shot and shell and small arms fire into the gunboat, notwithstanding that their own men were on board as prisoners. In the confusion, Westervelt, whom "Bohemian" described as a "grand rascal," either jumped or was blown overboard and subsequently expired.

The prize had become a trap. The intense fire from the shore gave Wood no choice but to burn the ship, but first he "calmly and clearly" ordered the Union prisoners and Confederate dead and wounded into the boats, the removal of which under heavy fire called for rigid discipline. After the doomed vessel had been quickly stripped and searched, Wood assigned Hoge to take fire from the boilers and set her ablaze. In the rush to leave the ship, some twenty Union prisoners were ordered into one of the *Underwriter*'s boats, and as they pulled away in the darkness it was discovered that there were only two raiders in the boat, so the Union prisoners lagged behind the other boats and, led by Engineer George E. Allen, who grabbed a cutlass, overpowered their two Confederate guards and escaped to shore.

When the raiders had withdrawn one-half mile from the ship, taking random shots from the Federals on shore, Wood, who did not think the ship had been properly fired from the looks of her, pulled up to Hoge's boat and asked him if he had set her on fire. Hoge said yes, but Wood sent him back on board to make sure. Without complaint, Hoge returned to the *Underwriter* as Wood's men lay on their oars. Ten minutes later the raiders saw fire leap out of a window forward of the wheelhouse where the engineer's supplies were stored. The great column of red flame outlined Hoge as he pulled away. The firing from the shore died away as the Federals, aware that the burning vessel contained several tons of powder, vacated their guns to escape the impending explosion. Wood and his raiders resumed their escape across the estuary, and as they turned up the Neuse, took a last look at the spectacle of the gunboat flaming into the sky and flashing light for miles across the water. Later, at 5:00 A.M., a tremendous flare-up followed by a dull, heavy boom assured Wood that the magazines had blown. The rain increased to torrents, wetting the men to the skin as they continued up the river to safety.

At sunrise, the Confederates pulled into Swift Creek, some seven miles up the Neuse. During the day, while Wood conferred with Pickett, the raiders tended the wounded and held funeral services for their fallen comrades. Wood lost five killed, fifteen wounded, and four missing. The enemy's losses consisted of about nine killed aboard the *Underwriter*, their bodies burning with the ship, some twenty wounded, and twenty-six carried off as prisoners, many of them without shoes or trousers against the February cold. Each of Wood's boarding cutters bore the marks of enemy balls; the white wooden plugs inserted averaged fourteen to each boat engaged, evidence of one of the most arduous cutting-out expeditions in naval history, especially in view of the proximity and intensity of enemy fire from shore. (In many respects, Wood's capture of the *Underwriter* was similar to an expedition of the British "Sea Wolf" Thomas Cochrane, Earl of Dundonald, who in the service of Chile in 1820 cut out the Spanish frigate *Esmeralda* in the harbor of Callao, Peru.)

In reference to the men killed in action, Wood stated that officers Gill and Saunders were a "loss to the service," and seamen Hawkins and Sullivan and marine Bell he termed "excellent men, tried and faithful." On the Union side, bodies and debris washed ashore for weeks after the attack, including the wheelhouse of the *Underwriter*, which Union soldiers used for firewood. Wood believed that Westervelt had escaped to shore, while Welles, thinking he had been carried off as a prisoner by Wood, prepared to greet him with a court of inquiry upon his release. But when Westervelt's body was among those recovered a month later, it was presumed that he had been killed defending his ship, so the Union commander was interred with "all the honors of war."[10]

Wood was eager to continue the assault of New Bern. His plan was to transport a force of Confederate infantry in his boats, which, with the assistance of his naval command, would attack the forts from the water side while pressure continued on the works from the land approaches. But at the time, Tuesday morning, February 2, Dearing had accomplished little, and Barton finally sent word that the mission assigned to him was "impracticable." Barton's uncooperative attitude cooled Pickett's enthusiasm for the entire project; there was now the probability of enemy reinforcements, and since Wood had been forced to burn the *Underwriter*, Pickett would not risk an amphibious assault because of the presence of other gunboats. The element of surprise was lost as well, so Pickett orderd his troops back to Kinston, saying there was "unfortunately no cooperation, the other parties having failed to attack, and I found we were making the fight single-handed." What seemed feasible to Wood did not appear prudent to Pickett.

In the entire land action, mostly by Hoke's brigade on February 1, the Confederates had killed or wounded 100 of the enemy, captured 300 men and rifles, 2 pieces of artillery, 4 ambulances, 3 wagons, 100 animals, a quantity of clothing, camp and garrison equipment, and 2 flags. Among the Union prisoners taken by Pickett outside New Bern and held in Kinston were several North Carolinians. Pickett later ordered them court-martialed as deserters, with the result that Hoke hanged up to 23 of these "buffaloes" to discourage Federal loyalty in the state, and most southerners considered the hangings justified. The Confederates lost about 45 killed or wounded.

The naval leader was critical of the general's decision to withdraw from New Bern. Wood had estimated enemy forces at four thousand, and believed the Confederate force was sufficient for a successful assault on the town from the waterfront. The two remaining gunboats, the *Lockwood* and the *Hull*, could hardly have frustrated Wood's plan, particularly if the troops were transported across the water at night, and in any event, Graves had stationed the two ships to resist a land assault. Commander Charles W. Flusser, captain of the U.S.S. *Miami* at Plymouth, was ordered to report "with all dispatch" to New Bern at the head of all available gunboats. Yet it was two days later, February 4, before Flusser arrived at New Bern, and considering Wood's determination and organizational ability, his plan probably would have succeeded, particularly since Federal strength at New Bern was only three thousand men.

Barton was severely criticized by his fellow army officers for failure to cooperate in the attack, and his subsequent wartime career remained undistinguished. Yet in spite of Barton's lackluster performance, Hoke believed that the Confederates had the situation in hand and should have succeeded: "We now know the place was within our grasp, which was seen before leaving the town. The enemy was thoroughly routed and demoralized." Admiral David D. Porter, USN, agreed, provided the attack had been carried out as suggested by Wood: "Had the enemy attacked the forts, the chances are that they would have been successful, as the garrison was unprepared for an attack on the river flank, their most vulnerable side."[11]

The situation for the Confederates was actually much better than either Wood or Hoke realized. While fighting was in progress around New Bern, the detached phase of the attack intended to draw the enemy's attention to Morehead City was proceeding smoothly. In accordance with Lee's instructions, General James G. Martin led a force out of Wilmington and on February 2 enjoyed complete success in a battle at Newport Barracks, a Federal depot on the Atlantic and North Carolina Railroad twenty miles below New Bern. Hence Martin accomplished much of what had been assigned to Barton, although Pickett was unaware that the railroad had been cut. Martin then drove the Federals to Beaufort, firing depots and bridges; seizing vast quantities of quartermaster, commissary and ordnance stores; and capturing four heavy dirt forts, three blockhouses, and some prisoners. This success, however, hardly compensated for Pickett's withdrawal from New Bern.

The Confederate operations in eastern North Carolina created great excitement among the Federals. General Benjamin F. But-

ler, commander of the Department of Virginia and North Carolina, hurriedly wired Gustavus B. Fox, Assistant Secretary of the
Navy, that the "Rebels are attacking New Bern," and that Flusser
was en route with reinforcements. Commander Benjamin M. Dove,
in charge of the U.S. Naval Station at Beaufort, reported disrup-
tion of telegraph lines and the Confederate occupation of Bogue
Island. Paymaster Charles C. Upham, at the U.S. Naval Depot on
Bogue Island, greatly overestimated Confederate strength at up to
25,000 men, and frantically shipped out or destroyed naval stores.
Union surprise and confusion was highlighted by the explosion of
the *Underwriter*, which was heard for miles and added to the
"consternation of the Yankee and Tory inhabitants of New Bern."[12]

The opportunity for successful continuation of the campaign
slowly slipped away during the two days following the destruction
of the *Underwriter*. Wood departed for Richmond on February 2,
apparently to appeal Pickett's decision, and ordered Loyall to
begin the withdrawal upstream after dark and await further orders
at Kinston. Traveling overland to Kinston, Wood boarded a train
and waited impatiently to reach the high councils of the Confederacy. He knew the fruit had been haphazardly plucked. Assuming the main prize, the town itself, could not be held indefinitely,
once inside, the Confederates could move out great quantities of
equipment and supplies by all available transportation, including
his boats. Lee had suggested as much himself, and a Raleigh newspaper soon prophesied that history would judge Pickett "unequal
to his opportunities." A Wilmington paper complained that "it is
time these failures in eastern North Carolina were put a stop to.
Last year we besieged Washington [North Carolina] for several
weeks, and came away without accomplishing anything. Now we
have witnessed a repetition of the same thing with regard to New-
bern, only it has not taken so long to do nothing."[13]

At Swift Creek, Loyall transferred the wounded and prisoners
to Dearing's command for land transportation to Kinston, while
the raiders built fires for cooking and drying out as they swapped
stories and waited for darkness. A weary Gift sat under a pine tree

with drops falling from the branches, and, writing atop a spyglass case, penned the first of a series of letters to his fiancée. That night and for the next two nights the party entered the boats and pulled against the current of the Neuse. When near Kinston they pulled in daylight, arriving on February 5, still tired from nearly a week of strenuous work. At Kinston, Loyall released Porcher's group to return to Charleston and waited for orders from Wood. As late as February 8 Wood telegraphed that the raid was not yet over, but the next day sent word to return to Petersburg. The boats were accordingly dragged up to the cars and again lashed on upright with ropes, after which the officers and men took their places as before.

En route to Petersburg the young midshipmen made miniature Union flags, and stopping at the same stations they had stopped at on the way to Kinston, called out the girls and claimed their rewards. There was much laughter and denial, and some kissing, before the train whistle called the men to their places in the boats. Wood met his men in Petersburg and ordered the boats into the Appomattox River. He instructed Loyall to strike Federal ships at City Point, where the Appomattox enters the James, if the situation offered an unusual opportunity for success. Gift's detachment apparently remained on the train because he left the rest of the group at this point. Wood returned to Richmond by rail. Loyall reached City Point after dark and was told by Confederate scouts that Union gunboats and transports were there in strength, so Loyall decided against an attack. He pulled into the swift current of the James, and keeping close to the Confederate side of the river, reached Drewry's Bluff the next evening without incident, where the men disembarked and returned to the ships of the James River Squadron.

The expedition to retake New Bern failed because of defective intelligence, lack of communication, the caution of Pickett (who overestimated Union capacity for reinforcements on the crucial second and third days), and the slowness of Barton. Then too, Dame Fortune helped the Federals as much as Confederate military ineptitude. Had the *Hull* not grounded, she would have been captured. Furthermore, it was probably Barton's presence which drew the *Lockwood* up the Trent and away from Wood's raiders. Wood had expected to find up to five gunboats in the estuary and certainly had ample forces to capture simultaneously the three actually in the area, had circumstances permitted.

Naturally disappointed with the overall outcome, Wood recommended Loyall for promotion and gave official praise to his command, writing in his official report, "I do not believe a finer body of young officers or men was ever brought together." He could indeed look with pride on the role of his raiders because, as he anticipated in such cases, the destruction of the *Underwriter* raised morale in the navy, and increased badly needed public appreciation of the service. According to Gift, the naval part of the raid was "a complete and thorough success," and southerners were congratulating the "gallant little navy." A North Carolina editor wrote that "this heroic deed adds lustre to our arms, invigorates the popular confidence in our cause, and reflects the highest honor on the gallant officers and men who executed it." The "warmest commendations" from civilians, however, came from those "who had felt the ravening hands of the [Federal] foraging parties." In New Bern, a "sinful town," where "full-scale race riots occurred almost every day," some of the citizens, especially the blacks, rejoiced at the Confederate military failure, while others, secessionists at heart, approved the limited Confederate naval success.[14]

After the New Bern raid, Wood's standing as a popular and influential Confederate officer soared. "We had the pleasure of meeting with Colonel Wood," declared one editor, "who adds to the quality of an excellent officer that of an accomplished and agreeable gentleman." Lee considered him the most successful leader of the expedition: "Commander Wood, who had the hardest part to perform, did his part well." Gift wrote that the raid "was a bold design, and well executed, and Wood deserves much credit. The weight of the fighting fell on Wood and Loyall, and right notably did they enact their parts. I am all admiration for Wood, he is modesty personified, conceives boldly and executes with skill and courage. He is a cool, determined man who acts and thinks quick." Gift concluded that "Wood's voice is all powerful now in naval affairs in Richmond." Fellow officer Robert D. Minor believed that "Wood's gallant affair in boarding, capturing and destroying the U.S.S. *Underwriter* under the enemy's batteries, had won for him another wreath, and I hope a step in rank." His raid, wrote Minor, "was the feature of the attack, and though not attended with all the results he had cause to expect, still it was a gallant act, well planned and boldly executed. He is surely one of our rising men, and I say Godspeed to him." In spite of the generous praise Wood gained from inside and outside the naval service, he refused promotion as a result of the raid. "The affair does not deserve it," he concluded.[15]

Wood could hardly decline the gratitude of the government, however, and on February 15 the Confederate Congress unanimously tendered a resolution of thanks to Wood and his command.

Resolved, by the Congress of the Confederate States of America, that thanks of the Congress of the Confederate States are due, and are hereby tendered, to Commander John Taylor Wood, Confederate States Navy, and to the officers and men under his command, for the daring and brilliantly executed plans which resulted in the capture of the U.S. transport schooner *Elmore*, on the Potomac River; of the ship *Alleganian*, and the U.S. gunboats *Satellite* and *Reliance*, and the U.S. transport schooners *Golden Rod*, *Coquette* and *Two Brothers*, on the Chesapeake; and more recently, in the capture from under the guns of the enemy's works, of the U.S. gunboat *Underwriter*, on the Neuse River, near Newberne, North Carolina, with the officers and crews of the several vessels brought off as prisoners.[16]

The enemy respected Wood as well. Admiral Porter commented on the capture of the *Underwriter*:

This was rather a mortifying affair for the navy, however fearless on the part of the Confederates. This gallant expedition was led by Commander John Taylor Wood. It was to be expected that with so many clever officers, who left the Federal navy, and cast their fortunes with the Confederates, such gallant action would often be attempted.[17]

United States Assistant Secretary of the Navy Gustavus Fox expressed an unusually keen interest in Wood's raids. Fox wrote a confidential letter to one of his admirals that it was a "pity" Federal raider William B. Cushing's "luck and dash" had yet to provide results "equal to the risk."

> You notice the Department never finds fault with these exploits. I believe they ought to be encouraged. To be sure the people will say when he is captured "damn fool." The Department will not. I have been reading this new English naval history, and I found their navy abounded in rash coast attacks and cutting out expeditions of all kinds. They were encouraged, and form a bright page of naval history. You may be very sure the Department will not find any fault with any dashing expeditions that give reasonable hope of a result injurious to the enemy, even though they fail occasionally. See how much they make out of John Taylor Wood's exploits, a solemn vote of thanks and everybody cheerful over the capture of three tugs. I am sure I do not blame them for being happy, for I have groaned over the loss constantly because it was disgraceful to us in each case.[18]

Fox wanted to promote (both publicly and in rank) his own raider, Cushing, and suggested the destruction of some blockade runner loaded with cotton and dispatches about to sail from a southern river. The secretary promised that the first officer who destroyed one would "go up several numbers" within a newly enacted system for promotion, especially if the officer was Cushing.[19]

Wood did not intend to abandon the eastern North Carolina campaign, but the next phase took a decidedly different hue. He notified Lee he would "press forward the completion of the gunboats [ironclads]. I think they can be ready for service in a month or six weeks."[20] Since the Federals as yet had no ironclads of light enough draft to cross Hatteras Bar, they had none in the sounds of North Carolina, and Wood believed the opportunity should not be lost. The best immediate hope for the Confederates was the ironclad under construction at Edwards Ferry on the Roanoke

River, sufficiently far upriver to be safe from the larger enemy gunboats that could only navigate a few miles above Plymouth. The construction site was more a cornfield than a naval yard, but Commander James W. Cooke, the "Iron-Monger Captain," exerted fantastic efforts to gather construction material, including the sending of foraging parties to all the neighborhood farms to gather scrap iron. The vessel's shield took an octagonal shape, 60 feet long (152 overall) with an 8-foot draft, and 4 inches of iron plating coated her pine timbers.

By April 10 the ironclad, christened the C.S.S. *Albermarle*, was almost finished, and Cooke promised to cooperate in the rapidly developing plans for the recapture of Plymouth. A strategic town that served as a Federal supply depot, Plymouth was situated on the south bank of the Roanoke, eight miles from its mouth at Albermarle Sound. While Union gunboats which cruised the river provided the chief deterrent to attack, General Henry W. Wessells commanded a garrison of about fifteen hundred men in Plymouth. General Braxton Bragg, recently made military advisor to Davis, tactfully disposed of Pickett and approved Hoke to lead the land assault, and Wood, in his capacity as aide to Davis, helped Hoke coordinate the army and navy elements for the offensive.

Moving from his headquarters at Kinston, Hoke opened the offensive on April 17, and after repeatedly throwing his division into the Federal battlements, drove Wessells into the fortifications inside Plymouth. Wood telegraphed to Davis that the Confederates had carried two strong outworks and that "the prospects are good for capturing the place." Then he added that "Captain Cooke is cooperating." But where was the *Albermarle*, which had the vital role of neutralizing the Union gunboats?

Cooke, like Hoke a North Carolinian, was as determined a sailor as Hoke was a soldier. The gallant captain had first proceeded upstream to Halifax to receive the ram's armament of two pivot guns, and was now slowly making his way downstream, workmen still swarming over the decks for the first few miles. Because of the many Loyalists in eastern North Carolina, Union forces had very accurate information concerning the ironclads, and when Cooke moved by the upper river obstructions and shore batteries and arrived at Plymouth on April 19, he found that he was expected. The two largest Union gunboats, the U.S.S. *Miami* and the U.S.S. *Southfield*, were bound together with timbers, waiting to trap Cooke and lash the *Albermarle* into captivity with heavy chains. After maneuvering to avoid the trap, Cooke rammed the *Southfield*, sending her to the bottom with most of her crew. Then the senior Union naval officer, the *Miami*'s Flusser, was killed by his own shot when it bounced off the *Albermarle* and exploded beside him on the deck. Their commander dead, the men of the *Miami* and lesser craft retreated to the sound, along with many Loyalists who were hurriedly escaping downriver in canoes.

Cooke then turned his guns to accompany Hoke's. The old soldier Wessells, with no hope for reinforcements, rode out on a beautiful coal-black horse on April 20 and presented his sword to Hoke. An elated Wood wired Davis: "Heaven has crowned our efforts with success." The Confederates had captured over two thousand prisoners, thirty pieces of artillery and a large stand of Springfield rifles, and two hundred tons of anthracite coal. Of particular significance were the vast quantities of stores that fell into Confederate hands. After obtaining instructions from Davis, Wood shipped badly needed commissary and quartermaster supplies up to the railroad at Weldon for movement to Lee's army. These included 100,000 pounds of meat, 1,000 barrels of flour, sugar, coffee, molasses, meal, bacon lard, and crackers. He also emptied a warehouse filled with calicoes, blankets, boots, shoes, stockings, and articles too numerous to mention. The recapture of Plymouth, moreover, opened two counties rich in agricultural produce and additional waters abounding in fish and fowl. The "well delivered blow," the first that was truly successful in eastern North Carolina, was one of the best combined land-sea attacks by the Confederates during the war.

Wood wired his wife that he would soon be in Richmond, adding that he was "hopeful" for continued success in eastern North

Carolina. Hoke soon captured Little Washington, but then the Confederate effort, so near success, ran into trouble. The ram C.S.S. *Neuse*, recently completed at Kinston, started downstream to aid Hoke in his attack on New Bern, and grounded so badly that she could not be moved. Then the *Albermarle* was called for, but while en route on May 5 she was crippled in a battle with the Union fleet on Albermarle Sound and could only limp back to Plymouth for repairs. Nonetheless, Hoke was on the verge of carrying New Bern without ironclad support when Grant opened his spring offensive in Virginia, forcing Hoke to rush northward to help defend Petersburg. So the Confederates held the territory won in eastern North Carolina for only six months. In October, Commander William B. Cushing, Wood's northern counterpart, ran up the Roanoke in a torpedo boat and sank the *Albermarle* (the only instance of a Confederate ironclad sunk by the enemy during the war), after which the Federals recovered Plymouth and Little Washington. Thus for the most part, this seaboard region remained in Union hands, denying the Confederacy inland waterways that could have relieved the overburdened southern railroads, and the large Federal blockaders could continue to concentrate on Wilmington, where "the very waves grew tired of holding up their ships."[21]

[7]

Havoc along
the North Atlantic
Coast

Wilmington was the staging area for Wood's next raid. During Grant's spring offensive, Wood had resumed his duties as aide to Davis, serving as a courier between the president and the generals as the Confederates rushed in reinforcements and set up defensive works at Petersburg. After the lines outside Petersburg stabilized, both sides sought to gain an advantage, perhaps to end the war— the Union by tunneling under the Confederate lines and exploding a tremendous subterranean mine, and the South by General Jubal A. Early's large-scale raid on Washington.

On the night of 2 July 1864 Wood appeared at Lee's headquarters near Petersburg to discuss a bold plan to release the Confederate prisoners at Point Lookout, Maryland. Composed of twenty-five acres on a promontory at the mouth of the Potomac River, Point Lookout held nearly twenty thousand prisoners-of-war. Wood, in a surprise waterborne attack, would run the Union blockade off Wilmington and throw troops on the Maryland beach at dawn on July 12 in cooperation with a simultaneous assault from the opposite direction by a detachment of Confederate cavalry under General Bradley T. Johnson. According to the plan, Wood's amphibious force would be equipped with extra arms for the prisoners, who, once released, would join Early's attack on Washington if feasible; otherwise they would pass to the north of the city and return to the South by a relatively easy crossing of the upper Potomac. A temporary capture of the Federal capital (which Grant would have soon reversed) would perhaps have an adverse effect upon northern morale in general and the 1864 presidential election in particular, as well as improving the southern bargaining position for negotiating a cease-fire in a forthcoming North-South conference.

On July 4, Independence Day for the United States, Wood received special orders from Davis which the southern leaders hoped would result in independence for the South. The following morning Wood departed Lee's headquarters for Wilmington, where the local commander, General W. H. C. Whiting, was instructed by Lee to furnish two Parrott rifles which could be used to provide covering fire for the amphibious landing at Point Lookout. Lee also ordered Whiting to cooperate in every way with Wood in organizing the mission, and added that there was "good ground to hope for the success of the enterprize."

But as Early, one of the South's ablest infantry generals, pressed up the Shenandoah Valley, creating wild excitement in the North, Wood's part in the raid ran into difficulty. He encountered a delay in getting the large number of weapons necessary to arm the prisoners, and, more seriously, there was a breach of security. Stringent efforts had been made for secrecy, but variations of the plan had been under consideration for months, and Davis notified Lee that "in this town I hear the expedition is spoken of on the street." Lee, already aware of the problem, responded that Wood's raid was discussed throughout the army, "information having been brought from Richmond." Yet both Davis and Lee were willing at this point to allow Wood to judge whether the expedition should continue. In Wilmington, Wood, with up to eight hundred soldiers and seamen, telegraphed Davis on July 9 that he was ready to attempt to run the blockade. Davis, growing increasingly doubtful, wired next morning suggesting "calm consideration and full comparison of views" with other leaders, and later that afternoon, to Wood's great disappointment, advised abandonment of the project.

The day Davis telegraphed Wood to abort the mission, Johnson's cavalry, badly pressed for time, was riding hell for leather day and night, cutting communications around Baltimore, which added to the uncertainty of news and panic in the North. With only seventeen hours to zero hour, Johnson was poised for the final non-stop race of eighty miles from near Bladensburg to Point Lookout when Early abruptly recalled him to join forces at Silver Spring. Grant had rushed a full corps and two divisions from Virginia to defend Washington. These Federal reinforcements arrived in time to drive Early from the suburbs of the city, causing him to order the Confederate army to withdraw to a point south of the Potomac.

Wood and Johnson would have found few prisoners at Point Lookout anyway, because the Federals, considering the possibility that Early could not be repulsed, had removed most of them by July 7 to Elmira, New York. However, by the time the Federal navy was alerted, Wood could have struck, since the usual series of messages among Union commanders—in this case, "be vigilant for Wood, on way to Pt. Lookout, he might try to attack blockading vessels off Wilmington," and "protect the entrance of the Chesapeake Bay from Wood"—were sent after the middle of July.[1]

Meanwhile, an English shipbuilding works on the Thames River near London, the J. and W. Dudgeon Company of Cubitt Town Yard, Millwall, had launched a new ship in March 1864 that was destined for an eventful career. The *Atlanta* was the finest of a series of vessels that represented the very latest in marine engineering and construction. Designed by Captain T. E. Symonds of the Royal Navy, she had a pair of propellers powered by two steam engines of 100 horsepower each, which turned the screws up to 120 revolutions per minute and could be operated separately or together; by reversing one screw, the ship could turn around on her center. The *Atlanta* was an iron vessel 220 feet in length, 24 feet in breadth, and 14 feet in depth. She weighed 700 tons gross, and unburdened drew only 9 feet of water. Painted gray with a red bottom, her silhouette showed two smokestacks and two sparsely rigged masts, used only for auxiliary power, which re-

C.S.S. TALLAHASSEE

(Official Records of the Navies)

flected the trend away from dependence on sail. But the most remarkable thing about the *Atlanta* was her top speed of 17 knots,
and it is doubtful whether any vessel then afloat could match her
speed and maneuverability.

The *Atlanta* was impressive from the start. As part of her shake-
down cruise, she raced the side-wheeler *Empress* across the English Channel. The fastest packet of the London, Chatham and
Dover Railway Company's line plying between Dover and Calais,
the *Empress* reached Calais in 107 minutes—30 minutes behind
the *Atlanta*. Since further tests were unnecessary, the *Atlanta*
returned to the Thames to "complete her outfit for the service
for which she had been built." Although constructed ostensibly
for the London, Chatham and Dover Railway Company, the
characteristics of the ship—long, low, of light draft, with powerful
motive power, and painted to blend with the horizon at night—
left little doubt that she was constructed to run the blockade. The
vessel was owned, perhaps originally, by a group of southern cap-
italists who had formed an Atlanta-based importing firm headed
by Richard Peters and Vernon K. Stevenson in Atlanta, Richard
T. Wilson in London, and James R. Crenshaw in Nassau. (The
blockade-runner *Atlanta*, also called the *Atalanta*, is not to be con-
fused with the ironclad C.S.S. *Atlanta*, formerly the *Fingal*, which
was captured near Savannah and became the U.S.S. *Atlanta*.)[2]

The United States Consul in London carefully watched the *Atlanta* and reported her movements to Union Secretary of State
William H. Seward. On April 1 he wrote: "The double screw is
called the *Atlanta*. Her sails are bent, and she appears quite ready
for sea." The *Atlanta* shortly moved down the Thames and set a
westward course along the southern coast of England. On April 9
she departed Falmouth with coal in ballast and eleven days later
arrived in St. George's, Bermuda. The United States Consul in
Bermuda took up the vigil and reported to Seward: "This vessel is
undoubtedly faster than any heretofore here." The *Atlanta* immediately began a regular series of departures and arrivals, and
John T. Bourne, Confederate agent in Bermuda, listed Nassau as

her destination in order to observe British clearance procedures, but her actual destination was Wilmington. From April to July 1864 the *Atlanta* logged four trips between St. George's and Wilmington, carrying mostly preserved beef and bacon for Lee's army. These trips allowed Union naval officers to become impressed with the ship's speed. Chasing her into Bermuda in June, Commander A. G. Clary of the U.S.S. *Keystone State* pressed hard at a speed of over eleven knots, but found that the *Atlanta* was "not even altering her course to avoid us, although we were running to head her off."[3]

The Confederate government was also interested in the *Atlanta*, and when she docked at Wilmington on her fourth voyage on July 15, only five days after Davis aborted Wood's Point Lookout mission, the Navy Department pressed her into service. Mallory was aware of the ship's propulsion apparatus. Early in 1863 he had written to James Dunwoody Bullock, naval purchasing agent in Liverpool, suggesting for conveyance of supplies that "a light draft, fast steamer is desirable, and I perceive that a new class of such vessel, with two propellers, has been successfully devised." The government compensated the *Atlanta's* owners, paying the blockade-running firm of Peters, Stevenson and Wilson Company $125,000, well above the ship's original cost of $85,000 (based on a conversion rate of five dollars to the English pound).[4]

Perhaps some of the political objectives southern leaders had hoped for as a result of Early's raid on Washington could still be attained. If the North could not be invaded by land, it was possible to carry the war to the enemy's coastal areas. Wood realized that commerce-destroying steam cruisers formed an important operation of modern warfare, and liked the idea of striking at the merchant marine of the North on the high seas. The *Atlanta* certainly seemed to be a suitable vessel for conversion into a sea raider, and Wood soon began to prepare for his most celebrated raid of the war.

Little time was lost in the conversion process. By July 23, the day Mallory named Wood commander of the ship, the *Atlanta* had been rechristened the C.S.S. *Tallahassee* and a battery of three guns mounted on deck: a rifled 32-pounder forward, a rifled 100-pounder amidship, and a heavy Parrott aft. Since the *Tallahassee* was a commerce destroyer, her armament would normally be used only infrequently since it would be useless for merchant ships to resist, and because the vessel was probably the fastest steamer afloat, she would rely on her speed to elude enemy warships. Yet for any brief hostile action, the *Tallahassee* combined several advantages developed since 1840 in addition to steam power. Her screw system replaced the vulnerable paddle wheel, and while the ship's scant fore and aft schooner rigging rendered sails of little value, the great hazard of spars falling on deck during an engagement was much reduced. Deck guns allowed her crew to use the new propulsion system to greater tactical advantage over the old line approach with broadsides, and the small amount of freeboard, especially when heavily loaded, reduced the silhouette available to the enemy as a target. As a former blockade runner, however, the boilers of the *Tallahassee* were not protected from enemy guns, and, designed for runs of less than one thousand miles, she had a limited range. Wood placed cotton bales on board to protect the boilers, and after filling the bunkers, stacked an extra supply of bagged coal on deck. He also ordered four barrels of turpentine placed on deck for use in firing captured merchant ships.

Wood's hand-picked crew of 120 officers and men, volunteers from the James River Squadron, included Lieutenant William H. Ward as his executive and boarding officer, John W. Tynan as his chief engineer, and Charles L. Jones as paymaster. As was usual on raiders, a complement of marines would act as sharpshooters, serve in boarding parties, or help repel boarders. Wood had little trouble recruiting because wages for service on cruisers were high and, by special permission of Mallory, paid in gold. Yet few of the officers and men had any sailing experience except on river craft. Even if they had, new training would be needed since Confederate ships varied so widely that men assigned to a different ship

WOOD KIDNAPPING WELLES

The artist of this cartoon gave Semmes's face to Wood, either because he did not know what Wood looked like, or because he was comparing Wood to Semmes. The incident is fanciful. (*Leslie's Weekly*)

usually had to be retrained. Strict discipline would also be required over the ragged and animated group to maintain the integrity of the navy. Thus Wood spent ten days drilling his crew, as
he had done with the gun sections for the *Virginia*, until he was
pleased with their performance.

On August 4, satisfied that all was ready, Wood took the pre-
liminary step of putting to sea by standing down the Cape Fear
River. Smith's Island at the mouth of the river created two en-
trances about six miles apart—New Inlet and Old Inlet. New Inlet
was protected by Fort Fisher while Fort Caswell guarded Old
Inlet, and both forts and outlying defenses were formidable works
as a result of Wood's 1863 inspection tour. The *Tallahassee*
steamed to Smith's Island and came to buoy near Fort Fisher.
That night Wood intended to run out through New Inlet.[5]

In addition to the usual difficulties of clearing the shifting sand
bars near the inlets of the Cape Fear, Wood also had to cope with
the increased draft of the *Tallahassee* from 9 to 13½ feet, a condition caused by the added weight of the crew, armament, and extra
supply of coal.

> Everything was secured for sea. The lights were all carefully housed,
> except the binnacle, which was shaded; fires were cleaned and fresh-
> ened, lookouts were stationed, and the men were at their quarters.
> The range lights were placed; these, in the absence of all buoys and
> lights, were necessary in crossing the bar, and were shown only when
> vessels were going in and out. The Mound, a huge earthworth [Con-
> federate battery below Fort Fisher], loomed up ahead, looking in the
> darkness like a black cloud resting on the horizon.[6]

On a high tide under a moonless sky, Wood quietly ordered the
raider forward. After moving only a short distance the vessel's
bow rose and the ship became immobile. She had grounded. Two
hours later the vessel was pulled free of a sand bar known as the
Rip, but the receding tide forced a 24-hour delay. The next night
the *Tallahassee* grounded so badly three steamers were required
to free her.

The following morning, August 6, Wood altered his exit route by crossing over to a point opposite Smithville, a dilapidated fishing spa. After dark the boatswain piped "up anchor" and at 10:00 P.M. the raider rounded Fort Caswell. The moon had gone down. A few black clouds in the sky and a vapor rising from the sea helped dim the stars. As the vessel steamed cautiously for Old Inlet, the leadsman chanted the depth of the rapidly shoaling water to a tense crew. The red bottom of the ship touched the Bar, a major underwater ridge of sand, tottering those on board as forward motion faltered slightly, but the dreaded rise of the bow did not occur. Then came the leadsman's welcomed call of deeper water. Wood's spirits rose as his thoughts turned to the task of running the gauntlet of Federal blockaders. When Lincoln had first proclaimed the blockade in the spring of 1861 the United States navy consisted of about forty vessels, but there were now more ships guarding Wilmington alone than were used to blockade the entire three thousand mile coast from Chesapeake Bay to the Rio Grande River during the first year of the war. Wood understood quite well what was expected of him as the *Tallahassee* steamed into the dark Atlantic.

> The captain of a successful blockade-runner needed to be a thorough seaman and a skillful navigator. His work required boldness, decision in emergencies, and the faculty of commanding and inspiring the confidence of his crew. . . . That absence of these qualities would invite loss was made apparent in a great number of instances, when the steamers were almost thrown away by bad landfalls, or by the captain or crew wilting at the first sight of a cruiser or the sound of a gun.[7]

Wood turned to Chief Engineer Tynan, who was standing beside him on the bridge: "Open her out, sir, but let her go for all she is worth." Tynan, who had served as an assistant engineer on the *Virginia*, knew that Wood did not issue idle orders. The engineer left for the engine room (where he probably ordered pork fat and pine knots into the boiler fires for quick heat) and soon the vessel tremored up to full speed. But a streak of flame from her stacks betrayed the presence of the raider. Attention immediately shifted from the leadsman to the lookouts as Wood called for sharp vigilance ahead. Soon two steamers were made out, one ahead and one off the starboard bow. Wood ordered the helm ported and veered between the blockaders while ignoring their signals. The *Tallahassee* was so close to the stern of the one ahead that "a biscuit could have been tossed on board" the blockader, and the commands of the Union officer in charge of her aft pivot could be heard by Wood: "Run out! Elevate! Steady! Stand clear!" The muzzle flash illuminated the sea as a shell whined between the pipes of the raider and trailed away like a comet. It was an excellent line shot that reflected the efficiency of blockading squadrons late in the war, and Wood knew that only the low silhouette of the escaping raider saved her from serious damage. Soon another blockader opened fire, guided by the initial firing and illumination rockets. But every shot went high as the *Talla-hassee*, steaming at fifteen knots, was quickly lost in the darkness. She passed three more blockaders unobserved. Since Wood did not respond to the fire of the enemy, it appeared that another blockade runner had escaped.[8]

Cruising southeastward at half-steam, Wood cleared Frying-Pan Shoals, which extended seaward from Smith's Island some eighteen miles, then wore around to the east into the coming dawn. Now came the real test of running the blackade, because the fastest and most efficient blockaders patrolled fifty miles off shore to snare outbound runners at daylight. Thus Wood was not surprised when a steamer was sighted five miles off the stern, her hull high in the water and smoke pouring from her funnel, indicating she was in full chase. The *Tallahassee*, outlined against the eastern sky, had been seen first. When a second steamer was reported off the bow, Wood altered course eight points toward the north to bring one pursuer off each beam. Considering the extra weight of the *Tallahassee*, it was fortunate that the wind was calm, denying the blockaders the use of their canvas, so that Wood was not forced to sacrifice any of his coal to lighten his ship. Engineer Tynan opened the engines for a sustained run of

eight hours, testing the raider's durability. Wood's admiration for
the *Tallahassee* rose even higher: "It was at times like this that the
ship and engines proved themselves reliable; for had a screw
loosened or a journal heated we should have been lost."

When it became apparent that the blockaders were not gaining, and since it was a beautiful Sunday on a smooth sea, Wood
mustered the crew on the quarterdeck and read Sunday services.
By late afternoon the first two pursuers fell astern and lowered
their hulls in despair. A third steamer was sighted from the raider's
masthead, but Wood easily kept her at a "respectful distance,"
and she chased only briefly. Then in the early darkness the *Tallahassee* almost ran into a fourth, which bore in hard, and when her
challenge was not answered, opened fire. The first shell screamed
overhead as Wood veered off and increased speed, and the remaining shots trailed off in the darkness. The outbound chase was
over. Wood had run a blockade of nearly fifty ships of all kinds
that extended well beyond one hundred miles from the coast.
Only the fastest blockade runners and most enterprising commanders could breach such a formidable seal.

Wood now prepared to take the offensive. The orders for his
mission as set down by Mallory contained the usual and necessary
authority to use individual judgment as contingencies might warrant. "Relying confidently upon your judgment and ability," wrote
Mallory, "and believing that the untrammelled exercise of your
own wise discretion will contribute to your success, it is deemed
unnecessary to give instructions in detail for your cruise." But it
was clear that Wood was to attack the northern merchant marine,
and since southern ports were blockaded, the prizes would have
to be destroyed. Wood was authorized to fit out prizes as cruisers;
to bond prizes, but only when destruction would be contrary to
the right of humanity and against the interests of the Confederacy;
to parole prisoners; to capture medicine chests, nautical instruments, and charts; and to draw up to $50,000 upon Bullock in
England through the Navy Department's agents in various neutral
ports. Mallory's instructions also cautioned Wood to observe

neutral rights, keep strict discipline over the crew to maintain the honor of the naval service, change his cruising area often to avoid capture, and to destroy prizes without fire if possible to avoid drawing attention to his work.[9]

The *Tallahassee* steamed northeastward in the swell of the Gulf Stream for the next three days. Wood spoke several vessels flying foreign (mostly English) flags, and sent a boarding party to check the registration papers of a few of them without incident. Running under easy steam to within eighty miles of New York on August 11, Wood scanned the horizon at first light with his glasses, identifying ship types at a glance. Soon the initial prize of the cruise came within his gaze. She was the coasting schooner *Sarah A. Boyce*, bound in ballast from Boston to Philadelphia for coal. Wood closed, flying the United States flag, but as he hailed her, she turned on the wind and fled. A musket shot from the raider ended the brief chase. The captain, crew, a few provisions, medicine chests, chronometers, and charts were taken from the victim, and since no cargo interfered with scuttling operations, Wood's men chopped holes in the hull of the new and valuable merchantman.

The Stars and Stripes successfully lured the next prize to the raider. Sleek pilot boats often cruised up to two hundred miles outside New York waiting to guide ships into the harbor, and at 9:00 A.M., within twenty miles of New York, the pilot boat *James Funk*, one of this fine class of schooners, approached the raider. The pilot lowered a small boat and pulled for the *Tallahassee*. Wood could see he was a large man, dressed in a black suit, with a high hat and heavy gold watch chain, who stepped over the side with a small valise and bundle of papers tucked under his arm. He evidently allowed his anticipation of a fee to cause his perception to be less than that of the master of the *Sarah A. Boyce*. Once on board, however, the feckless pilot sensed something amiss, and glanced upward to see that the United States flag had been replaced by the Stars and Bars. "My God! What is that? What ship is this?" he exclaimed, turning to Wood. "A more astonished man never stood on deck of vessel," Wood wrote. "He turned deadly pale, and drops of perspiration broke from every pore." Wood promptly informed his shaken visitor that he had boarded a Confederate cruiser and that his beautiful pilot boat would be burned.

But first the *James Funk* would serve the raider as a tender. After taking beef, vegetables, and other stores from her, Wood replaced the crew of the pilot boat with two officers and twenty men to overhaul enemy merchant ships and escort them to the raider, where Wood decided the fate of each vessel. The plan worked so well that forty prisoners, with their baggage, from a bark and two brigs began to crowd the *Tallahassee*. Hence, late in the afternoon, when the tender brought the schooner *Carroll* alongside, Wood bonded her for $10,000, which meant that the master of the vessel agreed in the name of the owner to pay that sum to the President of the Confederacy within thirty days after the conclusion of the war. Wood then paroled the prisoners and sent them ashore at New York in the *Carroll*.

The final victim of the day was another pilot boat, the *William Bell*, a splendid, speedy craft that ran away under full sail. The *Tallahassee* tore after her in an exciting chase. Wood hoisted fore and main sails for additional power, and soon the raider gained on the pilot boat. Once within range, Wood opened with his bow gun and after three shots the prey luffed to. The unhappy pilot was brought to Wood, who was seated in an armchair on the deck of the raider. The pilot offered to bond his boat for $30,000, but Wood refused. He ordered a boarding party over to the *William Bell* to "turpentine her and set her on fire."

Wood had sympathy for the pilot, but, for one thing, Mallory's orders prohibited unnecessary bonding. Then too, Wood wanted to keep pilots on board to pay or coerce one of them to serve as his guide during a midnight raid on New York. Wood knew the way into Long Island Sound via Sandy Hook and intended to proceed up the East River, set fire to ships on both sides, shell the navy yard, and, with a pilot's aid, exit via Hell Gate into the sound. He had learned from captured newspapers that no Union warships there could prevent the attack, but the pilots either did not know the way or refused to be coerced or bribed. Some of the prisoners who overheard Wood question the pilots added to the alarm on shore with stories that the raider would attack New York. Wood, however, was forced to abandon the plan.[10]

Among the six prizes Wood captured the following day, August 12, was the largest of the entire mission, the London to New York packet *Adriatic*. Most of the packet's 170 passengers were German emigrants, and when told that the *Adriatic* would be burned, they were terror-stricken. "It was some time before they could comprehend that we did not intend to burn them also," wrote Wood. Some southerners later suspected these emigrants were enlistees in the Union army, and suggested that Wood should have detained them for use as southern laborers; that was impractical due to lack of space aboard the cruiser.[11] Wood sent off the *Tallahassee*'s boats to transfer the emigrants and their effects to the *Suliote*, a bark captured by the tender and bonded for the purpose of conveying the Germans to shore. By the time the three-hour transfer operation was completed, it was late in the day and Wood decided to change his cruising grounds. In the gathering dusk, he fired the *Adriatic*, then ordered his tender in tow and set a course for the New England coast. In his wake, the burning packet "illuminated the water for miles, making a picture of rare beauty" as she burned to the water's edge.

Steaming near Boston on August 13, Wood captured his next ship and the second largest prize of the mission, the bark *Glenarvon*. Her papers showed a Thomaston, Maine, registration, and she was bound from Glasgow to New York with iron. After taking prisoners, nautical instruments, and provisions of chickens and pigs, Wood scuttled the *Glenarvon*: "We watched the bark as she slowly settled, strake by strake, until her deck was awash, and then her stern sank gradually out of sight until she was in an upright position, and one mast after another disappeared with all sail set, sinking as quietly as if human hands were lowering her into the depths. Hardly a ripple broke the quiet waters."[12] One of the passengers from the *Glenarvon* was the wife of a retired sea captain who, from all accounts, was a first-rate shrew. "She came on board scolding and left scolding. Her tongue was slung amidships, and never tired," lamented Wood. In a futile attempt to pacify her, Wood gave the elderly couple his cabin, then in desperation, he hailed a Russian ship and arranged passage for them. When the woman left the *Tallahassee*, "as a final effort to show how she would serve us, she snatched her bonnet from her head, tore it in pieces, and threw it into the sea."

Wood decided to burn his tender, *James Funk*, because she restricted his movement, although he later thought he should have sent her along the coast as a separate cruiser. At the time, Wood was more concerned about his dwindling supply of coal, and when he captured the large ship *James Littlefield* in an open pocket of fog off the Maine coast on August 14, he was pleased to learn that she carried anthracite coal in her hold. Yet the needed fuel eluded him. A persistent fog and heavy seas disallowed transfer of the coal at sea, and to have taken the prize into one of the small ports of Nova Scotia would have violated neutral territory, so Wood reluctantly ordered Ward to scuttle the *James Littlefield*, leaving her "to be a home for the cod and lobster."

During the next three days, the Confederate sea raider cruised through the mist off the Maine coast, striking hard at the New England fishing fleet and coastal trade. The astonished fishermen lost their ships partly because there was little Union-registered commerce remaining on the seas. When one captain of a small fishing vessel protested he was only a poor fisherman, Wood replied: "But you are the very fellows we are looking for." The game was indeed becoming scarce, forcing the cruiser to operate near land. A few of the prizes were captured within sight of Matinicus Island off Penobscot Bay and people on the shore of the island could be seen watching the movement of the *Tallahassee*. Finally on August 18, uncertain of his position in the ubiquitous summer fog, Wood accidently came upon a Nova Scotian pilot-fisherman who guided the raider into the neutral port of Halifax, where Wood hoped to obtain coal. He arrived with only forty tons on board.[13]

Wood's brief foray along the North Atlantic coast placed him in the elite company of such resourceful captains as James Waddell and Raphael Semmes. The *Tallahassee* was the chief reason for the continued success of Confederate commerce destroyers in wreaking havoc on Union shipping during 1864, since most of the approximately fifty-five merchantmen prizes taken that year were captured by Wood.[14]

[8]

Pursuit of the
C. S. S. *Tallahassee*

In Halifax Wood learned from late New York newspapers the full extent of the excitement and alarm the *Tallahassee* had caused in northern coastal cities. Released prisoners gave to eager newspapermen details of their capture which differed from the accounts given by their captors. The ever-present "Bohemian," now a *Tallahassee* crew member, wrote of the prisoners: "We have not yet found a single man who would acknowledge himself a Yankee." Instead, they claimed to be southern sympathizers who opposed Lincoln and the war. Once safely ashore, however, the parolees described for the press how they had been robbed of personal items, and then nearly died of exposure or drowning when sent off in overloaded ships without food or drink. Wood, who had been quickly identified and villianized by the northern press, regarded the published accounts of the parolees as "highly colored and sensational," and denied the reports that his crew robbed the prisoners. A strict disciplinarian who had been cautioned by Mallory to keep his crew in check, Wood punished a crew member for stealing a watch, and, in this single case that came to his attention, the watch was returned.[1]

By far the favorite expression used by northern editors and public officials to describe everything naval in the South was "pirate." Ranked fourth of all southern raiders in damages to Union shipping, the *Tallahassee* nonetheless operated under different circumstances from the *Alabama*, the *Shenandoah*, and the *Florida*, in that she cruised from a Confederate port, was armed there, was manned by Confederate servicemen, and was formally

commissioned by the Confederate Navy Department. Furthermore, the Tribunal of Arbitration at Geneva later disallowed the
United States' claims against England for damages by the *Tallahassee*. Of interest, however, is a comment by Wood that after
paying all claims for damages by the *Alabama*, the *Shenandoah*,
and the *Florida*, the U.S. still had half of the $15.5 million award-
ed at Geneva, and several years later the surplus was divided
among the victims of the other nine Confederate cruisers.[2]

Although the raider was not a pirate ship, the crew certainly
looked the part, a fact which had unnerved many prisoners. Wood
cheerfully admitted that his own appearance was less than regu-
lations prescribed because for three years he had been working
constantly, with no opportunity to replenish his wardrobe, and
during the cruise had slept in his clothes, either on the bridge or
in the chart-room. Before leaving ship in Halifax, Wood borrowed
different articles of clothing from his officers and pieced together
a uniform, and the crew could hardly be expected to be better
clothed than their officers. Furthermore, the Confederate seamen
were dirty as well as ragged because it was impossible to keep
clean on the *Tallahassee*. Coal dust from the firerooms filled the
air with a fine powder which settled "in and upon everything in a
most provoking and disgusting manner." To help alleviate the
clothing situation, Wood ordered the ship's complement be paid
a month's salary in gold.[3]

Some northern newspapers blamed England for the depredations of the *Tallahassee*. After parolees reported that the raider
was an English-built ship ("Tallahassee of London, 1864" was in-
scribed on the vessel's bell), a Philadelphia paper concluded that
"we are indebted to England for this new proof of the vigilance
with which she enforces her neutrality laws." As the supreme
maritime power of the day, England had little sympathy with
raider warfare, but admitted it as a right of belligerents. The
English press generally supported its government's policy of neutrality, but one paper, in a barb aimed at Secretary Welles, ex-

pressed "contempt for a system of naval administration which can permit one armed vessel to capture fifty [*sic*] craft almost within sight of New York."

The northern press also severely criticized Secretary Welles. With little appreciation of the difficulties of either maintaining a perfectly effective blockade or finding a ship in an ocean, a New York paper commented that "thanks to the vigilance of Mr. Welles" the Union was unprepared for the emergency, and consequently "the pirate has no doubt made good her escape." Had Welles dispatched naval vessels to blockade Nassau, Bermuda, and Halifax, as one newspaper advocated, success in capturing the *Tallahassee* would have been no more guaranteed than it had been at Wilmington.[4]

Welles, a busy man since he first learned of the raider at 5:00 P.M. on August 12, had ordered every available Union naval vessel on the eastern seaboard in pursuit of the *Tallahassee*. The practice vessels of the Naval Academy at Newport also joined the search. Within three days, sixteen ships were engaged. Even the ever-watchful Lieutenant Hooker of the Potomac Flotilla was warned: "Be on your guard against John Taylor Wood." Welles apparently had no strategy beyond having his commanders proceed on the latest information obtained from witnesses at sea. As a result his ships churned the water in a vain search among the wreckage left by the raider. Some nautical equipment was salvaged from scuttled ships, and the U.S.S. *Grand Gulf* recovered the *Billow*, which had not sunk.

The storming secretary learned at 10:00 A.M. on August 18 from the United States Consul in Halifax, Mortimer M. Jackson, that the *Tallahassee* had entered port. Jackson said he would protest against the raider's being coaled there. Welles then ordered the U.S.S. *Pontoosuc*, which had put into Eastport, Maine, the day before, to Halifax without delay as the vanguard of a sizeable fleet. The secretary finally had some definite information on the location of the raider, but as Wood's anchor went down at Halifax and Jackson's telegram went out to Welles, which happened almost simultaneously, diplomatic relations began to play a significant role in the situation.[5]

The first officer to lower a boat from the *Tallahassee* was Paymaster Charles L. Jones, ordered by Wood to go to B. Wier and Company, Confederate agents in Halifax, to purchase coal, some provisions, and a new mast; the aft mast had been carried away and lost over the side in an accidental collision with the *Adriatic*. Upon landing on the dock a throng of about a thousand people, some of them southern agents and naval officers but mostly English and locals, welcomed the ship. Jones wrote: "As I stepped from the boat it was with great difficulty that I could get away from the crowd who showed in their manner the greatest interest in our cause." Later Jones and a few of the ship's officers attended a ball sponsored by a local regiment and attended by British officers, where gray uniforms mingled with bright-colored British garb in a scene that, unfortunately for southern aspirations, was only too rare.

On the other hand, the official reception of the raider was exceedingly cool. Wood waited until mid-morning for British Admiral Sir James Hope, station commander, to pay the customary call to extend the courtesies of the port. When it was clear that the honors of the side would not be extended, Wood called on Hope aboard the admiral's flagship, H.M.S. *Duncan*. Wood knew of Hope from a story that apparently circulated in the Confederate navy involving an incident that occurred in the Far East during one of the Sino-British opium wars. Wood's commander on the *Virginia*, Franklin Buchanan, had been a neutral observer of a desperate battle between the English fleet and Chinese forts near Peking. Hope had been wounded and in need of assistance, so Buchanan had offered his services. When Hope had expressed surprise, Buchanan's classic reply had been "blood is thicker than water."[6] Buchanan was now the Confederacy's only admiral, but Hope was in no mood to inquire after old acquaintances. On the contrary, Wood found the British admiral rude and disagreeable.

When Wood entered his cabin, Hope did not rise, shake hands, nor offer his visitor a seat. After quizzing Wood about the latter's orders regarding neutrals, and lecturing him to be wary of molesting any ships of British registry, the admiral referred Wood to the provincial governor on the questions of stay in port and refueling.

Lieutenant Governor Richard Graves MacDonnell of Nova Scotia received Wood more cordially at Government House at 11:00 A.M., and routinely cited the Queen's Neutrality Proclamation, allowing belligerents in port only twenty-four hours, or longer if repairs were needed, and taking in only enough coal to enable the belligerent to reach the nearest home port. Soon after Wood left Government House, the consul, Jackson, called to request that the *Tallahassee* be detained in port without coaling rights until he could furnish proof that Wood had violated international law and intended to load munitions of war. MacDonnell refused. He was now the middleman between Wood and Jackson. Wood's postwar writings were seldom critical of his former enemies, but he maintained a genuine dislike for Jackson.

> From the time of our arrival, Judge Jackson, the energetic American consul, had not ceased to bombard the authorities, both civil and military, with proofs, protests, and protocols in regard to our ship. He alledged general misdemeanors, that we had violated all the rules of war, and protested against our taking in supplies. The provincial government acted as a buffer, and I heard of the protests only in a modified form.[7]

In order to determine the amount of coal on board the *Tallahassee,* and the amount needed to reach Wilmington, Jackson induced Hope to send three officers on board the raider ostensibly to study her new twin-screw system. As a result of this duplicity, MacDonnell sent Wood a note restricting the purchase of coal to one hundred tons, and at the same time requested Hope to enforce the order. Hope overreacted by sending an officer on board backed by eleven armed boats that congested the waters around the raider. Wood considered the presence of the British offensive, especially since they had come from a ship quarantined by smallpox. At his urging, MacDonnell ordered the British away and relieved the cruiser of further surveillance, but made it clear that Wood was not to exceed shipping the stipulated quantity of fuel. Wood now understood for the first time that MacDonnell intended to enforce the coaling order.

On the afternoon of August 19, his second day in port, Wood requested additional time to take in a new mainmast. Since the request complied with the Queen's mandate allowing repairs, MacDonnell granted the extension. But Wood knew from northern newspapers that Union vessels were in pursuit, and believed a few had arrived outside the harbor. He therefore used the time to plan his departure. He took in the new mast without installing it, ceased coaling at 80 tons (120 tons total), and requested Confederate agent Wier to send aboard the best local pilot to discuss the least conspicuous route for leaving the harbor. Wier sent Jock Fleming, who knew the harbor "as well as the fish that swam its waters." Wood and Fleming studied a chart of a small and obscure eastern inlet. Wood believed he could make the necessary sharp turns, but realized the vessel could easily run aground in the shallow water. "Don't be 'feared; I'll take you out all right," boomed Fleming. "As he spoke," Wood wrote, "he brought his hand down on my shoulder with a thud that I felt in my boots." Fleming's confidence caused Wood to make the attempt on the next high tide.

At 1:00 A.M. on August 20, after forty hours in port, Wood ordered an exit through the narrow, unlighted, and little-used eastern passage to the sea, which, for a ship the size of the raider, was possible only because of the twin-screw system. Dark clouds chased one another across the sky as the cruiser's keel glided through the underwater eelgrass toward the "pulsating bosom" of the ocean. The *Tallahassee* was in the Atlantic at 2:00 A.M. and Wood set a southern course. The more difficult exit was unnecessary since the *Pontoosuc* did not arrive at Halifax until 6:15 A.M., but the raider had sailed none too soon. To cover his escape, Wood had left the impression in Halifax, which Consul Jackson promptly relayed to Commander George A. Stevens of the *Pontoosuc*, that the raider was bound for the Gulf of St. Lawrence to attack a northern fishing fleet. Stevens accordingly weighed anchor in the wrong direction, and over a week later Welles was still dispatching ships to the Gulf of St. Lawrence.[8]

The *Pontoosuc* left Halifax less than twenty-four hours after the sailing of the *Tallahassee*, which was as much a violation of the Queen's Neutrality Proclamation as the loading of an excessive quantity of coal would have been in the case of the raider. MacDonnell had not only unevenly applied British neutrality laws, he had presided over what must have been a singular instance of the British favoring the North over the South in provincial ports. This was partly the result of a changing British attitude toward the Confederacy, and partly due to the efficient Union diplomatic efforts, including Consul Jackson's strong protests against the *Tallahassee*'s taking in supplies. In addition, the close proximity of Halifax to the United States could have influenced the British attitude. A factor which apparently weighed heavily with MacDonnell was the destructive capacity of the raider: "It was clear that a cruiser reported to have captured or destroyed between thirty or forty vessels in about twelve days, and said to have a speed exceeding by five knots that of the *Alabama*, was the most formidable adversary which the Federal commerce had yet encountered." He believed that as little as five tons of extra coal would insure "a heavy loss to Federal shipping." It also seems probable that MacDonnell received directions to apply the neutrality laws strictly against Wood after Wood's visit to Government House in Halifax. According to Wood, when he first saw MacDonnell on the morning of August 18, "I stated that I was in want of coal, and as soon as I could fill up I would go to sea; that it would take from two to three days. No objection was made at that time." But the next day MacDonnell had changed his policy, saying he must "carry out the instructions he had received."

The episode shocked Confederate leaders. Mallory regarded the official reception of the raider at Halifax incredible, and Wood

submitted a supplemental report after the cruise detailing his
interview with Hope. Secretary of State Benjamin suspected
Union Secretary of State William H. Seward had persuaded the
British minister to Washington, Lord Lyons, to send pro-Union
instructions to Admiral Hope. Benjamin soon initiated diplomatic
correspondence in an effort to ascertain any change in the British
position on neutrality. He referred to Wood as "one of our most
accomplished and dashing naval officers . . . a most modest and
meritorious gentlemen," and criticized Hope as "arrogant and
offensive." Benjamin's letters produced no official response since
the British government had evidently become totally inaccessable
to Confederate agents.[9]

After leaving Halifax, Wood reluctantly headed for Wilmington.
He could not resume the raid along the Delaware coast as he had
intended without the needed coal. He also chose to avoid the yel-
low fever outbreak in Bermuda, and could not risk steaming off
course in an attempt to capture coal at sea. Wood hailed a few
ships en route to North Carolina, most of which showed a foreign
register, probably "whitewashed," but he captured and burned the
brig *Roan,* the single victim of the return voyage, after taking the
prisoners on board for Wilmington.

Steaming down the coast on a straight course, the raider was
chased briefly on August 25 by two steamers of the outer blockading force as she approached North Carolina. As he drew near
the Cape Fear, Wood decided to run for New Inlet after dark by
steaming near the shore from northward, a favorite method of
approach, because soundings could easily be made. When darkness set in, he called the crew to quarters and ordered the *Tallahassee* under full steam just outside the breakers. Suddenly, the
U.S.S. *Monticello* loomed ahead. Wood attempted to pass inside,
a familiar but (this late in the war) impossible maneuver, because
the *Monticello* was almost in the surf. Veering seaward as two
other blockaders joined the first, Wood gained a few minutes during the signaling process. Satisfied the intruder was a blockade
runner, the Federals opened fire. Wood replied with his entire

battery, directing his guns by the enemy's muzzle flashes. Since blockade runners did not return fire, the Federals ceased firing and resumed signaling. In answer Wood delivered another salvo, to which the blockaders gave a spirited response. Confederate batteries along the beach north of Fort Fisher joined the action to support the raider. As the *Tallahassee*'s twin screws propelled her toward the Bar at fourteen knots, the U.S.S. *Britannia*, the final obstacle, exchanged rounds with the raider. A howitzer shell from the *Britannia* burst just over the *Tallahassee*, lighting up her decks, but like most night firing, the random shots caused almost no damage. Wood signaled Fort Fisher, and the range lights were set for crossing the Bar, which was easily accomplished because the incoming raider rode higher in the water.

Wood anchored close under the fort at 10:30 P.M. on August 26; he then mustered the crew and read prayers of thanksgiving for their safe return. At sunrise he ran up the Confederate flag, exchanged a 21-gun salute with the fort, and stood up the Cape Fear to Wilmington, leaving the blockaders in a bunch five miles offshore, their officers and men discussing the events of the night. From Wilmington Wood telegraphed President Davis that the *Tallahassee* had returned safely, and a few days later was detached from the ship to return to Lola in Richmond and resume his duties as aide to Davis.[10]

Some results of the raid were to increase Wood's popularity in the South, vindicate to some extent the sinking of the *Alabama*, and bring cheering news in the wake of the southern defeat at Mobile Bay. Typical of the southern response was the comment of a South Carolina newspaper which called the *Tallahassee* a "saucy, rollicking craft" that avenged the gallant Semmes. A Virginia woman wrote to Davis praising Wood as the president's "brave and high-toned nephew," and even the anti-administration *Richmond Examiner* chorused that Wood was "as enterprising and intrepid an officer who ever trod a quarter-deck." President Davis himself expressed gratification that the extemporaneous sea raider had lit up the northern coast with burning prizes. Considered a success by most southerners, the cruise was seen as retaliation for excesses and cruelties by Union troops on land.[11]

But such tactics were less popular among those concerned with preserving the Confederacy's single remaining lifeline to the outside world. Zebulon Vance, Governor of North Carolina, maintained that Wood had only irritated the enemy, which in turn brought a "swarm of enemy gunboats" off the coast. Editorials in a Wilmington newspaper expressed reserve about the raider: "She certainly kicked up a fuss, but we doubt very much whether she weakened the military resources of the Yankee Government to any appreciable extent." The paper also correctly predicted that the raider's presence would cause a heavier blockade, and a week later another editorial cried: "There is a thundering blockade off here now." Wilmington's military commander, General W. H. C. Whiting, complained that the *Tallahassee* was unsuitable as a warship and her guns and men were needed in naval batteries to defend the entrance of the Cape Fear. Futhermore, continued Whiting, within a month of the return of the raider, seven of the fastest blockade runners were lost to the enemy as a result of the expedition of the *Tallahassee*. The raider had taken hard coal and left soft coal for runners. They then trailed black smoke while their speed was reduced by one-half, and this "in a sea swarming with cruisers." Since no hard coal was mined in the South, anthracite was obtained only by capture or importation, and Vance was indignant over the raider's use of the precious fuel, especially since the blockade runner *Advance*, the pride of his state and apparently named in his honor, was lost in September while burning soft coal. The governor condemned Wood for taking anthracite to capture a few "smacks."

Wood had already recommended, however, that the ship be retained as a cruiser. Davis agreed, and allowed Mallory to put the case for the government. Mallory said the general cause was the most important, called runners "gamblers," and said soft coal could be used at night. Mallory also made clear that coal used by the *Tallahassee* came from a common heap of Welsh and not from any individual ship.[12] The Secretary pointed out that the *Talla-hassee* had captured many vessels, cargoes and prisoners; caused detention and delay in ports of northern sea commerce because of insecurity; and driven up insurance rates which added millions to the cost of commerce and navigation. In addition, Welles was forced to redouble his efforts to track down Confederate cruisers and extend the naval convoy of California steamers to and from New York. Mallory believed, incorrectly as it turned out, that another cruise would draw some of the blockaders from Wilming-ton in pursuit.[13] The controversy demonstrated that when Davis was forced to intervene in naval affairs, he supported Wood and Mallory.

Davis forwarded the Government's case to Vance and a few days later directed General Braxton Bragg, the new commander at Wilmington, to send the *Tallahassee* to sea. With her name changed to the C.S.S. *Olustee,* the raider made a brief cruise along the North Atlantic coast under Lieutenant Ward and de-stroyed six vessels, four of which were over three hundred tons. Reconverted to a blockade runner named the *Chameleon,* she left Wilmington in late December 1864 under Captain John Wilkin-son to import food from Bermuda, but was unable to reenter Wilmington or Charleston and reached Liverpool the day Lee surrendered. Seized by the British Government after the war, the vessel was turned over to United States authorities and sold to Japan as a cruiser.[14]

A weaker adversary naturally resorts to raiders and guerrilla tactics, and the cruise of the *Tallahassee* reflected the desperation of the South. Any of the political objectives hoped for as a result of Early's raid on Washington that might have been salvaged by the raid along the North Atlantic coast were quickly negated by General William T. Sherman's capture of Atlanta. There is some evidence that the cruiser was on a secret mission to participate in one of the many conspiracy schemes against the North. According to the confession of Francis Jones, one of three Confederate agents captured while attempting to rob a bank in Calais, Maine, a month earlier, the *Tallahassee* was to play a role in the proposed invasion of Maine. Jones said five thousand Confederate troops were to be transported through the blockade to Canada, and from there the force would strike south and put Maine to the torch. At the same time the *Tallahassee* and the *Florida* would convoy troop-laden sailing ships for a Confederate beach landing in Maine and also shell and burn Maine's coastal cities. Confederate engineers and topographers, disguised as artists, had already sketched the Maine coast and located isolated inlets where the two ships could hide and refuel. The entire Maine venture was to be a diversionary eastern facet for the Copperhead uprising in Chicago (Northwest Conspiracy) planned by Confederate agent Jacob Thompson in Canada. Both schemes aborted—victims of betrayals, lack of military leadership, and counterespionage.[15]

Wood's cruise further crippled Union sea commerce, but, except for raising southern morale, hardly aided the Confederate war effort. Since the *Atlanta* brought in mostly meat, she would have served the Confederacy better had she continued as a blockade runner, while the raider's operation out of Wilmington pointed up the need for the Union to close the port entirely. Worst of all, the cruise dashed an already fading hope that England would extend further recognition to the Confederacy, and without English aid the South had no more chance of winning the Civil War than the Americans had of winning the Revolutionary War without French aid.

[9]

The Confederacy Topples

In the fall of 1864 Wood engaged in liaison work along the James River. Lee's strategy was to deny Grant the use of the upper river and if possible to operate against the Federals' movement through Dutch Gap. Grant had ordered obstructions placed in the channel at Trent's Reach in June because he considered the river too important as a base of operations and means of communication to risk it in a naval contest with the James River Squadron. The result was only desultory action on the part of the opposing forces on the river, and by the end of the year all Federal ironclads except the U.S.S. *Onondaga* were withdrawn to take part in the assault on Fort Fisher.

Mallory considered the time opportune for an attack, and early in 1865 urged Commodore John K. Mitchell, commander of the squadron, to get underway as soon as the water depth permitted. Wood conferred with Mitchell concerning details and on January 23 the flagship *Virginia II*, along with sister ironclads *Richmond* and *Fredericksburg*, and the gunboat *Drewry*, one torpedo boat, and three torpedo launches, steamed down the river. From the Confederate battery at Howlett's Wood soon telegraphed Davis the bad news that on reaching Trent's Reach during the night half the force grounded, and that the *Onondaga*, which had retreated, then returned and joined the Federal shore batteries in shelling the squadron from daylight until mid-morning. The badly mauled Confederate vessels withdrew on the first high tide, the *Virginia II* damaged and the *Drewry* and one of the torpedo launches destroyed.[1]

The Confederate attack caused the Federals to strengthen the obstructions at Trent's Reach and again increase their fleet on the river, after which the James River Squadron rode at anchor at Richmond or Drewry's Bluff. This inactivity, coupled with defeatism among the southern people and the army,[2] helped demoralize the navy. On 10 February 1865 Wood was promoted to captain in the provisional navy for "gallant and meritorious conduct" in the *Underwriter* capture and the *Tallahassee* cruise; he declined command of the James River Squadron. Raphael Semmes, who replaced Mitchell as commander of the squadron in mid-February, complained that "great discontent and restlessness" prevailed during the last few weeks of the war, and sailors defected from the squadron by the "boat loads."[3]

In addition to the general decline in southern morale near the end of the war, the Confederate navy had another problem. Throughout the conflict the navy was unpopular chiefly because it blew up ironclads. Of twenty-two armored vessels completed during the war and over thirty unfinished (including one at Halifax, North Carolina, which was to replace the *Albermarle* and to be powered by the engines Wood had taken from the *Satellite* and the *Reliance*), four were captured and one, the *Albermarle*, was destroyed by the enemy, and the remainder were destroyed by the Confederates to prevent capture. The *Virginia II* and other ships of the James River Squadron suffered the same fate as the original *Virginia*. Advancing enemy land forces, not the Union navy, again forced not only this destruction but also that of the other major Confederate squadrons. Although most of the latter were destroyed during the last six months of the war, still the process adversely affected the morale of Confederate seamen, as reflected in the prediction of a crew member of the *Savannah* that "if we are attacked we will follow the course of the other ironclads and either blow up or get captured."[4]

Sunday, April 2, dawned bright and beautiful in Richmond amid rumors that things were not going well in Dinwiddie County beyond Petersburg. John B. Jones, a Government clerk, wrote in

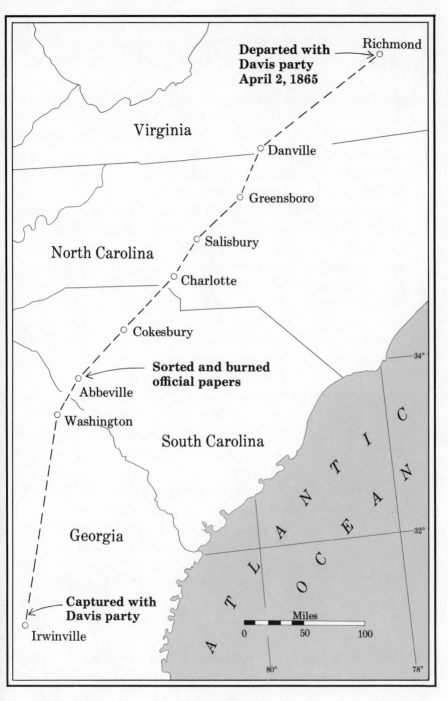

Wood's escape route from Virginia to Georgia

his well-known diary: "Certain it is, the marching of veteran troops from the defenses of Richmond, and replacing them hurriedly with militia, can only indicate an emergency of alarming importance." Wood was with Davis in St. Paul's Church when a message came from Lee with the news that the Confederate lines had given way and could not be reestablished. The government would have to evacuate Richmond that night, and although such an eventuality had been discussed by Davis and Lee for weeks, it had come sooner than they had expected.

When the news spread through the city there was no panic—rather, a measured hurrying—as men, many in uniform, moved about carrying trunks to the railroad depot. Mallory ordered Semmes to blow up the James River Squadron at dawn the following day. Captain William H. Parker and the midshipmen of the *Patrick Henry,* charged with guarding the government specie and private coin from Richmond banks, loaded a total of some $500,000 on the Confederate treasure train. Wood, after packing some personal belongings, worked most of the day boxing papers at Davis's home and office. That night he boarded a train with the president and Cabinet members for the 140-mile journey to southwestern Virginia where they would set up a new capital at Danville. Eight trains in all, carrying leading Confederate figures and government supplies sorted according to department, chugged away from the station at 11:00 P.M. with men clinging to the cars. At one station along the way, an observer commented after the trains had passed: "I saw a government go by on wheels."

The explosions of the ironclads at Drewry's Bluff shattered the early morning air in Richmond. The Confederates also fired the tobacco warehouses and all the bridges over the James. Ammunition storehouses went up in tremendous blasts that accidentally caused disastrous fires. Much of the city was consumed by the flames amid wild looting by local citizens. At 4:00 P.M., the hour the Confederate government arrived in Danville, Lincoln, announced by a 34-gun salute, landed at Rocketts Navy Yard and walked into the smoking city. Sitting in Davis's chair in the deserted Executive Mansion, he said he intended to "let the people down easy." Then Lincoln took a carriage ride to view the ruins, and Jones described the scene: "He flitted through the mass of human beings in Capitol Square, his carriage drawn by four horses, preceded by out-riders, motioning the people out of the way, and followed by a mounted guard of thirty. The cortege passed rapidly, precisely as I had seen royal parties ride in Europe."

The melancholy leaders of the Confederacy, save Benjamin, who maintained a buoyant spirit, were welcomed by a large crowd of citizens at the station in Danville. From there, Wood accompanied Davis and other staff members to the expansive home and hospitality of Major W. T. Sutherlin on Main Street. During the next few days, Wood helped to prepare the large Benedict House for Cabinet offices, and aided in fitting up the president's office and arranging his papers. There was no word from Lee, but Davis remained resolute, and on April 5 issued a proclamation with the words: "Let us not despond, my countrymen, but meet the foe with fresh defiance, with unconquered and unconquerable hearts." At the time he was confident that Lee would link with Johnston, defeat Sherman, and then turn on Grant, but in view of the events of the next few weeks, the proclamation was, as Davis himself later wrote, "oversanguine."[5]

On April 8 Wood journeyed to Greensboro, North Carolina, to visit Lola, who had left Richmond ten days earlier as a precautionary measure. General Joseph E. Johnston was near by and Wood sent him a message that he had not heard from Lee, but "all private accounts [are] cheering and represent the army in good condition and spirits." However, the following day, while Wood was spending a quiet Sunday with his family, Lee surrendered. On April 10 Wood received the shocking news in a telegram from Davis's headquarters, and learned as well that the president would soon leave Danville for Greensboro. Amid rumors of an impending collapse of the first magnitude, the commander of the North Carolina militia asked Wood to take command of local troops, but Wood declined in deference to his staff duties, and was on hand on the morning of April 11 as Davis's train crept into town. Davis, who had narrowly escaped capture by a unit of General George Stoneman's cavalry division, received an unfriendly reception in North Carolina. The people of Greensboro refused to open their houses to the president; pro-Union sentiment was strong among some natives of the Old North State while others feared reprisals from Stoneman, only a few miles to the west, and from Sherman, who was in Raleigh, all of which contributed to an attitude by the North Carolinians of "sullen indifference."

Stoneman, after destroying the Virginia and Tennessee Railroad west of Lynchburg, on April 9 had led his column southward some distance west of Danville into North Carolina. Just north of present-day Winston-Salem, he divided his force, sending one brigade to the east under Colonel William J. Palmer to tear up the rails between Danville and Greensboro. That done, Palmer, who had just missed Davis's train, reined southward toward Salisbury and destroyed the line below Greensboro. Meanwhile, Stoneman continued directly to Salisbury with the main body of two brigades, entering the city on April 12 and capturing fourteen pieces of artillery and 1364 prisoners. The cavalry general then withdrew to Tennessee.[6]

Wood had rented half a modest house for his family, and in spite of the protests of the frightened landlord, prepared for the president a small second-story room containing a bed, a few chairs, and a desk. (The house was on the site later occupied by the National Theater.) Secretary of the Treasury George A. Trenholm, ill since leaving Richmond, was invited into the mansion of John Motley Morehead, who perhaps expected to trade Confederate bonds for gold from the treasure train, but all the other Cabinet members were forced to set up quarters in a dilapidated railroad car which they dubbed the "Cabinet Car."

On the afternoon of April 12 Davis was speaking to a group of officers in Wood's lodgings, suggesting that the cause was not lost

DAVIS PARTY IN GEORGIA

Sketch of Davis (*left center*) and his escort moving along a Georgia road on May 5, five days before his capture (from a sketch by an artist of the *Illustrated London News*). (*Confederate Soldier in Civil War*)

because the South could rally west of the Mississippi River and continue the struggle for independence. As he spoke, the official communication of surrender from General Lee was brought in and handed to him. Although Davis had received reliable information in Danville concerning Lee's surrender, he was much moved by this official document. He read the dispatch slowly without comment, then turned away and "silently wept bitter tears." Wood and Robert E. Lee, Jr., were standing by the president's side, and young Lee recalled: "He seemed quite broken at the moment by the tangible evidence of the loss of his army and the misfortunes of its General. All of us, respecting his great grief, withdrew, leaving him alone with Colonel Wood." A sympathetic Davis biographer commented: "Jefferson Davis was fortunate in having his first wife's nephew with him at this crushing moment. He had loved Sarah Knox Taylor profoundly and her death three months after their marriage had transformed the gay young man into something of a stoic. Now, with Lee's official notification of surrender clutched in his hand, Davis again had an acute intimation of heartbreak."[7] Wood himself could "hardly realize this overwhelming disaster. It crushes the hopes of nearly all."

At mid-morning the following day, Davis convened a solemn Cabinet meeting, or more appropriately a council of war, in the small upstairs room at Wood's quarters. Wood, who understood quite well the personal and professional relationships of those in attendance, watched the proceedings with great interest and growing dismay. After the amenities were dispensed with, Davis turned to his generals, Johnston and Beauregard. "I think we can whip the enemy yet, if our people will turn out," the president began. "We must look at matters calmly, however, and see what is left to do. We have not a day to lose." Then Davis called for the views of his longtime antagonist, Johnston, whose reply, according to Mallory, was "almost spiteful." Johnston's words came in a rush as he said the cause was lost, the people regarded the war at an end since Lee's surrender, and "my small force is melting away like snow before the sun and I am hopeless of recruiting it." There

followed a tense silence. Finally, Davis, in a measured tone, called
on his other senior general: "What do you say, General Beauregard?" When Beauregard concurred with Johnston, followed by a
like vote by the Cabinet members (Benjamin abstained and Trenholm was absent), Davis had little choice but to reluctantly dictate
a note, written by Mallory and signed by Johnston, asking Sherman for terms. After the meeting, Wood sadly wrote in his diary
that "depression is universal and disorganization is setting in."

Davis's private secretary, Colonel Burton N. Harrison, wrote
of the situation in Wood's family lodgings:

> The Woods were boarding. They had but few and small rooms. The
> entertainment they were able to offer their guest was meager, and
> was distinguished by very little comfort either to him or to them,
> the people of the house continually and vigorously insisting to the
> Colonel and his wife, the while, that the President must go away,
> saying they were unwilling to have the vengeance of Stoneman's cav-
> alry brought upon them by the presence of Mr. Davis in their house.
> The alarm of these good people was not allayed when they ascer-
> tained, one day, that General Joseph E. Johnston [and the others],
> were in Col. Wood's rooms, holding a council of war there.[8]

Plans were made for the president and his party to continue
toward the southwest. (Mrs. Davis, who had left Richmond for
Charlotte a few days before the president, now continued to
Chester, South Carolina, on the treasure train, which, after $39,000
had been removed for payment of Johnston's troops, was sent
ahead before Stoneman's cavalry could cut the rails.) Wood was
"debating anxiously" what to do with his family. He soon learned
that the rails had been broken below Greensboro by Stoneman's
men and, refusing to subject Lola and his family to the rigors of
the trail, left them in Greensboro under the care of one of Davis's
servants, Spencer. Then Wood secured a horse and prepared to
depart. The Confederate government, with cavalry escort, now
took to horseback and wagons, and on April 15 left Greensboro
and the demoralized remnant of Johnston's army. It rained hard
as the party moved south of Greensboro, and the wagons bogged

in the mud, to be pushed free with the aid of the younger officers. Adding to the misery were the locals who refused to take Davis into their homes, and as a consequence, the president, Cabinet, and staff members began camping out for the first time since leaving Richmond. As if to demonstrate that matters could get worse, Wood's horse began to limp.

The president's party pushed on through Lexington to Salisbury, where they saw the still smoldering fires of the prison, depot, arsenal, and other public property burned by Stoneman's cavalry. Wood and the other aides were able to find an overnight home for Davis—the rectory of Reverend Thomas G. Haughton of St. Luke's Episcopal Church. Then it was on to Concord and the home of Judge Victor C. Barringer on Union Street, and next to Charlotte on April 19, Wood's lame horse showing gradual improvement.

Several days were spent in Charlotte awaiting the outcome of the Johnston-Sherman peace negotiations. Wood helped fit out an office for Davis in a branch of the Bank of North Carolina (later the site of the *Charlotte Observer* building). The president was offered only one house, that of L. F. Bates, located on the corner of Tryon and Fourth streets. Bates, from Massachusetts, was a local agent of the Southern Express Company, and later thought to have been a Union spy. Wood, Colonel William P. Johnston (son of General Albert Sidney Johnston), and Colonel Frank R. Lubbock (ex-governor of Texas), all Davis aides, took up quarters in the Bates house with the president. While in Charlotte, the party learned of Lincoln's death, which Davis realized was unfortunate for the South. There also came news of the Confederate loss of Mobile and Columbus, after which many military officers started for home, eager for paroles. Wood wrote that "disintegration is setting in rapidly, everything is falling to pieces." The only consoling factors were church services and Bates's bountiful table, the latter providing Wood the best food he had taken since the beginning of the war.

As soon as it was learned that the Johnston-Sherman peace terms had been rejected by Washington, Davis ordered Johnston, whose army was not surrounded, to retreat to the southwest and draw upon the military supplies which would be stored at various points. Then the government, amid Cabinet resignations, headed into South Carolina, the various elements of the cavalry escort held together with some difficulty by Secretary of War John C. Breckinridge. Before long came the crushing news that Johnston had surrendered anyway, rendering the Confederate leaders little more than a group of fugitives. Ironically, Davis, still the hope of the Confederacy, was traveling through an area of South Carolina untouched by the war, and he was received as a conquering hero. Women met him with flowers and wreaths, and children scattered flowers in his path. Wood considered such incidents "flattering but sad . . . in our present state of affairs. My heart rises to my throat whenever I see it."

When the party pulled into Abbeville on May 2, Davis entered the rose-covered home of Colonel Armistead Burt, an old friend whose wife was a niece of John C. Calhoun, and was given the same room Mrs. Davis had recently vacated. That afternoon Davis called in the five brigade commanders who led his cavalry escort—S. W. Ferguson, George G. Dibrell, J. C. Vaughn, Basil W. Duke, and W. C. P. Breckinridge—for consultation concerning the "plan upon which the further prosecution of our struggle shall be conducted." It was rather a junior group of officers for such high-level talks. Davis began by pointing out that another southerner, George Washington, had continued in the face of the "most disheartening reverses of the Revolutionary struggle." Further, Davis stressed that the 3,000-man escort could form the nucleus for another southern army. The astonished cavalry leaders told Davis that the South could not support further warfare, and to continue was out of the question. They made it clear that they were there merely to provide for his personal safety. Secretary of War Breckinridge and General Braxton Bragg, in attendance at the meeting, silently approved the position taken by the five cavalry officers. Davis turned pale, rose with difficulty, and left the room. In reality, he was no longer the president of the Confederacy.

An increasing sense of urgency swept through the president's entourage. For the next few hours following the meeting, Wood, Johnston, and Captain Micajah C. Clark, a clerk in the Executive Office, began sorting and burning official papers. A number of the Davis papers which Wood and Clark had packed in Richmond were destroyed, many of them from Lee. Wood's policy was to burn "all applications for exemptions, detail appointments, and promotions, but retain all letters and telegrams from generals, governors, members of the Cabinet, and prominent senators and members of Congress, all papers relating to the organization of the army, and such other records as would likely be of value in recording the life of the Confederacy."[9]

While the papers were being destroyed, General Duke and fifty picked cavalrymen took charge of the specie on the treasure train. Parker and his young midshipmen had been moving from place to place to elude the Union cavalry, but now the rails were broken to the south. After dark, Duke and his men loaded the treasure onto wagons, using candlelight to seek out the small iron chests, money belts, and various boxes scattered in the dirty boxcars. Parker, glad that his duty was completed, disbanded the midshipmen, thus putting an end to the Confederate naval school.

At midnight the Davis party, accompanied by "a few demoralized soldiers, and a train of camp followers three miles long" resumed the march southward. They crossed the Savannah River on pontoon bridges early the next morning, May 3, and took breakfast at a nearby farmhouse, their first stop in Georgia. Here the corpulent Benjamin, sensing capture, left the party disguised as a French traveler. He set out in a buggy for Florida, guided by Colonel Henry J. Leovy and financed by Confederate gold.

Pushing on in stormy weather, the party reached Washington, the home town of Robert Toombs, former Secretary of State and himself soon to be a fugitive. Davis and his staff found shelter in a local branch of the Bank of Georgia (later site of the county courthouse), where Davis held his last official meeting. The president did not believe he had authority to dissolve the Confederacy, and refused to leave the country or surrender himself while Confederate troops were in the field. He continued to express the belief that he could unite scattered Confederate forces in the West, but hinted that an alternate eventuality, his capture, would not be dishonorable.

Wood and other aides hoped to prevent Davis's capture by reducing the train and blending with the soldiers returning home. The reluctant cavalry escort, which was not large enough to fight off the Union cavalry, yet was too large for inconspicuous travel, was dismissed. Cabinet members were not entitled to paroles, and could not simply quit the cause as could soldiers, but Mallory resigned to take his chances with his refugee family in LaGrange, Georgia, leaving only two Cabinet members—Postmaster General John H. Reagan, and Breckinridge. In his last official act, Davis appointed Clark to the position of Acting Treasurer. The portion of the treasure belonging to the Richmond banks, some $230,000, was deposited in the Washington bank. Of the Confederate part, $40,000 in silver was issued to Major R. J. Moses for soldiers' provisions; James A. Semple, a naval paymaster who had served with Wood on the *Virginia*, was to take $86,000 in gold, concealed in a false carriage bottom, to an eastern port city to be shipped to a Confederate agent abroad; while Clark took charge of the remaining $35,000 in gold specie.

Wood gave his sword to a kinswoman, the wife of General Lafayette McLaws, for safekeeping, then sat impatiently on his horse while Davis concluded a brief parting ceremony in the town square. When the trek southward resumed, the company consisted of Reagan and Clark, aides Wood, Johnston, and Lubbock, a twenty-man cavalry escort, Davis's servants Robert and James, and four wagons. Breckinridge remained behind to disperse the disbanded cavalry in different directions in an attempt to confuse any Union cavalry that might be on Davis's trail.

Avoiding settlements now, the party crossed the Georgia Railroad west of Warrenton. Most members of the group traveled incognito as returning soldiers, while Davis assumed the role of a Texas member of the defunct Confederate Congress and Reagan played a Texas judge. Reagan's assumed identity was especially logical since he actually was a judge from Texas, and the latter probably explains why he was still with the Davis party.

On May 5, ten miles north of Sandersville, they divided part of the treasure and split into two groups, with each taking a different route. Clark doled out part of the remaining specie for the journey to the West—$1500 in gold for "safekeeping" and $10 in silver for "small uses" to each aide, and about double that to the higher officials. Then Clark, with the remaining $25,000 and most of the party's personal belongings in the wagons, made a dash with the cavalry escort for Madison, Florida, about fifty miles east of Tallahassee. He was eventually to deliver the specie and baggage to the Confederate government in Texas. Wood gave his voucher for the coin consigned to him, strapped his saddlebags on his horse, which he fondly called "Old Tom," and rode out in the lead of the Davis party. Davis still intended to swing west and cross the Chattahoochee River "below the point at which the enemy had garrisons." Since Clark took most of the cumbersome articles and equipment to Florida, leaving Davis only a pack mule, Wood considered the situation improved because the group could travel faster. Escape now seemed probable as the small band of horsemen ranged southward through sparsely inhabited pine forests.[10]

Suddenly, however, the cheering prospect of escape was complicated by the proximity of Mrs. Davis, who had left Washington with her wagons one day ahead of Davis. With roads and towns from North Carolina to the Gulf states full of soldiers going home through a section where rails were broken, horses and mules were at a premium and "few had any scruples as to how to get one." Near the Oconee River, Davis heard that a group of disbanded soldiers intended to rob his wife's train that night. He mounted his horse and said: "This move will probably cause me to be captured or killed. I do not feel that you are bound to go with me, but I must protect my family." He rode off, followed by the entire party, and overtook his wife's train in camp after midnight. At their approach, Burton Harrison, on picket, heard the soft tread of horses' hooves on the sandy road. He challenged and was astonished to hear the voice of Davis. They were in time, according to Wood, to prevent the theft of Mrs. Davis's stock. She was apparently en route to Florida to embark for a foreign port, a scheme which, with a train of eight wagons and volunteer cavalry escort, Wood considered "a most quixotic enterprise and cannot be carried out."

As Davis resumed the march toward the south, traveling with or near his wife for the next few days, other circumstances that were unknown to the party combined to make his capture almost a certainty. A few days earlier on May 4, Davis's brother-in-law and Wood's uncle, General Richard Taylor, had surrendered all Confederate land and naval forces in Alabama and Mississippi, virtually sealing that escape route. Then too, the new president of the United States, Andrew Johnson, had signed a proclamation erroneously linking Davis with the assassination of Lincoln. Federal handbills distributed in Macon on May 6 offered $100,000 reward in gold for the capture of Davis, and Secretary of War Edwin M. Stanton issued orders to "intercept the rebel chiefs and their plunder" of, he believed, "between $6,000,000 and $13,000,-000 in specie." The northern press and pulpit joined the politicians in crying for the revenge of Lincoln. Thus Federal troops in Georgia were thoroughly alerted, and soon learned that Mrs. Davis's train had been recognized as it passed through the tiny village of Abbeville, Georgia. Although the Davis party did not realize how highly motivated their pursuers were, Wood wrote in his diary on May 7 that according to rumor "Union troops were leaving Macon for us, but nothing reliable." The next day's notation said "enemy reported in Hawkinsville, 25 miles away."

Meantime, Colonel Benjamin D. Pritchard, commander of the

Fourth Michigan Cavalry, was riding at the head of his column from Hawkinsville to Irwinville by a parallel road. Pritchard, who perhaps was not yet aware of the proclamation but nonetheless wanted to participate in the capture because of the alleged treasure, led a detachment belonging to General R. H. G. Minty's division of General James H. Wilson's cavalry corps. Moving south along the west bank of the Ocmulgee from Macon on May 7, Pritchard struck the trail and rushed to Irwinville, then swung back northward.

Sometime after the Davis party left Greensboro, Wood and Colonel Charles E. Thorburn, a naval purchasing agent, blockade runner, and secret agent for the Confederate State Department, had planned an escape for the president and Cabinet by water. Thorburn was to ride to Florida and prepare a boat for the cruise down the east coast of the peninsula and across the Gulf of Mexico to Galveston or Matamoros. Thorburn left the Davis camp on his mission before dawn on May 10, accompanied by a black servant. The two ran into Pritchard's men, but both escaped during an exchange of fire, Thorburn shooting one of his pursuers from the saddle in the process. Upon reaching Lake City, Florida, Thorburn had a meeting in an old railroad car with Captain Louis M. Coxetter, an experienced blockade runner, and arranged for Coxetter to ready a boat the latter had hidden in the Indian River.

Shortly before dawn on May 10 Pritchard moved up to the Davis camp, located in a wooded area by a small stream one mile north of Irwinville, and after deploying part of his troops in front of the site, sent the remainder across the stream in the rear to block escape back to Abbeville. At the same time, another detachment of Union troops, the First Wisconsin Cavalry, under Colonel Henry Harden, had been on the heels of the southern high command down the direct road to Irwinville. Harden's cavalry rode up from the opposite direction as Pritchard's troopers took up their position in the rear of the camp, and each mistaking the other for Confederates in the predawn gloom, blasted away with repeating rifles.[11]

Wood described May 10 as an "unfortunate day." The din of battle created by the clash of Michigan and Wisconsin cavalry awakened the fugitives. Davis was sleeping in his wife's tent, the children in another tent, and the others in the open air. Wood, asleep near the horses, was roused by James H. "Jim" Jones, a Davis servant, and arose to the clatter of hooves on the Irwinville road. Before he could move, a hundred bluecoated troopers surprised the camp, seizing weapons and horses. Wood instinctively jumped for his mount, but a Union cavalryman on the other side of the horse's head grappled with him for control of the animal, and Wood released him only for fear of his life. "I gave him up reluctantly," Wood wrote, "I never rode as game a horse."

While the Federals were distracted by the heavy firing from the direction of Abbeville, Wood cautiously moved through the darkness to Davis's tent, and finding Mrs. Davis outside, suggested to her that the swamp was not more than one hundred yards away, and Davis, not yet known to the Union troops, might escape in the confusion. She, much alarmed, said if he could engage the attention of some Union troops near the tents, she would do so. Davis's well-known account of the next few minutes was that he mistakenly put on his wife's light overcoat, and she threw a shawl over his head. Wood described the scene in his diary:

> Some time was lost; it was becoming more light and the enemy were posting sentries around the camp. The President came out of the tent with a gown and hood on [,] a bucket on his arm, with Helen the mulatto nurse. They advanced some distance toward the stream. A Yankee guard guided them in another direction as the balls were flying where they wished to go. They pushed on, Mrs. Davis in her over-anxiety from the tent saying they were only going after water, they were not afraid of the balls. Another Yankee rode up, ordering them to halt, saying he knew who it was, recognizing a man but not the President; they walked on, and again he ordered them to halt, pointing his Carbine at the President's head. Then Mrs. Davis by her appeals, the children by crying, the servants by fear and howling destroyed all. Others rode up and the President was obliged to make his identity known. This attempted escape in disguise I regret ex-

ceedingly. Only Mrs. Davis's distress could have ever induced him to adopt it.[12]

The notion that Davis wore a hoopskirt is fanciful. "Jim" Jones, Davis's servant, present when the capture occurred, denied the hoopskirt story. Nor was it likely that Davis was actually wearing a woman's dress; rather, as one newspaper surmised, he quite probably fastened the waterproof around his waist so that the garment reached to his heels, then placed the shawl over his head and the upper part of his body, making "as complete a womanly garb as there was time to improvise." Wood's diary makes clear his conviction that Davis was dressed as a woman, and there could hardly be a more reliable source. If so, with respect to the methods adopted, Davis's effort to reach Texas at the end of the war was not unlike Lincoln's secret entry into Washington at the beginning of the conflict.

The boat that was being held in readiness in Florida was destroyed after the capture of Davis. Wood perhaps would have had difficulty persuading Davis to leave southern soil anyway, even for a brief sea voyage to Texas. As for the Confederate treasure, of the private portion left in the Washington bank, the bulk was taken by the Federal government or stolen by stragglers while it was en route back to Richmond. The fate of the rather large part of the public treasure entrusted to Semple for shipment abroad apparently remains unclear (as does, according to Parker, a heavy box which contained jewelry contributed to the cause by Confederate women and left on May 3 at the farmhouse near the pontoon bridge across the Savannah River). Clark divided the specie he had among the men of the cavalry escort that accompanied him to Florida. He then quietly returned to the home of Henry J. Leovy in Abbeville, South Carolina, where the official papers of the Confederacy had been secreted, and over a five-day period sorted and destroyed more of the documents according to the guidelines set up by Wood.[13]

Davis had planned to gain some concessions from the North after he reached the Trans-Mississippi West. A large Confederate military department stretching from Missouri beyond Texas, the Trans-Mississippi West was presided over by General Edmund Kirby Smith. Because of lack of rails to move Federal armies and supplies, and Kirby Smith's promising courtship of Mexico, the Union conquest of "Kirby Smithdom," as the western Confederacy was sometimes called, could have been troublesome.[14] However, Kirby Smith, following the examples of Lee, Johnston, and Taylor, surrendered on 26 May 1865, thus insuring continued northern economic domination of the South for at least another century, but more importantly, bringing peace to the country on what eventually proved to be acceptable terms. The fact that the Civil War was brought to a close according to traditional standards of warfare, and did not degenerate into a lingering separatist struggle carried on by terrorists, is indeed significant.

[10]

Escape to the
Florida Coast

When Davis's escape attempt failed, Wood quickly reviewed his own situation. He believed his close association with Davis during the war, combined with the northern newspaper coverage of his raids, would cause him to be treated with special severity by his captors. Besides, it was his nature to attempt to escape. After consulting with Davis, who advised him to try, Wood walked slowly about the camp as the Federals plundered the wagons for treasure. Studying the faces of the enemy, he selected a guard who seemed especially interested in booty and motioned him aside. Using mostly sign language on the trooper, who turned out to be a German who spoke little English, Wood produced a twenty-dollar gold piece and pointed toward the stream. The guard took the coin, tested it between his teeth, and with his carbine escorted Wood to the small creek. Once among the undergrowth and thick grass which lined the banks of the stream, Wood motioned for his guard to return to camp, but the trooper replied "nein, nein," so Wood gave him another twenty-dollar gold piece and turned his pockets inside out. Satisfied that Wood had no more gold, the guard turned and walked back alone.

After bribing the guard, Wood crept a little further into the swamp, and lay concealed for three hours, crawling about to escape notice as soldiers passed within a few yards of him when they came to the stream to water their horses. Finally, as Wood watched from his hiding place, bugles sounded and the wagons started off, followed by the Davis party and guards on horseback. Wood then returned to the abandoned camp and picked up from

among the debris a small derringer, which he thought had been
dropped by either Reagan or Davis. A young Confederate cavalry
lieutenant named Barnwell, who apparently had not been captured, also came into the camp. Patching a saddle and bridle from
scraps of leather, Wood fitted out a "sad and war-worn" horse that
had been left behind. Since the animal was unfit for riding, Wood
led his mount out of the camp, heading south with Lieutenant
Barnwell.

Wood traveled as a paroled soldier returning home. The next
day he met former Secretary of State Benjamin, alias M. Bonfals,
still under the guise of a French traveler. "With goggles on, his
beard grown, a hat well over his face, and a large cloak hiding his
figure," mused Wood, "no one would have recognized him." Wood
told Benjamin of Davis's capture and, since Benjamin was eager
to push on, arranged to meet him in a few days near the refugee
town of Madison, Florida. There they would decide what to do.

Before his escape, Wood had asked Reagan and Lubbock to
take charge of his saddlebags and clothes, but Wood evidently
still carried some specie. Since he had no baggage, Wood chanced
an entry into Valdosta, Georgia, on May 13 and bought two "hickory" shirts and a pair of socks.[1] Outside Valdosta, he stopped at
the large log cabin of Osborne Barnwell, an uncle of Wood's
young friend. The elder Barnwell had moved his family to south
Georgia to escape the occupied coast of South Carolina. Wood remained at the cabin two days, enjoying the company of Osborne's
family as he rested himself and his horse. On May 15, with Lieutenant Barnwell remaining with his uncle, Wood rode out alone
toward Madison. He was about to enter the Florida "underground
passage" for fleeing ex-Confederates, where he would continue to
travel incognito, known only to a few southerners who would send
him from one place to another.

Cautiously, Wood guided his nondescript mount through the
pine forests of south Georgia, ever watchful for Federal patrols.
He crossed into Florida without challenge and near Madison
reined in at the home of General Joseph J. Finegan. The hero of

the Battle of Olustee (in honor of which Wood's cruiser *Tallahassee* had been rechristened), Finegan had been in charge of most Confederate forces in the state, and was well qualified to give advice on the best escape routes through Florida. Here Wood met not Benjamin but Breckinridge. Benjamin had arrived in the area two days before, but upon learning of Federals in Madison, continued southward in his new disguise as a farmer. Wood and Breckinridge quickly conferred with Finegan upon "the most feasible way of leaving the country." Breckinridge, a general since 1861 and a fine leader, had been involved in many major engagements in both theaters during the war, and received an injury at Cold Harbor. He had been Confederate Secretary of War less than two months. In spite of his many high offices in the United States and Confederate governments, he was only forty-five years old, and physically able to withstand the rigors of the trail.

Wood assumed, quite correctly, that the Federals in Florida were alerted for escaping ex-Confederates. Union Admiral Cornelius K. Stribling, in charge at Key West, had already issued orders to guard the southern coasts of the peninsula. The Florida keys seem to have been most carefully watched, but Federal commanders in other parts of Florida were aware that attempts would be made to reach nearby islands. Wood favored sailing to the Bahamas from the east coast, and since he was an experienced seaman, Breckinridge tentatively agreed, hoping eventually to reach the Trans-Mississippi Department. Crucial to their plans, of course, was obtaining a boat.

A small party was formed, consisting of Breckinridge, his aide and fellow Kentuckian, Colonel James Wilson, and his black servant, Thomas Ferguson, who had been with the general throughout the war. The horse Wood had been riding was spent, and he acquired a better mount by trading it to Finegan with fifty dollars to boot. Then after gathering some supplies, the men mounted and rode eastward twenty-five miles to the home of Lewis M. Moseley, who ran a ferry across the Suwannee River.

On the morning of May 16 the men rose early, crossed the

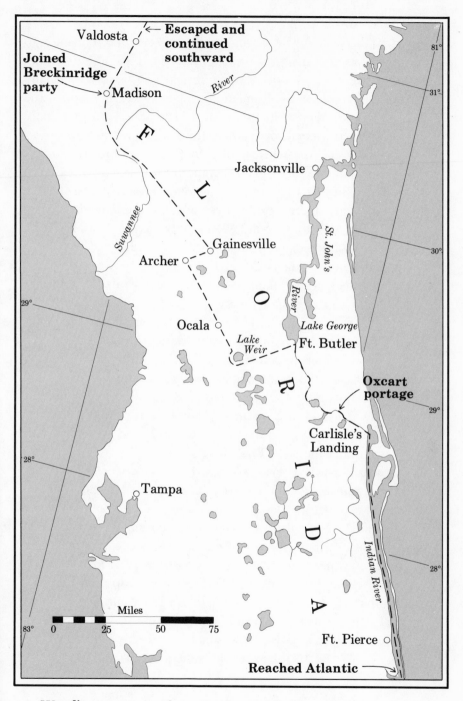

Wood's escape route from Georgia to Florida

limestone-banked Suwannee on Moseley's Ferry, and rode out into
an isolated region along the St. Augustine road. Right away it became apparent that Florida's summer heat and insects, especially
mosquitoes, would cause torment, and the riders also sampled the
loneliness and deprivation to come. Mile after mile the only
sounds were the creak of leather, the rhythmic tread of horses
across sandy soil, the whisper of a light breeze through the tall
pines above, and an occasional scamper of a wild hog or call of a
quail. The Santa Fe River ran underground for a distance of three
miles, forming a natural bridge over which the unknowing horsemen jogged, and they found water only at the Double Sinks,
which Wood sampled and pronounced of "bad quality."

Upon reaching Gainesville on the night of May 18, the tired
riders, who had been looking forward to the hospitality of former
Confederate Congressman James B. Dawkins, learned with dismay that his house was already filled with guests for the night.
Their single opportunity for accommodations was the floor of a
local tavern, which Wood dismissed as a "filthy hole." Taking
breakfast at Dawkins's table the following morning, however, they
found him not only a splendid host but an important source of
information for their escape plans. They had to work fast because
Federal patrols had recently ridden through and were expected
to return at any moment. First, Captain J. J. Dickinson, who was
in the nearby town of Waldo where his command was being paroled, was summoned to the secret conference at Dawkins's home.
Dickinson, known as the "Francis Marion of Florida," knew the
country well. He confirmed Wood's inclination toward the east
coast because, although several Federal blockade camps remained
there, it could not be as closely guarded because of inland waterways and keys. During the war Dickinson had captured the Federal gunboat *Columbine* on the St. John's River and had retained
one of her lifeboats which could be raised from its hiding place in
the river. Dickinson offered the small boat to his fellow ex-Confederates, and the St. John's would provide an avenue southward.

Wood and Dickinson were kindred spirits, and it is small wonder that Wood termed him "a most valuable friend."

While Dickinson set about readying the boat, Breckinridge, with his aide Wilson and servant Ferguson, hurried from Gainesville twenty-four miles south to Millwood Plantation, the home of Colonel Samuel H. Owens, guided by Dickinson's son. Wood separated from them and rode southwest in search of Benjamin, who had passed Moseley's Ferry only two days ahead of them, to see if the former Secretary of State wanted to join the group. Better armed now with a revolver Dickinson had given him, Wood followed the Cedar Keys and Fernandina Railroad tracks to Archer, where he was heartily welcomed at Cottonwood Plantation by the charming and beautiful wife of former United States and Confederate Senator David L. Yulee. Wood wrote that the jovial Benjamin was "too wily to be found at the house of a friend." (Benjamin made good his escape, although most of the ex-Confederates considered it unlikely because of his rotund figure, and after passing down the west coast of Florida and through the Bahamas and Cuba, settled in England, where he became a distinguished attorney.)

Although he did not locate Benjamin, the side excursion provided Wood with information on the thinking of northerners regarding the former Confederate states. Yulee returned during the evening from Jacksonville, where he had gone to discuss the status of the postwar South with United States Supreme Court Chief Justice Salmon P. Chase. The attitude of Chase gave Yulee a disturbing vision of the new era. Chase had said that Rebels might be dealt with for treason; certainly they would not have the same rights under the United States Constitution as Loyalists. Freedmen, all considered Loyalists and in some places the majority of the population, might well control public offices. Wood also learned that Davis was aboard a ship off the South Carolina coast, en route northward to an uncertain fate in a Federal prison. (Davis was imprisoned for two years at Fort Monroe, where for a time he was shackled. His treatment aroused the sympathy of even those southerners who had opposed him.)

The visit to Yulee's Cottonwood Plantation afforded Wood his first reliable information about public affairs for some time, and he would have been convinced by this visit, if not by the capture of Davis, that his flight was purely an escape, not a retreat. A disillusioned Yulee advised Wood to seek terms with the Federals, but this latest news only reaffirmed Wood's intention of evading the enemy. He was more convinced than ever that punishment awaited him if recaptured. He had completed many missions more dangerous than his present flight, and was confident of his ability to get out of the country. He therefore disregarded Yulee's counsel.

On May 20 Wood rode eastward to rejoin his fellow fugitives at Millwood Plantation. Unknown to Wood, Mallory was arrested late that night at the LaGrange, Georgia, home of former Confederate Senator Benjamin H. Hill. Mallory was spirited away half-dressed, charged with treason and with "organizing and setting on foot piratical expeditions." Five days later, Yulee himself was arrested for treason, and at the same time a grand jury in Washington indicted Davis and Breckinridge for treason.[2]

At Millwood, Wood learned that Dickinson had been hard at work arranging for the escape. Dickinson himself visited the plantation and told the party that in a few days the boat, manned by three of his men, would be ready at Fort Butler on the St. John's River. To coordinate the timing of the rendezvous at Fort Butler, Dickinson left at Millwood Lieutenant William H. McCardell, who would guide the fugitives eastward at a leisurely pace to allow time for the boat to be raised, repaired, and moved to Fort Butler. The journey could continue at a more relaxed pace in central Florida because Federal patrols were not likely to penetrate the remote interior around Ocala.

For a few days the travelers assumed a holiday air. On May 21 they ventured a short distance to Rutland Plantation, the home of Owens's brother, Captain William A. Owens, who had been a

COLUMBINE LIFEBOAT

Wood (*unidentified*) and his companions as they would have appeared launching their boat in the Indian River (*Century Magazine*)
(from a sketch by Wood).

leading Confederate in local organization and supply. Rutland was the most comfortable Florida home to receive the party so far, and Wood noted that the Owens brothers were "very wealthy, until this present issue of affairs." Yet Wood's adventurous spirit called him away on another side excursion. While Breckinridge and the others engaged in overnight hospitality at Rutland, Wood set out with their guide, McCardell, to Silver Springs, six miles northeast of Ocala, where they were the guests in the "log cottage hotel" of wartime Florida legislator Hiram T. Mann, McCardell's father-in-law. Silver Springs, formed by an underground river, was already something of a tourist resort. Wood marveled at the transparency of the springs, noting that at a depth of several hundred feet, the crystal waters could be viewed "almost as distinctly as though seen through air," and that it was the "most beautiful submarine view I have ever seen."

After leaving the springs, Wood rode southward and rejoined Breckinridge at Wauchula Plantation, the home of the former Confederate Quartermaster General of Florida, Colonel A. G. Summer. Here the group lingered during May 23 and went deer hunting. The mosquitoes were becoming almost unbearable, and red bugs added to the misery as the men slowly became acclimated to the simmering heat. Moving on the following day, the men dismounted at Lake Weir and spent the night along its banks. Wood called it "a fine sheet of water, some five or six miles across." The lake was so inviting he went for a swim, which provided him temporary relief from the heat and mosquito bites. Wood enjoyed this landscape more than the nearly three hundred miles of uninteresting pinelands he had passed through; he found middle Florida was better watered, and the forests more diversified.

Passing along the south side of Lake Weir on May 25, McCardell swung eastward and pulled up at the plantation of Major Thomas Stark, which brought the party within a day's ride of the St. John's River. The mood turned serious once again as the ex-Confederates made final preparations for travel by water. Since they could not depend on obtaining food to the south, they had gathered a two weeks' supply of stores from friends along the way, including salt, meal, grits, and sweet potatoes. Breckinridge had a small pocket compass, and they obtained a map of Florida (ordered prepared and published by Jefferson Davis when serving as Secretary of War under Franklin Pierce) and information concerning routes and Federal patrol stations. Their movements through the "underground passage" of the settled areas of north and central Florida were kept secret by their faithful hosts. Wood considered this trustworthiness characteristic of the general population of central Florida, where he believed Breckinridge had been recognized several times.

Early on the morning of May 26 the party mounted for a ride of thirty-two miles into the wilderness. This final leg of their long journey on horseback lay through a region of heavy sand, dwarf pine, and scrub oak. Arriving at Fort Butler on the St. John's shortly after noon, they found the lifeboat *Columbine* waiting. On hand with the boat were Sergeant Joseph J. (Jerry) O'Toole, and Corporal Richard R. Russell, paroled soldiers from Dickinson's command who were ready to hire out their services. These men turned out to be experienced beachcombers, and Wood heartily approved of them: "Most valuable and trustworthy comrades they proved to be, either in camp or in the boat, as hunters or fishermen."[3] A third paroled soldier, Private P. Murphy, accompanied the party for three days, then left to return home.

The boat was a small man-of-war's gig, only some seventeen feet in length, open, and with little freeboard. It was powered by four oars and a small mast which allowed the use of a sail by holding the sheet in the hand. "Her outfit was scanty," explained Wood, "but what was necessary we rapidly improvised." After loading provisions, camping equipment, firearms, and ammunition, the boat's company took their places and noted with some dismay that the gunwales almost touched the coffee-colored water of the river. Wood remarked that "it was a tight fit to get into the boat," and there was no room to stretch. Breckinridge considered it serviceable for the river, but thought it "a very frail thing" for ocean travel. Nonetheless, the escaping Confederates manned the oars and sail, and late in the afternoon began their ascent of the river between banks covered with cypress, palmetto, water oak, and maple trees.

The first night was passed in an extremely uncomfortable manner, an indication of the coming trials of the journey. They anchored in midstream because the mosquitoes seemed fewer there than on shore, but there was no room to lie down in the boat, and about midnight a severe thunderstorm came up, sending rain down in torrents, which dissolved a large part of their salt and ruined much of their other provisions and powder. "Morning broke on a thoroughly drenched and unhappy company," Wood observed, "but a little rum and water, with a corn-dodger and the rising sun, soon stirred us." Breckinridge was able to find some good in the rain—"it cooled the air a little."

Wood noted that the boat sailed well, and with a fair wind to aid the oars, the boatmen logged thirty-five miles the first full day. The riverbanks were uninhabited, because the occasional visit of a Federal gunboat during the war had driven off the few settlers, leaving only the ruins of their cabins. A small savanna here and there contained a feeding herd of wild cattle and deer. A few shots at the deer went wide. Wood saw hundreds of alligators, twelve to fifteen feet long, and when passing them "uncomfortably near, we could not resist, even with our scant supply of ammunition, giving them a little cold lead between the head and shoulders, the only vulnerable place." Wood added to the food supply by catching bass, which bit well in the quiet waters. Figs, bananas, guavas, and citrus began to appear in the deserted orchards, and after experimentation the men found that sour oranges and dirty brown sugar made a "miserable" fruit drink.

Near its headwaters, the St. John's formed two lakes, Monroe and Harney, with a narrow and tortuous connecting stream that divided into many branches and cul-de-sacs, which made navigation difficult. At times the boat headed for every point of the compass, and instead of wasting more time under these conditions, Wood and O'Toole disembarked and hiked five miles inland to Saulsville (later Osteen) on the evening of May 28 to get a team and wagon to haul the boat overland to the Indian River, down which they would continue. Wood engaged a local man, George Sauls, who agreed to meet the group twenty miles upstream at Cook's Ferry, near the mouth of Lake Harney.

The next morning Private Murphy left the party, probably to help conserve precious supplies and lighten the overloaded lifeboat. (Murphy had somehow laid claim to the boat, so Breckinridge paid him $100 for it.) Hence from the morning of May 29 the group consisted of six men—Breckinridge, Wood, Wilson, Russell, O'Toole, and Ferguson. The day was hot and windless, causing hard pulling through grassy tropics full of blue and white herons, snowy egrets, water turkeys, and ducks. The tired fugitives reached Cook's Ferry that night and found Sauls waiting for them. After loading the boat on the cart so that it would be ready for an early departure in the morning, the river travelers spent a rare night indoors at the Cook home, protected from the heavy rain outside and oblivious to the hoot of owls, croak of frogs, and loud bellow of bull alligators.

At sunrise on May 30 the adventurers were ready to begin their overland trek of about twenty-eight miles. The course lay southeast through sandy palmetto barrens, broken by an occasional thicket and grassy swamp. Travel for all was by foot under a boiling sun. The boat had to be guarded against upsets, for their escape depended on getting it safely across, but in spite of their efforts it thumped to the ground several times. From the start Wood was critical of the draft animals, a pair of bulls, and their owner, Sauls, whom Wood described as "a compound of Caucasian, African, and Indian." The bulls would neither gee nor haw, and one frequently started forward while the other began backing. Time after time progress was halted when their heads ended up on opposite sides of a tree. Reflecting on the situation, Wood concluded that "it would have been less labor to have tied the beasts, put them into the boat, and hauled it across the portage." The animals were probably distracted by the large flies which bit them savagely around their heads and necks, saturating them with blood. Sauls loitered behind, coming up only for meals, but pitched in when told: "No work, no grub; no drive bulls, no tobacco." The day's travel, a disappointing eighteen miles, placed them at Six Mile Creek, two miles west of the present town of Mims, where they camped for the night. An evening meal of bacon, eggs, and sweet potatoes cooked over a cheerful lightwood fire was consumed with the comforting assurance that no Federal pursuers were on their trail. When the sun went down, however, the mosquitoes came out in force; the smoke from the campfire only partially deterred them, and sleep was impossible.

The wayfarers finally reached Indian River the following day, and Wood took a deep breath of the familiar salt air and commented that the waters were "a most welcome sight." He was very much relieved as they lowered the boat into the river at Carlisle's Landing opposite Cape Canaveral, some three miles north of Titusville, and dismissed Sauls and his team of oxen to the wilderness. The constant pounding the boat had received during the overland passage necessitated some caulking and pitching to repair leaks. An inventory of provisions gave cause for anxiety; the meal was wet and worthless, and all the salt had dissolved, leaving only bacon and their mainstay of sweet potatoes. But the new water route appeared alive with fish, and perhaps there was game on shore.

Actually, Indian River was not a river, but an inland waterway which extended more than two hundred miles from Cape Canaveral to Key Biscayne. Averaging a mile in width, it was separated from the Atlantic Ocean by a narrow sand ridge. The waterway was found to be very shallow, and upon embarkation the boat was pushed out almost half a mile before it would float. This near the ocean there was a good sailing wind almost daily, and once afloat the fleeing men headed southward under full sail, hoping most of their troubles were behind them. They realized, however, that they were once again subject to capture since several camps of Federal guards were stationed along the Indian River.

The first night on the waterway, Wood and his companions camped on the west bank, and finding the river too brackish for drinking, dug in the sand for "indifferent" water. They made good progress for the next two days, taking advantage of every wind day or night, but the bothersome mosquito problem continued. Without a breeze during the day, the heat was suffocating, and when shade was sought the mosquitoes drove them back into the sun's glare. "When sleeping on shore," Wood wrote, "the best protection was to bury ourselves in the sand, with cap drawn over the head, if in the boat to wrap the sail or tarpaulin around us." Wood's buckskin gauntlets proved invaluable against the pests, and at times he wrapped his head in a towel. He believed he could fill a bucket with mosquitoes by swinging it around his head a couple of times, and Breckinridge was of the opinion that a man with his hands tied behind his back and his face exposed would die from them after two nights. "Besides this plague," Wood added, "sandflies, gnats, swamp-flies, ants, and other insects abounded. The little black ant is especially bold and warlike." If disturbed, "they would rally in thousands to the attack." Some relief came on the afternoon of June 2 when, near the present city of Vero Beach, rain lashed the forlorn band of travelers so fiercely that visibility was reduced to twenty feet.

When the mariners approached to within ten miles of a Federal camp at Indian River Inlet, they pondered how to avoid these blockaders who waited to intercept escaping ex-Confederates. The answer, so familiar to Wood, was to slip by at night. Most of the fugitives must have been apprehensive as their boat moved silently closer to the point of danger. Soon they could see a fire on the bank, indicating that the camp was indeed occupied. Keeping to the middle of the stream, they glided by in the dark without detection, and continued ten miles farther before landing a short distance south of Fort Pierce.

After sunrise the peripatetic band again dug in the sand for water and visited a deserted orange grove. Oranges were out of season, but the men took on board a supply of lemons and coconuts which Wood termed "a most welcomed addition to our slim commissariat." Continuing southward they found the channel broadened for an easy thirty-mile run to Juniper Narrows, but there they experienced another serious navigational problem similar to that encountered on the upper St. John's River. The Narrows was crooked as well as narrow, and a dense growth of juniper and tall grass combined with shoals confounded reckoning within the intricate channel. A half day was lost in these everglades. Wood had expected to turn into the ocean at Juniper Inlet some twenty miles further south, but late in the afternoon they stumbled upon a short haulover only fifty yards wide and decided to drag the boat over the dunes to the sea. "What a relief it is," declared Wood, "to get out of the swamps and marshes of Indian River into the blue waters of the old Ocean and the freedom from mosquitoes; what enjoyment to us, who have been punctured and bled for the past two weeks."[4] From this point on, Wood, with his success in dealing with the enemy in various waters during the war and as one of the most skillful and resourceful seamen in America, was to prove crucial not only to the escape of the ex-Confederates, but to their very survival.

〖11〗

Voyage into
Exile

Wood was particularly grateful to reach the Atlantic because the possible haven of Nassau was near, but there were two known hazards: the *Columbine* was very small for the ocean, and they might now be captured by Federal patrol ships. He believed that another camp of Federal guards was located at Juniper Inlet, which would render that area extremely hazardous. Resuming the voyage immediately in order to pass the critical inlet at night, the little boat braved the ocean just offshore. Wood watched with anxious eyes as first one and then another steamer went by a mile from the beach, but both ships continued on course. As the men made their way past Juniper Lighthouse, it sent forth no beacon, having been put out of operation by Confederates during the first year of the war. No campfire was visible, nor was there any sound of the enemy. Relieved that their luck was holding, the voyagers sailed on southward for fifteen miles, and at sunrise on May 4 landed at the present site of Palm Beach.

Fresh water was obtained from Lake Worth, but food had become a very serious problem. Only a few sweet potatoes remained. Fortunately, it was the time of year when the green turtles deposited their eggs under the sand just above the high-tide mark, and Russell and O'Toole had hunted for them before. "Sharpening a stick," Wood explained, "they pressed it into the sand as they walked along, and whenever it entered easily they would dig." After a few hours' search, aided by turtle tracks, they found a nest that bears from the Everglades had not destroyed. A single nest yielded several dozen eggs, and the beachcombers dug them with the eagerness of prospectors digging for gold. They were literally "scratching for a living," according to Wood. The green turtle's egg was about the size of a walnut; the yolk cooked hard, but the white became softer with prolonged boiling. Wood found their taste pleasant, especially when they could be varied with a few shellfish or snails.

The little band was now in position to sail for freedom across seventy miles of ocean to the Bahama Islands. But first they rested because the sleepless voyage of the previous night and the search for food had made them weary. Then they indulged in a refreshing swim off the beach. As they entered the boat at 5:00 P.M. all were aware of the danger that such a small craft on the open sea afforded. Wood pointed out that "it was of course a desperate venture to cross this distance in a small open boat, which even a moderate sea would swamp." After a prayer by Wood, they set out, the sunset at their backs and a strong wind blowing in from the bow. Wood struggled against the headwind all night, but at daybreak the boat was not even out of sight of land.

Soon a more urgent problem forced a quick change of plans. Wood's resourcefulness and coolness were put to the test when the would-be emigrants sighted a big ship heading directly toward them from the north. Wood saw that she was cruising close to the beach to avoid the four-knot current of the Gulf Stream, and from her sparse yards and general appearance, he promptly made her out to be a United States naval steamer. With great alarm the ex-Confederates rowed to shore, pulled the boat onto the beach and turned it on its side to blend with flotsam scattered about, and took cover back among the palmettos. The cruiser, with colors flying, steamed abreast so close to land that the fugitives could see the officer of the deck scanning the shore. "To our great relief," Wood wrote, "the cruiser passed us, and when she was two miles or more to the southward we ventured out and approached the boat, but the sharp lookout saw us, and, to our astonishment, the steamer came swinging about, and headed up the coast." She came within three hundred yards and lowered a

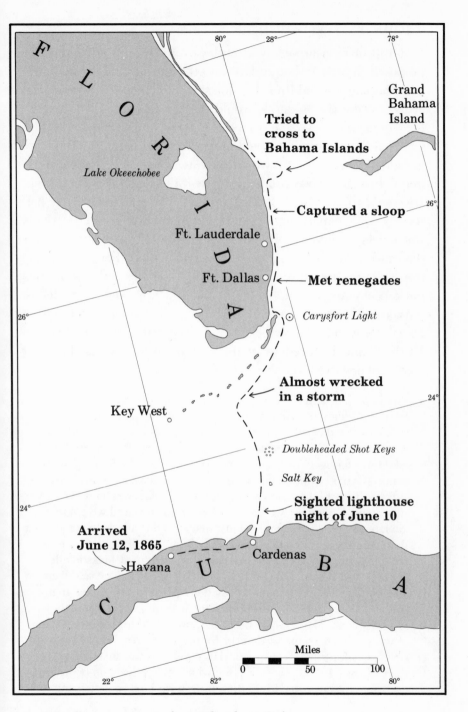

Wood's escape route from Florida to Cuba

boat full of men armed with cutlasses and pistols. Breckinridge proposed that they should dash into the swamp and abandon the boat, hoping it would not be molested. Wood, more experienced at this, knew the Federals would destroy or carry off the craft, leaving no way to escape from the country, and that many a ship-wrecked Spaniard had starved to death in the swamps. "Besides," he said, "the mosquitoes would suck us as dry as Egyptian mum-mies." Instead, Wood proposed to meet the Federals with a bluff. He would row out with Russell and O'Toole, who fortunately had their parole papers with them, and see what could be done. Breckinridge agreed, and taking his pistols and satchel, went over the sand ridge with his aide Wilson and servant Ferguson to the brush. The other three men launched the boat, threw in two buckets of eggs, and pulled out to meet the approaching Federals.

Wood prepared himself by assuming the role of the "roughest longshore woodsman, wrecker, and fisherman that ever lived in Florida," and his account of the confrontation reveals the inner contempt he felt for the young Federal officer.

I had one oar, and O'Toole the other. To the usual hail I paid no attention except to stop rowing. A ten-oared cutter with a smart-looking crew dashed alongside. The sheen was not yet off the lace and buttons of the youngster in charge. With revolver in hand he asked us who we were, where we came from, and where we were going. "Cap'n," said I, "please put away that-ar pistol; I don't like the looks of it, and I'll tell you all about us. We've been rebs, and there ain't no use saying we weren't; but it's all up now, and we got home too late to put in a crop, so we just made up our minds to come down shore and see if we couldn't find something. It's all right, Cap'n; we got our papers. Want to see 'em? Got 'em fixed up at Jacksonville." O'Toole and Russell handed him their paroles, which he said were all right. He asked for mine. I turned my pockets out, looked in my hat, and said: "I must er dropped mine in camp, but it is just the same as theirn." He asked who was ashore. I told him "There's more of we uns b'iling some turtle-eggs for dinner. Cap'n, I'd like to swap some eggs for tobacco or bread." His crew soon produced from the slack of their frocks pieces of plug, which they passed on board in exchange for our eggs. I told the youngster if he'd come to camp

we'd give him as many as he could eat. Our hospitality was declined.
Among other questions he asked if there were any batteries on shore
—a battery on a beach where there was not a white man within a
hundred miles! "Up oars—let go forward—let fall—give 'way!" were
all familiar orders; but never before had they sounded so welcome.
As they shoved off, the coxswain said to the youngster, "That looks
like a man-of-war's gig sir"; but he paid no attention to him.[1]

The Federals pulled briskly to the davits, the boat was lifted
aboard, and the steamer continued toward the south. When Wood,
Russell, and O'Toole returned to shore, they found Breckinridge,
who had been standing in the brush with pistols in hand, very
much relieved at the success of Wood's scheme. It had been a
narrow escape.

After the Federal steamer was out of view, the men again attempted to get to sea toward the Bahamas, but the headwind
remained too strong, so they decided to resume the voyage southward along the coast to the tip of Florida, and from there try to
sail to Cuba. About mid-morning they saw a cluster of tents on
shore and landed to find a group of peaceful Seminole Indians
dressed in calico shirts, loincloths, and turbans. Only a few hundred descendants of this once powerful and warlike tribe, which
Zachary Taylor had helped decimate, remained in the Florida
Everglades. Wood could be thankful that the ancestors of these
Seminoles had escaped his fighting grandfather, because this small
party of redmen had some fish and *koonti* (or *kuntee*) left over
from their breakfast, which the fugitives ravenously consumed.
Koonti, a substance pounded from the roots of a fernlike plant
and baked in ashes, was Indian bread. This "palatable but tough
cake," as Wood termed it, was well received since the mariners
had no bread, and they wanted an extra supply to take with them.
The aging Seminole chief, who spoke some English, proved an
astute bargainer. He wanted powder for their antique rifles, and
could not be tempted by an old coat, fish hooks, or even a cavalry
saber. There was no alternative, short of hostilities, to dividing
the small amount of powder in exchange for some Seminole flour.

Upon completion of the negotiations, the chief produced the peace pipe for a friendly party, and after it made the rounds, the ex-Confederates manned their boat with this slight increase in provisions.

So far June 6 had been an eventful day for the ex-Confederates, but it was not over yet. Wood was about to take full advantage of their greatest opportunity of the entire journey. Just north of the present city of Delray, Wood spotted a sail coming north toward them. With the early morning encounter with the Federals fresh in their minds, the men were exasperated at this new threat, presumed to be a Federal guard boat. But their consternation changed to bewilderment when the approaching vessel altered course by standing to seaward, obviously to avoid them. As Wood watched, he suspected the crew consisted of Union naval deserters or escaped convicts from the Dry Tortugas, an island prison off western Key West, and that they were themselves fearful of capture. He judged from the expanse of sail on the distant boat that it was a larger and better seacraft, and quickly convinced Breckinridge that the fleeing vessel should be captured. There was only a light breeze, giving oars an advantage, so Wood lowered the small sail and gave chase, slowly overhauling the sailing craft until a shot caused its canvas to drop.

Pulling alongside, Wood noted the three crewmembers were dressed in man-of-war uniforms, and considered them deserters. "They were thoroughly frightened at first," he wrote, "for our appearance was not calculated to impress them favorably." The former Confederates assumed a bloodthirsty air, an easy task considering their appearance—unkept whiskers, deeply sunned, and bodies growing gaunt from exhaustion and malnutrition. Wood told the deserters that as far as he was concerned the war was not over, and they were prisoners and their boat a prize; they would be paroled but the boat would be kept. The deserters, sullen and evasive, objected to an exchange of boats. Wood could see that they were desperate and that the issue would be decided by force. Should the strangers draw weapons first, although outnumbered,

A FINAL
CAPTURE BY WOOD

Wood and Breckinridge force an exchange of their boat for the
more seaworthy sloop of the Union deserters (from a sketch by Wood).
(*Century Magazine*)

the fight would be about even. Thus Wood and Breckinridge pulled their revolvers, disarmed the opposing crew of pistols and knives, and went through the delicate operation of changing from one boat to another. That done, Wood searched the new boat for provisions and found a small supply of sea biscuits and a breaker of fresh water, part of which he took in exchange for *koonti* and turtle eggs. Next, in order to set the prisoners in the proper frame of mind—probably to preclude their attempting a future sneak attack to regain their boat—Wood threatened them with every-thing his active imagination could invent, particularly immediate execution as deserters and pirates, then said on second thought he would let them off with the exchange as it stood. The strangers, hearing all this, were relieved at Wood's final offer and became communicative, asking directions to Jacksonville or Savannah. Wood complied and returned their arms, while Breckinridge gave them a twenty-dollar gold piece difference for the trade. The grateful victims, submitting to the inevitable, headed north in the lifeboat from the *Columbine*. For the first time, Wood had lived up to his northern reputation as a pirate (or perhaps more ac-curately a receiver of stolen goods), but the fugitives, unlike the deserters, needed the new boat to escape the country.

Wood was quite pleased with the newly-acquired craft. It was a nameless sloop not much longer than the gig, but it had more beam and plenty of freeboard, and the bow was decked over to the mast. Well-found in sails and rigging, the sloop worked and sailed well after Wood added a little ballast, and could make some progress even when standing into a light wind. Long oars, or sweeps, added some auxiliary power. More confident now, Wood could forget to some extent a possible fate when they next at-tempted to get to sea, of which "a great deal of derelict stuff—the remains of vessels and their cargoes" along the beach served as a constant reminder. The new boat lifted the spirits of all aboard, especially after Wood pointed out that the sloop presented a good chance of crossing the heavy Gulf Stream to Cuba.

The hungry seafarers next turned their attention to the chronic problem of food, particularly a few days' rations of some kind which Wood said would be necessary to sustain them on the passage across the Gulf Stream. They hoped to acquire the needed supplies without stopping at Fort Dallas (Miami), an abandoned Seminole War fort where there was still a small trading post. They suspected the last Federal patrol station they would have to pass was in that vicinity. Before reaching Fort Dallas, they landed on the beach and searched for more turtle eggs, but the many bear tracks they saw told them why they were unsuccessful. When under sail, they "scanned the washings along the strand in vain for anything that would satisfy hunger." At one place a few onions, washed from some passing ship, were eagerly devoured. As a well-informed seaman, Wood realized that these landings on shore were becoming dangerous since the lower east coast of Florida attracted lawless "seacoasters" who preyed on the misfortunes of seamen. Yet in spite of hazards from Federal patrols or reckless adventurers, the fugitives would be forced to seek supplies at Fort Dallas.

Working hard through the night of June 7, the men pulled the sloop over sand bars and reefs from the ocean, and sailed across the clear waters of Key Biscayne. During the approach to Fort Dallas they gazed upon a picturesque view of the old limestone walls of the fort, set in a small clearing dotted with coconut trees, all outlined by a background of tropical greenery. A black column of smoke began to rise into the air near the fort. "We approached cautiously," Wood explained, "not knowing with what reception we should meet." Moving slowly against the current of the Miami River toward the small wharf, the former Confederates found waiting twenty or thirty armed men of various nationalities. Wood observed that "a more motley and villainous-looking crew never trod the deck of one of Captain Kidd's ships. We saw at once with whom we had to deal—deserters from the army and navy of both sides, with a mixture of Spaniards and Cubans, outlaws and renegades." Hence the stage was set for a propaganda pirate to match wits with the genuine article.

Maneuvering the sloop to within hailing distance without standing in to the wharf, Wood allowed a tall, burly black, obviously the local leader, to begin the parley. As the leader hailed the newcomers in broken English, he must have considered the sloop's crew "motley and villainous-looking" as well, and first wanted to know who they were. "Wreckers," replied Wood. Then he added: "We left our vessel outside and came in for water and provisions." The spokesman on shore, obviously suspicious, asked the location of the ship. Wood said she was northward a few miles, that a gunboat had overhauled them a short time earlier and found their papers in order. This produced a noisy conference on shore, followed by a demand that the boat pull to the wharf so that the papers could be examined. "No," Wood responded, "send off a canoe and one of our men will go on shore and buy what we want." Soon a canoe came off, paddled by two blacks, who announced that only the captain (i.e., Wood) would be allowed ashore. O'Toole volunteered to go, but the two boatmen objected to anyone except Wood. "I told them," wrote Wood, "to tell their chief that we had intended to spend a few pieces of gold with them, but since he would not permit it, we would go elsewhere for supplies." Confident the lure of gold would cause the renegades to reconsider, Wood set the sloop in motion down the river.

The canoe returned to shore, and as the ex-Confederates watched, fifteen to twenty renegades jumped into four or five canoes and dugouts, and started for the sloop. As the sloop's crew quickly checked their weapons, Wood considered the odds: "Though outnumbered three to one, still we were well under cover in our boat, and could rake each canoe as it came up." Even Breckinridge's servant Ferguson became a fighting hand, and the crew opened fire when the attackers came into range. Paddles were shot away and two renegades tumbled over as the leading canoes were driven back, while the fire of the pursuers went wild from the motion of their small crafts. Soon the canoes stopped and formed into a bunch so that another powwow could be held. Then

DIFFICULT SAILING

Jetsam and a pursuit vessel are astern as the fleeing ex-Confederates push their sloop over a coral reef (from a sketch by Wood).

(*Century Magazine*)

three men in a single canoe, holding aloft a white flag, came toward the sloop. Wood hove to and asked what was wanted. He
was determined not to go near their lair again, but the urgent need
for supplies necessitated some terms if possible. After some parley,
it was decided that O'Toole would go ashore with them to purchase some provisions. When Wood said O'Toole must return in
two hours, the renegades thought the time too short. "But I insisted," Wood recalled, "that if O'Toole were not back in two
hours, I would hail the first gunboat I met, and return with her
and have their nest of freebooters broken up." O'Toole was given
five of Breckinridge's twenty-dollar gold pieces, partly tribute
money, and instructed to be "dumb as an oyster" in regard to the
sloop's crew. The Irishman hopped into the canoe, and all the
buccaneers returned to the fort as Wood dropped anchor to await
the return of O'Toole.

The time element was important. Wood's suspicion that the
rising column of smoke near the fort was a signal for the return
of a ship in the vicinity seemed borne out by the renegades' desire
to detain the sloop. Convinced that the renegades had a larger
craft, all hands maintained a sharp lookout for sail, while indul-
ging in pleasant anticipation of what O'Toole would fetch in the
way of food. Two hours passed, then another half-hour. The sloop's
company began to despair of a feast, not to mention O'Toole, of
whom they had grown fond. Wood reluctantly weighed anchor
and with a slight breeze stood out the mouth of the river. After
sailing three or four miles and debating what to do, they saw the
welcomed sight of a canoe astern. It was O'Toole with a bag of
rations—hard bread, two hams, rusty salt pork, sweet potatoes,
fruit, two breakers of fresh water, and a keg of rum. Sailing off in
high spirits, the crew assaulted the provisions, enjoying a feast of
ham biscuits washed down with water and rum, and a dessert of
oranges and bananas, all the while entertained by O'Toole's account of his experience ashore.

O'Toole's report to his shipmates revealed that both sides in this
encounter had surmised with surprising accuracy the position of

the other. The renegades had heard of the end of the war, but not of Davis's capture, and suspected that notable Confederates, probably escaping with treasure, were in the sloop. The marauders were looking for the return of a schooner as Wood had expected— hence the smoke signal—and were playing for time. O'Toole had been cross-examined and threatened, but divulged nothing, and was allowed purchases and released only after the renegades saw the sloop leaving.[2]

Sailing down Key Biscayne, Wood hoped to avoid detection inside the reefs, but soon made out a schooner of thirty to forty tons off the stern which was quickly overhauling the sloop. Realizing that the schooner had a deeper draft, Wood intended to draw his pursuer into shoal water. By the color of the water he located a reef ahead, just awash, which seemed to extend across the channel. Wood made for it, at the same time ordering the ballast overboard. As the fugitives anxiously looked down into the shoaling water, the keel grated over the coral, moved off, then came up hard. All six men quickly jumped overboard and pushed the sloop forward a few yards, but there was not enough water. Astern, the schooner bore in, only a mile away. To shove off the reef, Wood ordered everything out of the sloop—anchor, chains, spare rope, even the provisions, except for a few biscuits. Keeping all sail on, the men pushed for a hundred yards before passing over the coral. Exhausted, they climbed back aboard, safe for the moment. To the delight of all, Ferguson opened the transom, took out a jug of rum he had secreted there, and poured each man a measure. But the chase continued when the schooner, her skipper familiar with the waters, found an opening through the coral. Another reef was off the sloop's bow, but instead of crossing over, Wood hauled eastward into the wind and ran alongside the reef as the schooner, taking advantage of the resulting angle of chase, closed within range and opened with a deck gun and small arms. Spotting a break in the coral, Wood upped the helm, took the wind and shot through, discouraging the schooner from further chase.

Although free from pursuit, the little expedition was now low on provisions once again. From the time of their drenching on the St. John's River that first night in the gig, the former Confederates had encountered difficulty maintaining a food supply. "Really a fatality appeared to follow us as regards our commissariat," observed Wood. At Key Elliott, some twenty miles south of Fort Dallas, Wood brought the sloop to anchor by making fast to a long oar. The crew attempted to rest, but the mosquitoes were worse than ever. All wrapped themselves completely in sail with only their nostrils exposed, and tried to ignore the swarming insects. "Their buzzing was like the roaring of the wind," complained Wood.

Continuing southward after the fitful respite, the determined little band searched for new ballast and supplies. Finding a small rise of ground above the swamp, they waded ashore on a little stretch of sand. Wood carried the sail ashore and, improvising a canvas sack, filled it with sand to ballast the sloop. Without ballast it was a cranky sailer, which lessened their chances on the open sea. The sand strip contained a half-dozen coconut trees, and while Wood readied the boat, Ferguson, using a strip of canvas between his feet, climbed fifty feet to the green fruit. Breckinridge went hunting in the swamp and returned with two pelicans and a crane. Ferguson soon cooked one of the pelicans and served it to Breckinridge, who after considerable exertion cut off a mouthful. While the others looked on anxiously, Breckinridge rose and without a word walked into the bushes. When he returned a few minutes later, his expression satisfied all that the bird would not keep them from starving. The crane proved no better. The only edible morsels from Breckinridge's hunt were a dozen recently swallowed small mullet in the stomach of one of the pelicans. Cleaned, wrapped in palmetto-leaves, and roasted in the ashes, they were delicious. Yet the fugitives had added only a few coconuts to their supplies, and Wood realized that it would require three to four days' sailing to reach Cuba, considering the winds that usually prevailed at that time of the year. "With the strictest

economy," Wood wrote, "our provisions would not last so long."
But the travel-weary men wanted no more of Florida swamps and
reefs, and were determined "to face almost any risk to escape from
those shores."

Setting sail for the open sea was no easy task. Wood found that
their chart was not sufficient to navigate the keys, and for several
hours they ran aground repeatedly, forcing them to wade and
pull the sloop over one reef after another. It was nightfall before
they sailed through the numerous inlets of swift-flowing Caesar's
Creek at the lower end of Biscayne Bay, and stood down the
ocean side of the keys. By 10:00 P.M. the ex-Confederates passed
Carysfort Lighthouse opposite Key Largo, and slowly the dim
shoreline of Florida receded from view.

Wood had little time to consider that he was leaving his native
land for exile, because he was busy working the sloop among the
submerged reefs that border the keys. Shortly before morning a
squall blew up, lashing the sea into deep troughs and sending
salt spray over the crew. The small craft began to creak as if it
might fly apart. "I knew from experience" (while serving aboard
the U.S.S. *Wabash* before the war), Wood wrote, "what we might
expect from summer squalls in the straits of Florida."[3] He quickly
ordered the boat made trim. After reducing sail he took the helm,
giving Breckinridge the sheet and Wilson the halyards, while
Russell and O'Toole prepared to bail. Ferguson could only remain
on the bottom of the boat, immobile from sea sickness. At first,
however, there was nothing any of them could do. As Wood told
it:

> Great drops of rain fell like the scattering fire of a skirmish line, and
> with a roar like a thousand trumpets we heard the blast coming,
> giving us only time to lower everything and get the stern of the boat
> to it, for our only chance was to run with the storm until the rough
> edge was taken off, and then heave to; I cried "all hands down!" as
> the gale struck us with the force of a thunderbolt, carrying a wall of
> white water with it which burst over us like a cataract. I thought we
> were swamped as I clung desperately to the tiller, though thrown
> violently against the boom. But after the shock, our brave little boat,

though half filled, rose and shook herself like a spaniel. The mast bent like a whip-stick, and I expected to see it blown out of her, but, gathering way, we flew with the wind. The surface was lashed into foam as white as the driven snow. The lightning and artillery of the heavens were incessant, blinding, and deafening; involuntarily we bowed our heads, utterly helpless.[4]

When the rain began pouring down, Wood, during flashes of lightning, motioned for Russell and O'Toole to begin bailing. Tied to the thwarts, the two men set to work. From the direction of the wind, Wood realized they were headed westward toward reefs, where the violent sea would pound the boat into splinters. He had to attempt to bring the sloop under control. Exchanging positions with Wilson, he unfastened the mainsail, then at a slight wind lull, shouted for Wilson to put the helm to starboard in order to port the boat southward, while at the same time Wood made a small "leg-of-mutton" sail of the mainsail. The delicate maneuver worked perfectly as the sail took the wind without shipping water, but as Wood was tying the halyards, Wilson, frozen at the helm, soon turned the craft completely around, bringing the wind off the other bow. The boom flew around, knocking Wood's feet from under him. He tumbled overboard and disappeared below the raging waters.

For an instant the craft was motionless, and as Wood surfaced, he grabbed the sheet. Then, with Breckinridge's assistance, he scrambled back on board, ascribing his rescue to "Divine Providence." A near disaster had occurred in the predawn storm. Wood's genius as a seaman had repeatedly saved them all, and had he been lost, the escape expedition undoubtedly would have come to a watery end. "Col. Wilson," wrote Breckinridge, "expressed his gratification at the general result and explained that he had thought it his duty to hold everything lest 'it might get some advantage of him.'"

Wilson, sometimes too enthusiastic and rather bumbling, had provided welcome levity for the group from time to time on their travels. He was, by common consent, the least experienced out-

doorsman, but was well-liked in spite of his misadventures. Breckinridge made fun of his aide occasionally, always in a goodnatured
way, as in this description of the accident (Breckinridge forgetting
for the moment that it was his duty to handle the sheet which
controlled the boom):

> I was tired and just losing myself in a daze—and the celebrated Col-
> onel Wilson was steering. Suddenly I was roused by a wave going
> over me and half filling the boat, which leaned over until the gun-
> wale was under the water. At the moment I observed that Capt.
> Wood was overboard, and looking around I saw Col. Wilson as stiff
> as a staunchion holding on like grim death to the rudder and [sheet].
> It was his grip on the latter that was about to sink us. I knew just
> enough to shout to him to let go the [sheet] which he did, and the
> strain being taken off, the boat finally righted.[5]

Wood took the helm and for many hours trusted it to no one
else. Using the North Star and Breckinridge's small pocket compass, he steered toward Cuba through the storm-driven Gulf
Stream. After daylight on June 9 the sea moderated a little as the
storm passed to the west, but frequent gusts from the east whipped
up heavy seas which kept Wood uneasy and prevented him from
adding more sail. All aboard began to suffer from exposure, and
their bread was soaked. During the day Wood rested briefly as
Breckinridge doled out a small, precious ration of rum and water.

In the evening the wind and sea increased. Wood again took
the helm and found himself battling for their lives against twenty-
foot waves in a nerve-racking ordeal that lasted through the
night. A wave crashing broadside would have been fatal; only by
keeping the boat's bow into the waves did he keep it from filling.
Between the mountainous waves the craft poised motionless, then
it would rise on the crest where even the little sail set was strained
to the limits. "She had to be nursed carefully," Wood explained,
"for if she had fallen off, one breaker would have swamped us, or
any accident to sail or spar would have been fatal." Breckinridge
thought the boat must go under: "Capt. Wood looked very grave,
but he held the helm himself through the night, cool and col-

lected. He told me afterwards that the chances were against us that night—that we certainly would have perished in the other boat—and that in nineteen years' experience of the sea he had never felt in so great peril."

Dawn of June 10 peeped over the horizon on a moderating sea, and at noon Wood put on more sail. The escaping ex-Confederates had crossed most of the Gulf Stream in rough weather, but now the sun came out and added to the growing problem of exhaustion. Supplies were down to a pint of rum in water and two water-soaked biscuits for each man a day under a tropical sun. Several sails were visible at a distance, and Wood became determined to hail a ship, even at risk of capture, and ask for food and water. Presently a brig drifted toward the little craft and they pulled for her with the long oars, waving at the figures gathering on her deck. As the escaping men neared her stern, they could see she was a United States merchantman, the *Neptune*, of Bangor, Maine. Wood noted that her crew was armed and at quarters. Her captain, extremely wary of their appearance, hailed the boat from the taffrail and ordered them to keep off. Wood replied that they were shipwrecked men and in need of provisions. The captain at first refused, but after Wood accused him of being "no sailor," he threw off a breaker of water and a bag of sea biscuits, careful all the while not to allow the boat alongside his ship. Ironically, Wood, who had burned many ships like the *Neptune*, was now unwittingly given crucial aid by a Yankee skipper.

Continuing southward under a boiling sun, the men lay in the rolling boat, cramped and feverish. Ferguson's severe seasickness continued, and Breckinridge began to develop a loud ringing sound in his right ear. During the afternoon, Wood noticed a change in the color of the water, which meant that they were on soundings. Soon he recognized some small rocky islands as the Doubleheaded Shot Keys. Located on the northwest edge of Salt Key Bank, the barren islands gave Wood his first sure fix on their position, and assured him that they were out of the jurisdiction of the United States. The thirty-mile stretch of water over Salt

Key Bank was very clear and only fifteen to thirty feet in depth. The shells, marine flowers, and fish underneath seemed within arm's reach, and Wood recalled that the "display of food was tantalizing." Russell, an expert swimmer, volunteered to dive for some shellfish. Among the samples he brought up were some thin-shelled bivalves shaped like a large peapod which Wood considered "tolerable." Amazingly, the emigres had secured food on two occasions while en route from Florida, without which they probably would have perished.

The tropical night closed in with the anxious crew straining their eyes in vain for some glimpse of their destination. A few hours after dark they spotted a lighthouse off the Cuban coast. At last they were within reach of a friendly shore. Wood gave up the helm for a well-deserved rest; he had been on the alert continually as the only navigator aboard. Wilson was steering, when, as Breckinridge recalled, "that enterprising officer ran the boat nearly on the lighthouse and then concluded to wake us up for consultation." After moving clear of that hazard, Wilson struck a coral reef. The boat "thumped heavily" and almost capsized. With difficulty they hauled off again, and sailed westward outside the reefs along the coast during the night, Wood looking for some suitable place to enter the country.

On June 11 the rising sun revealed several vessels at anchor on the blue waters of a bay some ten miles away, and as the starving men sailed nearer, they made out a city at the head of the bay, with mountains towering beyond. It turned out to be the bay at Cardenas, a city of thirteen thousand on the northern coast, seventy-five miles east of Havana. Moving into safe harbor that Sunday morning they heard church bells pealing in the distance. Wood must have thought of that Sunday when the long trek by rail, horseback, and boat had begun from St. Paul's Church in Richmond, and, at Breckinridge's request, he gave a prayer of profound gratitude for their deliverance.[6]

[12]

Expatriate

Since pratique was not forthcoming, Wood ventured ashore to report to the local customs officers, and it was some time before he could make them understand that he and his companions had come from Florida and wanted to land. The little boat soon produced as much excitement as the arrival of a liner, and because the astonished officials could hardly believe the small craft had crossed from Florida, their demeanor grew overbearing and suspicious. The ex-Confederates might have been lawless adventurers in disguise, so the local officials requested instructions by telegraph from the Spanish Governor General in Havana, Domingo Dulce.

By this time a large crowd had gathered on the wharf to watch the armed men disembark from the miniature craft. Many of the onlookers were Americans who believed Davis had eluded his captors and was in the boat. John Cahill, a resident of Cardenas by way of Kentucky, offered to act as interpreter, and this, combined with Breckinridge's former high status as a government leader (and the offer to surrender their arms), paved the way to better relations with custom officials. As they had no passports a number of papers had to be made out and signed for the irregular entry, including a registry for the sloop, which was duly entered as the *No Name*, although the boat certainly deserved an appellation more in keeping with its recent service.

After clearance had been granted them, the men took coffee and a light breakfast at the Fonda del Almirante Colon near the customs house, and were shown lodgings at El Hotel Cristobol Colon.

The excitement of their arrival continued as Governor General Dulce sent instructions that the former Confederates were to be treated as representatives of a friendly, though fallen, government. Southerners in Cardenas also took the group in hand. Wood, gaunt and blistered, took a bath and donned a linen suit provided by Gumersindo A. Pacetti, a refugee and former mayor of St. Augustine. Continuing with his diary entries, Wood wrote that "the transition from a small open boat at sea, naked and starving, to the luxuries and comforts of civilized life was as sudden as it was welcome, and thoroughly appreciated." That evening Pacetti gave them all a banquet, after which a musical group called the Cardenas Volunteers, sponsored by Cubans who had served in the Confederacy, provided entertainment. The reception was evidently nonpartisan, since by request the band played the "Star-Spangled Banner" as well as "Dixie."

Governor General Dulce sent an aide to escort the new arrivals to Havana, and San Martin, the Spanish president of the local railroad, not only insisted that they travel in his private railroad car, but he also purchased the *No Name*, with Breckinridge, Wood, and probably Wilson, sharing the proceeds. The following morning at 6:00 the men boarded Martin's private car for the trip to Havana. After stopping at Matanzas for breakfast, they moved on through fine cane country and reached Havana's Regla Station, across the bay from the city, at noon. On entering the capital city, where the Confederacy had been strongly favored, an enthusiastic throng of ten thousand (many thinking Davis was in the party) greeted them as they moved through the streets to the Hotel Cubano, which was run by a southern woman and known as a place where Confederates congregated. Dulce was as friendly as the citizens of Havana. Two days later, on June 14, after the group had rested from their fatigue, Wood, Breckinridge, and Charles J. Helm, former Confederate purchasing agent in the West Indies with headquarters in Havana, rode out to Dulce's country palace for dinner and a long interview, in the course of which Dulce offered them asylum in Cuba for as long as they wished.

Wood was grateful for Dulce's considerate offer, but he had no intention of remaining in Cuba. Yet where would he go? Letters from Lola revealed that the political news from the United States was "not pleasant." President Johnson's proclamation of amnesty of 29 May 1865 excepted, among others, officers of the Confederate service above the rank of lieutenant in the navy, and those educated at the United States Naval Academy. Undoubtedly learning of the surrender of Kirby Smith, Wood no longer had either cause or country, and decided to find a new country and send for his family. The Havana climate was relatively healthful at the time, but the sudden change in diet, which must have been accompanied by some mental depression as he reflected on his situation, caused him a few days' illness which he cured by fasting and rest. Then he began making plans to leave Cuba, saying he was "anxious on every count to reach Canada as soon as possible."[1]

A number of blockade runners were riding at anchor in the harbor at Havana, and among the southern captains Wood met George E. Shryock, recently of the Confederate navy. Wood booked passage with Shryock aboard the *Lark*. The ship was bound for England, probably to be sold, but en route would put in at a Canadian port. On June 23, the *Lark*, with Wood aboard, stood out of Havana for Halifax, Nova Scotia. During his stay in Havana, Wood had seen the last great hope of the Confederacy, the French-built ram *Stonewall*, still flying the Stars and Bars as she rode at anchor in the harbor. The ram served as a fitting denouement to the ironclad program of the Confederate navy, a final case of not being able to get the ships into action in time.

The other members of the escape party were also making plans to leave Cuba. Wilson boarded another blockade runner and made his way to Toronto for a temporary residence, and then moved on to Henderson, Kentucky, where he ran a hotel. Russell and O'-Toole returned to Florida via Mobile, and although Breckinridge gave them a letter explaining that they participated in the escape only by his fervid entreaty, both men were imprisoned for two months. Breckinridge's servant, Thomas Ferguson, sickest of all on

WOOD IN CANADA, CIRCA 1867
(Evans, *Confederate Military History*)

the crossing, had taken an oath against future ocean voyages and could not accompany Breckinridge further. With a letter of recommendation from Breckinridge, he left with Russell and O'Toole to return to his family. (Since Trenholm was captured near Columbia, South Carolina, and Attorney General George Davis was captured at Key West as he attempted to flee the country, only Breckinridge and Benjamin of the Cabinet at the end, escaped into exile.) Breckinridge first went to England, then to Canada, where he was joined by his wife and two of their children. For the next two years he toured Europe and the Middle East with his family, before returning to Canada in 1868 to settle in the southern colony on Lake Ontario, and finally in 1869 he moved to Kentucky, where he quietly practiced law. Only one remnant of the group, the intrepid little sloop *No Name*, remained in Cuba, a constant reminder of a great adventure.[2]

Wood's whereabouts were well known in the North as no attempt at secrecy had been made while in Cuba; indeed, he had granted interviews to reporters about the recent escape. There was therefore some risk of capture while aboard the *Lark*, especially since she had a reputation for being rather slow for a blockade runner. The voyage required seven days, but the *Lark* went unchallenged and steamed without incident to Halifax. Arriving on June 30, she almost ran aground in the heavy fog on Devil's Island at the entrance to the harbor, and the hazardous entry was made worse, according to Wood, by the compass's being off two points. The circumstances of his arrival, except for the ubiquitous fog, were much different from the time, less than a year earlier, when he had visited Halifax in command of a Confederate commerce raider, but he welcomed the cool weather and was glad to be in port, where he was finally safe from capture.

Wood immediately began making arrangements to continue to Montreal, and during the next four days, while waiting for sea passage, he quartered on board the *Lark* to reduce living expenses, while former Confederate agent Wier turned over to him one hundred dollars left from the *Tallahassee* account. On the afternoon

of July 4 (no holiday for him) Wood boarded the steamer *Queen
Victoria* and arrived in Montreal on the morning of the eleventh,
after stopping for a day or two en route. He had spent a day in
Quebec, where he visited the Plains of Abraham, site of one of the
most glorious victories in British military history. In Montreal,
Wood checked into the Donegana Hotel, a "good house," where
he waited for his family to join him. On July 15 Lola, Zach, and a
new baby daughter named Lola arrived from Elk Ridge, Maryland, in what must have been the happiest family reunion since
Lola met him in 1859 at the Astor House in New York.[3]

Lola felt as he did about the war. After a few days in Montreal
spent discussing their future with her, Wood returned with his
family to settle in Halifax. The port appealed to Wood. Nova
Scotia was somewhat like the South in that geographical and political isolation caused the province and its seaport to develop
slowly, yet Halifax was a growing resort area with a healthful
climate and plenty of boating. There Wood could maintain his
closeness to the sea, and his wide travels before the war doubtless
made living outside the United States easier. Besides, he could
enjoy the friendship of the congenial local inhabitants as well as
fellow southerners.

Before long Wood became a leading citizen of the port city. He
established a merchant commission house with Captain John
Wilkinson, the famous blockade runner who had commanded the
Chameleon (formerly the *Tallahassee*) at the end of the war. The
firm of Wilkinson, Wood and Company flourished, doing business
mostly with Baltimore and Richmond. Later when Wilkinson retired to his farm in Virginia, Wood continued the firm as Wood
and Company. He was also active in the Church of England in
Canada, maintaining thereby what had been the one constant
among the changing circumstances of his early life.

Other business ventures Wood entered into were shipping and
marine insurance. As foremost promoter, manager, and director of
the Eastern Steamship Company, created to increase trade for
Halifax by plying between Halifax and St. John's, Newfoundland,

Wood purchased the ship *Virgo* to begin operations. A used but well-fitted screw steamer weighing eleven hundred tons and costing $45,000, she would allow Halifax "to supply those places which have hitherto been supplied by strangers" from the North. Wood was also agent for the Cromwell Line, and in that capacity had to deal with a number of losses suffered by the company. (Two vessels, the *George Washington* and the *George Cromwell,* were both wrecked off Newfoundland with "not a soul saved," and the *Cortes,* from New York to Halifax to Newfoundland, grounded in the same area, although in the latter case Wood rushed to the scene and removed the passengers and cargo in small boats.)

As secretary of the Halifax Pilot Commission, Wood maintained a keen interest in developing the strategic value of the city. He offered a resolution in the Merchant's Reading Room before his fellow members of the Chamber of Commerce, calling for the Canadian government to speed completion of the Intercolonial Railway. The road was designed to connect Halifax with Canada's interior ports and cut two days from transatlantic shipping. Another pet scheme of his was to connect New York and Halifax by rail, saving one day over the all-water route to London and Liverpool. Wood also supported sending a delegation to Ottawa to lobby for Halifax as a winter port, and bombarded the editor of the Halifax *Morning Chronicle* with other suggestions for attracting more transatlantic vessels. He proposed, for instance, that port charges be reduced to draw big ships from the ocean lanes less than one hundred miles from Halifax, thus making the port important to England in wartime, like Malta and Gibraltar. He particularly favored the construction of a large dry dock, and advocated the purchase of a training ship for underprivileged boys—pointing out that almost every seaport in the United Kingdom had one. Although Wood worked hard to promote the maritime city, not all the local citizens agreed with him. Some of his projects met opposition from petitioners who did not want increased taxes to help pay for improvements. Thus while the development of Halifax was sometimes slow, Wood gave impetus to building his adopted city into Canada's leading winter port.[4]

Wood soon made peace with his father, sending him an over-coat for Christmas the same year the war ended. The reconciliation was by mail since Wood, Sr., believed "explanations" would be required by his military superiors should he visit Halifax. But Wood was much more reluctant to reconcile his differences with the American government. Subsequent amnesty proclamations by President Johnson (7 September 1867 and 25 December 1868) removed the earlier sanctions applicable to him as well as the requirement of an oath, but Wood did not respond. He was still barred from any civil or military office, Federal or state, by Section 3 of the Fourteenth Amendment to the United States Constitution. This could be removed only by two-thirds vote of both houses of Congress, and it was thirty years after the war before Wood asked Congress for removal of his political disabilities. Congress hesitantly complied, but still Wood remained on British soil, living out his life in permanent exile in Halifax.[5] His visits to the United States were infrequent until long after the war, and then they were usually for the purpose of attending some function sponsored by former Confederates. He visited Virginia several times, once in May 1890 at the request of the Lee family to witness the unveiling of the Lee statue in Richmond, and again in March 1892 to visit Norfolk on the thirtieth anniversary of the battle between the *Virginia* and the *Monitor*. Some members of the press in Virginia remembered the "strong-handed, cool-headed amphiboid" who had been three decades in a foreign land.[6]

During all these years, Wood found great pleasure in boating on the waters near Halifax. He could be seen sailing his seventeen-ton yacht, *Whisper*, in the annual Aquatic Carnival, a three-day regatta of the Royal Halifax Yacht Club for the Prince of Wales Challenge Cup. As his yacht raised a spray across the harbor, Wood must have remembered the time the *Tallahassee* stood across the same waters, the times he approached enemy ships in small boats on the waters of Virginia and North Carolina, and his struggle across the Gulf Stream at the helm of the fearless *No Name*. After the twelve-mile race for the Prince of Wales Cup, which Wood won more than once, club members took their places at their fifty-seat banquet table. An officer of the club, "Vice-Commodore" Wood did the honors at one end of the table, while from the verandah of the clubhouse could be heard the airs of Her Majesty's Sixty-first Regimental Band.

Northern newspaper correspondents watched Wood's activities in the early postwar years, and usually found him "perfectly quiet, attends to his own business, has little to say about public affairs, but . . . is far from being 'reconstructed' as yet." According to the northern press, he continually fostered "a bad feeling against the country from which he had to flee [and] has, like a good many other disaffected southern refugees, a spite against everything Yankeeish." Reporters knew that Wood was an unreconstructed Rebel, not by his words, but by his deeds. Among his more reprehensible acts, northern readers learned, was the failure to invite his wartime antagonist, United States Consul Mortimer M. Jackson, on board the *Virgo* for the gala which accompanied her maiden voyage from Halifax: "We understand that although Mr. Wood's invitations to the excursion were generally circulated among the business men of Halifax, he intentionally omitted our popular Consul, Judge Jackson." Even more outrageous was the Confederate flag that often fluttered in the breeze above Wood and Company.[7]

Appendix

Vessels Captured by the C.S.S. *Tallahassee*

Date	Name	Type	Tonnage	Cargo	Disposition
1864					
Aug. 11	Sarah A. Boyce	schooner	382		scuttled
"	James Funk	pilot boat	121		burned
"	Carrie Estelle	brig	249	logs	"
"	Bay State	bark	199	'wood	"
"	A. Richards	brig	274	coal	"
"	Carrol	schooner			bonded
"	William Bell	pilot boat			burned
Aug. 12	Atlantic	schooner	156		"
"	Adriatic	ship	989	emigrants	"
"	Suliote	bark			bonded
"	Spokane	schooner	126	lumber	burned
"	Billow	brig	173	"	scuttled
"	R. E. Packer	schooner	222	"	bonded
Aug. 13	Glenavon	bark	789	iron	scuttled
"	DuPont	schooner	194	coal	burned
Aug. 14	J. Littlefield	ship	547	"	scuttled
Aug. 15	M. A. Howes	schooner	61		"
"	Howard	"	148	coal	"
"	Floral Wreath	"	54	wood	"
"	S. B. Harris	"			bonded
"	Restless	"	50	(fisherman)	scuttled
"	E. Caroline	"	39	"	"
Aug. 16	P. C. Alexander	bark	283		burned
"	Leopard	schooner	74	wood	"
"	Pearl	"	42	(fisherman)	"
"	Sarah Louise	"	81	wood	"
"	Magnolia	"	35	(fisherman)	"

Date	Name	Type	Tonnage	Cargo	Disposition
Aug. 17	*North America*	"	82		scuttled
"	*Neva*	brig	286	coal	bonded
"	*Josiah Achom*	schooner	123		burned
"	*Diadem*	"		mackerel	released
"	*D. Ellis*	"		"	"
Aug. 20	*Roan*	brig	127		burned

burned	16
scuttled	10
bonded	5
released	2
total	33

Report of Wood, *Official Records of the Navies.*

Notes

Chapter 1

1. Family Notes, John Taylor Wood Papers, Southern Historical Collection, University of North Carolina, Chapel Hill; Register of the Commissioned and Warrant Officers of the Navy of the Confederate States to 1 January 1863, Special Collections, Woodruff Center, Emory University, Atlanta.

2. For an entertaining and highly informative account of Wood's exploits while on duty guarding against the African slave trade aboard the *Porpoise* see J. Taylor Wood, "The Capture of a Slaver," *Atlantic Monthly* 86 (1900): 451–63.

3. *Dictionary of American Biography*, s.v. "Wood, John Taylor."

4. Series of letters from Wood to Lola, 1858–59, Wood Papers.

5. Wood to Lola, 12 August 1859; 11 September 1859, Wood Papers. One notable achievement resulted from the seniority system: Annapolis had been established in 1845 after a series of naval disasters caused by incompetent naval authorities. See Theodore Roscoe and Fred Freeman, *Picture History of the United States Navy* (New York: Scribner, 1956), pp. 486, 504.

6. Wood, Diary, Wood Papers; William H. Parker, *Recollections of a Naval Officer, 1841–1865* (New York: C. Scribners' Sons, 1883), p. 200.

7. Quoted in T. Harry Williams et al., *A History of the United States,* 2 vols. (New York: Alfred A. Knopf, 1967), 1: 634.

8. Family Notes, Wood Papers. Wood's father, Robert C. Wood, Sr., assistant surgeon-general, did much to persuade Lincoln to create the United States Sanitary Commission. Stewart Brooks, *Civil War Medicine* (Springfield, Ill.: Charles C. Thomas, 1966), pp. 10–11.

9. *Dictionary of American Biography*, s.v. "Rodgers, Christopher R. P." and "Rodgers, George W."

10. James G. Randall and David Donald, *The Civil War and Recon-*

struction (Lexington, Mass.: D. C. Heath and Company, 1969), pp. 195–96, 231–33.

11. Wood, Diary, Wood Papers; *Register of Officers of the Confederate States Navy* (Washington: U.S. Government Printing Office, 1931).

12. Wood, Diary, and Family Notes, Scrapbook, Wood Papers.

Chapter 2

1. Randall and Donald, *Civil War and Reconstruction*, pp. 208–9.

2. Ibid., pp. 209–10.

3. John Taylor Wood, "The Fight Between the Monitor and the Merrimac," in *Battles and Leaders of the Civil War*, ed. Robert U. Johnson and Clarence C. Buel, 4 vols. (New York: Castle Books, n.d.), 1: 693–94.

4. *Battles and Leaders*, 1: 715–17; 2: 267.

5. Scrapbook, Wood Papers; *Battles and Leaders*, 1: 692, 717; J. Thomas Scharf, *History of the Confederate States Navy* (Albany, N.Y.: Joseph McDonough, 1894), pp. 708–9; *Journal of the Congress of the Confederate States of America*, 7 vols. (Washington: U.S. Government Printing Office, 1904–5), 1: 536; Clement A. Evans, ed., *Confederate Military History*, 12 vols. (Atlanta: Confederate Publishing Co., 1899), 1: 626.

6. *Battles and Leaders*, 1: 695–96; Wood to Buchanan, 22 January 1862, Mallory to Benjamin, 25 January 1862, *Official Records of the Union and Confederate Navies in the War of the Rebellion*, 30 vols. (Washington: U.S. Government Printing Office, 1894–1922), ser. 2, 2: 137; Report of Mallory, 5 November 1864, Special Collections, Woodruff Center, Emory University; Tom H. Wells, *The Confederate Navy: A Study in Organization* (University, Ala.: The University of Alabama Press, 1971), pp. 33–34, 148.

7. Wood to Lola, 9 August 1858, Wood Papers; John R. Eggleston, "Narrative-Merrimac," *Southern Historical Society Papers*, 38 vols. (Richmond: Virginia Historical Society, 1876–1910), new series, 13 vols. (1914–1959), 41: 167–68; Scharf, *Confederate States Navy*, pp. 153–58; William N. Still, *Iron Afloat: The Story of the Confederate Armorclads* (Nashville: Vanderbilt University Press, 1971), pp. 22–24.

8. *Battles and Leaders*, 1: 696–98, 713–14; Scharf, *Confederate States Navy*, pp. 158–65; William C. Davis, *Duel Between the First Ironclads* (Garden City, N.Y.: Doubleday, 1975), p. 99.

9. *Battles and Leaders*, 1: 713.

10. Ibid., pp. 692, 714–15. Perhaps the men aboard the *Virginia* had some advance notice of the arrival of the *Monitor*. "In a postwar article [Jones] stated that they were not surprised to see her that morning since a pilot had observed the vessel the night before in the light of the burning *Congress*." Still, *Iron Afloat*, p. 33.

11. *Battles and Leaders*, 1: 727.

12. Wood to Lola, 20 March 1862, Wood Papers; Eggleston, "Narrative-Merrimac," *Southern Historical Society Papers*, 41: 176; William Norris, "The Story of the Confederate States Ship *Virginia*," *Southern Historical Society Papers*, 42: 205, 211–12; *Battles and Leaders*, 1: 698–703, 718–19; Davis, *Duel Between Ironclads*, pp. 131–35; Still, *Iron Afloat*, p. 34; Bern Anderson, *By Sea and By River: The Naval History of the Civil War* (New York: Knopf, 1962), p. 76.

13. Scrapbook, Wood Papers; Scharf, *Confederate States Navy*, p. 208.

14. Scrapbook, Wood Papers; *Battles and Leaders*, 1: 703–5; David D. Porter, *The Naval History of the Civil War* (New York: The Sherman Publishing Co., 1962), p. 76.

15. Rembert W. Patrick, *Jefferson Davis and His Cabinet* (Baton Rouge: Louisiana State University Press, 1944), pp. 266–67.

16. Wood to Lola, 18, 20, and 26 March 1862, Wood Papers. William N. Still wrote that Wood's visit to Richmond at this time was a quick overnight trip on the eve of the battle with the *Monitor* (*Iron Afloat*, p. 33).

17. Randall and Donald, *Civil War and Reconstruction*, p. 210.

18. Wood to Lola, 11 April 1862, Wood Papers.

19. Ibid; Scharf, *Confederate States Navy*, p. 208.

20. Wood to Lola, 4 May 1862, Wood Papers.

21. Wood to Lola, 4, 6, and 7 May 1862, Wood Papers.

22. Wood to Lola, 8 May 1862, Wood Papers; *Battles and Leaders*, 1: 706–9.

23. *Battles and Leaders*, 1: 709; 2: 151–52, 268.

Chapter 3

1. *Battles and Leaders*, 1: 694.

2. Ibid., p. 710; Norris, "*Virginia*," *Southern Historical Society Papers*, 42: 223.

3. *Official Records of the Navies*, ser. 1, 7: 788; *Battles and Leaders*, 1: 710–11; *Richmond Examiner*, 13, 14 May 1862; Scharf, *Confederate*

States Navy, pp. 236–37; Davis, *Duel Between Ironclads,* pp. 154–55.

4. Scharf, *Confederate States Navy,* pp. 708–9, 712.

5. *Battles and Leaders,* 2: 440–41.

6. *Battles and Leaders,* 1: 711.

7. Buchanan to Catesby Jones, 19 June 1862, *Official Records of the Navies,* ser. 1, 7: 789; *Battles and Leaders,* 1: 711; *Richmond Examiner,* 16 May 1862; Scharf, *Confederate States Navy,* pp. 709–16, 724; Davis, *Duel Between Ironclads,* p. 155.

8. *Battles and Leaders,* 2: 207–8, 263, 446–47.

9. Randall and Donald, *Civil War and Reconstruction,* p. 212.

10. Wood to Lola, 24, 28 May 1862, Wood Papers.

11. *Battles and Leaders,* 2: 443.

12. Wood to Lola, 1 June 1862, Wood Papers; Randall and Donald, *Civil War and Reconstruction,* p. 213.

13. Wood to Lola, 1, 3, and 5 July, 4 August 1862, Wood Papers; *Battles and Leaders,* 2: 174–79, 214–19, 270, 437–38.

14. Wood to Lola, 11 August 1862, Wood Papers; Randall and Donald, *Civil War and Reconstruction,* pp. 214–18.

Chapter 4

1. Wood to Catesby Jones, 30 August 1862, *Official Records of the Navies,* ser. 2, 2: 137; *Journal of the Confederate Congress,* 2: 402.

2. Scrapbook, Wood Papers; Davis, *Duel Between Ironclads,* pp. 130–31; Wells, *Confederate Navy,* p. 60.

3. Douglas S. Freeman, *Lee's Lieutenants,* 3 vols. (New York: Charles Scribner's Sons, 1942–44), 3: 335n.

4. Scrapbook, Wood Papers; Wood to Lola, 1, 2, 3, 5, and 6 October 1862, Wood Papers; *Official Records of the Navies,* ser. 1, 5: 118, 346; William H. Parker [commander of the navy schoolship *Patrick Henry*], *Questions on Practical Seamanship, together with Harbor Routine and Evolutions* (Richmond: MacFarlane and Fergusson, 1863), pp. 36–37; Parker, *Elements of Seamanship* (Richmond: MacFarlane and Fergusson, 1864), pp. 154–55; *Richmond Dispatch,* 10 October 1862; *Richmond Examiner,* 10 October 1862; Scharf, *Confederate States Navy,* p. 122.

5. Scharf, *Confederate States Navy,* p. 719.

6. Wood to Lola, 14 August, 24 October 1862, Scrapbook, Wood Papers; *Official Records of the Navies,* ser. 1, 5: 119, 137–41, ser. 1, 7:

61, ser. 1, 8: 165–69; Wood to Catesby Jones, 30 August 1862, *Official Records of the Navies*, ser. 2, 2: 137; *Richmond Dispatch*, 1 November 1862; *Richmond Examiner*, 1 November 1862; *Raleigh Register*, 5 November 1862; Scharf, *Confederate States Navy*, p. 719.

7. Report of Mallory, 1 January 1863, Special Collections, Emory University; *Richmond Dispatch*, 28 March 1862; *Journal of the Confederate Congress*, 3: 33, 59–60; Wells, *Confederate Navy*, pp. 21–22.

8. *Official Records of the Navies*, ser. 1, 2: 828–29.

9. Scrapbook, Wood Papers; Wood to Davis, 14 February 1863, Wood to Catesby Jones, 24 March 1863, *Official Records of the Navies*, ser. 1, 8: 163–64, 859; Report of Mallory, 5 November 1864, Confederate States Navy Register, 1 June 1864, Special Collections, Emory University; Davis to Beauregard, 13 December 1864, in Dunbar Rowland, ed., *Jefferson Davis, Constitutionalist: His Letters, Papers and Speeches*, 10 vols. (Jackson, Miss.: Mississippi Department of Archives and History, 1923), 6: 415; Naval History Division, Office of Chief of Naval Operations, comp., *Civil War Naval Chronology, 1861–65*, 3 vols. (Washington: U.S. Government Printing Office, 1961–66), 1: 78; Wells, *Confederate Navy*, p. 7; Still, *Iron Afloat*, pp. 133–34.

10. Randall and Donald, *Civil War and Reconstruction*, pp. 451–52.

Chapter 5

1. Wood to Hoge, 7 July 1863, *Official Records of the Navies*, ser. 1, 9: 180; Davis to Lee, 16 September 1863, *Official Records of the Union and Confederate Armies in the War of the Rebellion*, 128 vols. (Washington: U.S. Government Printing Office, 1880–1901), ser. 1, part 2, 29: 726–27.

2. Report of Wood, 7 September 1863, *Official Records of the Navies*, ser. 1, 5: 344–45; Flag Officer French Forrest to all commanding officers of the James River Squadron, 30 December 1863, *Official Records of the Navies*, ser. 1, 8: 853; "Bohemian" in *Richmond Dispatch*, 2 September 1863.

3. Davis to Lee, 16 September 1863, *Official Records of the Armies*, ser. 1, part 2, 29: 726–27.

4. Scrapbook, Wood Papers; Report of Wood, 7 September 1863, *Official Records of the Navies*, ser. 1, 5: 344–45; Reports of Union naval officers, *Official Records of the Navies*, ser. 1, 9: 160–61; "Bohemian" in *Richmond Dispatch*, 2 September 1863.

5. *Richmond Dispatch,* 2 September 1863; Report of Thomas L. Rosser, 5 September 1863, *Official Records of the Armies,* ser. 1, 29: 76–77.

6. Report of the Board of Officers to Harwood, 25 September 1863, *Official Records of the Navies,* ser. 1, 5: 333–34; Report of the Court of Inquiry, Navy Department, Washington, 21 October 1863, *Official Records of the Navies,* ser. 1, 5: 334–38; Walters to Welles, 2 December 1863, *Official Records of the Navies,* ser. 1, 5: 342–43; Scharf, *Confederate States Navy,* p. 123.

7. Scrapbook, Wood Papers; *Richmond Sentinel,* 26, 27 August 1863; *Civil War Naval Chronology,* 2: 298.

8. Wood to Davis and Mallory, 25 August 1863, *Official Records of the Navies,* ser. 1, 5: 344; Davis to Lola, 25 August 1863, Wood Papers; Report of Wood, 7 September 1863, *Official Records of the Navies,* ser. 1, 5: 344–45; John McCabe, from Philadelphia, to Welles, *Official Records of the Navies,* ser. 1, 5: 344.

9. Wood to Lola, 27 August 1863, Scrapbook, Wood Papers; Report of Rosser, *Official Records of the Armies,* ser. 1, 29: 76–77; "Bohemian" in *Richmond Dispatch,* 2 September 1863.

10. Harwood to Lee, 1 October 1863; Hooker to Harwood, 1, 5, and 28 October, 18 November 1863, Harwood to Welles, 31 October 1863, Welles to Harwood, 4 November 1863, Harwood to Hooker, 2, 16 November 1863, *Official Records of the Navies,* ser. 1, 5: 359, 368–72; *Civil War Naval Chronology,* 1: 132–33.

Chapter 6

1. Davis to Wood, 6 January 1864, Scrapbook, Wood Papers; *Battles and Leaders,* 4: 625; *Journal of the Confederate Congress,* 3: 461; *Philadelphia Inquirer,* 31 August 1863; *New York Tribune,* 7 March 1864; Hudson Strode, *Jefferson Davis: Tragic Hero,* 3 vols. (New York: Harcourt, Brace, 1964), 3: 5.

2. Lee to Wood, 20 January 1864, Scrapbook, Wood Papers; Lee to Davis, 20 January 1864, Lee to Pickett, 20 January 1864, *Official Records of the Armies,* ser. 1, 33: 1101–2.

3. John K. Mitchell, commander of the Office of Orders and Detail, to French Forrest, naval commander, Richmond, 27 January 1864, Wood to Gift, 20 January 1864, Mallory to Gift, 21 January 1864, Wood to Gift, 25 January 1864, Wood to Davis, 11 February 1864, *Official Records of the Navies,* ser. 1, 9: 449–52; Gift to Ellen A. Shackelford,

7 February 1864, George W. Gift Papers, Southern Historical Collection, University of North Carolina, Chapel Hill.

4. Daniel B. Conrad, Confederate surgeon, "The Capture and Burning of the *Underwriter*," *Southern Historical Society Papers*, 19: 93–100; also in *Blue and Gray* (1894 clipping), Trist Wood Papers, Southern Historical Collection, University of North Carolina.

5. Benjamin P. Loyall, "Capture of the *Underwriter*," *Southern Historical Society Papers*, 27: 139; "Bohemian" in *Richmond Dispatch*, 10 February 1864.

6. Wood to Davis, 11 February 1864, Report of Mallory, 30 April 1864, *Official Records of the Navies*, ser. 1, 19: 451–52, 454; Report of Pickett, 15 February 1864, *Official Records of the Armies*, ser. 1, 33: 58; *Battles and Leaders*, 4: 625; Report of Barton, 21 February 1864, *Southern Historical Society Papers*, 19: 8; John G. Barrett, *Civil War in North Carolina* (Chapel Hill: University of North Carolina Press, 1963), pp. 211–12. Bachelor's Creek was often spelled Batchelor's Creek and Batchelder's Creek.

7. "Bohemian" in *Richmond Dispatch*, 12 February 1864.

8. Gift to Shackelford, 7 February 1864, Gift Papers.

9. G. W. Graves to H. K. Davenport, commander in North Carolina waters, 12 February 1864, Davenport to Admiral Samuel P. Lee, commander of the North Atlantic Blockading Squadron (relieved Goldsborough 5 September 1862), 17 February 1864, *Official Records of the Navies*, ser. 1, 19: 441–44.

10. Wood to Davis, 4, 11 February 1864, S. P. Lee to Welles, 10, 15 February 1864, Welles to S. P. Lee, 17 February 1864, Davenport to S. P. Lee, 25, 28 February, 1 March 1864, Allen to Graves, 2 February 1864, *Official Records of the Navies*, ser. 1, 19: 440–48, 451–52; Conrad, "*Underwriter*," *Southern Historical Society Papers*, 19: 93–97; Gift to Shackelford, 7 February 1864, Gift Papers; *Southern Historical Society Papers*, 27: 136–44; "Bohemian" in *Richmond Dispatch*, 10, 12 February 1864; Scharf, *Confederate States Navy*, pp. 397–402; Barrett, *Civil War in North Carolina*, p. 431n; J. P. W. Mallalieu, *Extraordinary Seaman* (New York: Macmillan Co., 1948), pp. 138–45.

11. Wood to Lee, 8 February 1864, Report of Pickett, 15 February 1864, Report of Hoke, 8 February 1864, *Official Records of the Armies*, ser. 1, 33: 58, 95, 101–2; Report of Barton, 21 February 1864, *Southern Historical Society Papers*, 19: 10; Gift to Shackelford, 5 February 1864, Gift Papers; Douglas S. Freeman, ed., *Lee's Dispatches* (New York: G. P. Putnam's Sons, 1957), p. 137n; Porter, *Naval History of the Civil War*, p. 472; Rush C. Hawkins, *An Account of the Assassinations of*

Loyal Citizens of North Carolina (New York: J. H. Folan, 1897), pp. 12–13; Barrett, *Civil War in North Carolina* p. 208n.

12. Graves to Davenport, 12 February 1864, Davenport to S. P. Lee, 2 February 1864, Davenport to Flusser, 2 February 1864, Butler to Fox, 4 February 1864, Dove to S. P. Lee, 3 February 1864, Upham to S. P. Lee, 4 February 1864, *Official Records of the Navies,* ser. 1, 19: 439, 441–42, 454–59; Barrett, *Civil War in North Carolina,* pp. 211–12.

13. Lee to Wood, 20 January 1864, clipping, n.d., Scrapbook, Wood Papers; "Lee's Endorsement of a Report of the Expedition, 7 February 1864," in Freeman, ed., *Lee's Dispatches,* p. 136; *North Carolina Standard,* 9 February 1864; *Wilmington Daily Journal,* 6 February 1864; Walter Clark, ed., *North Carolina Regiments and Battalions,* 5 vols. (Raleigh and Goldsboro: E. M. Uzzell, 1901), 5: 333n.

14. Scrapbook, Wood Papers; Report of Wood, 11 February 1864, Wood to Colonel L. J. Beall, 16 February 1864, *Official Records of the Navies,* ser. 1, 19: 451–54; Gift to Shackelford, 5 February 1864, Palmer to Major R. S. Davis, 2, 5, 7, 8, and 10 February 1864, Gift Papers; *Southern Historical Society Papers,* 27: 142–43; Barrett, *Civil War in North Carolina,* p. 225n.

15. Wood to Catesby Jones, 26 February 1864, Gift to Catesby Jones, 13 February 1864, Minor to Catesby Jones, 23 March 1864, *Official Records of the Navies,* ser. 1, 19: 180–81, 453, 806; Minor to Buchanan, 17 February 1864, *Official Records of the Navies,* ser. 1, 2: 827–28; Gift to Shackelford, 5 February 1864, Gift Papers; "Lee's Endorsement of a Report of the Expedition, 7 February 1864," in Freeman, ed., *Lee's Dispatches,* p. 136. A few days after his return from the New Bern expedition, Wood became embroiled in a dispute with a bitterly anti-administration newspaper, the *Richmond Examiner,* which an impartial observer termed "a common sewer of falsehood and infamy." The editor of the *Examiner,* John Daniel, accused Davis of using his position to preserve his own cotton when much of the Mississippi crop was burned by Confederate military authorities to keep it from falling into enemy hands. Wood took offense at the editorial, and fired off a lengthy letter to Daniel supported by evidence, denying any wrongdoing by the president. The editor referred to Wood's correspondence as "morsels of hard language written on different pieces of paper, the whole forming an abusive but unsatisfactory contradiction" to the charge. When Daniel refused to print Wood's material, Davis's private secretary, Burton N. Harrison, a young Mississippian, wrote a private letter to Daniel (which the editor published) charging him with "petty

personal malignity." Daniel responded in print: "If he [Harrison] will tell the editor which of Davis's or the late Genl. Taylor's family is not holding any office anywhere, we shall not only print it with pleasure, but the public will receive this information with a gratification heightened by surprise." At this, Mary Boykin Chesnut, wife of another Davis aide, Colonel James Chesnut, penned in her famous diary: "Today [February 15th], a terrible onslaught upon the President for nepotism. Burton Harrison's and John Taylor Wood's letters denying the charge that the President's cotton was unburnt, or that he left it to be bought by the Yankees, have enraged the opposition." The incident probably helps explain why Wood opposed a promotion at that time, because, should Davis promote a relative, "family reasons might be thrown in his teeth," but more importantly it demonstrates that while Davis and his staff attempted to foster discretion in publishing sensitive military information, southern newspapers remained unmolested. Scrapbook, Wood Papers; Mary Boykin Chesnut, *A Diary from Dixie* (Boston: D. Appleton Co., 1949), pp. 380–81; Strode, *Davis: Tragic Hero,* 3: 7, 14; Patrick, *Davis and His Cabinet,* pp. 39–40n.

16. *Journal of the Confederate Congress,* 3: 747.

17. Porter, *Naval History of the Civil War,* p. 472.

18. Gustavus B. Fox to S. P. Lee, 8 April 1864, *Official Records of the Navies,* ser. 1, 9: 589.

19. Ibid.

20. Wood to Lee, 8 February 1864, *Official Records of the Armies,* ser. 1, 33: 101–2.

21. Hoke to Wood, 7 April 1864, Wood to Davis, 20, 21 April 1864, Davis to Wood, 20 April 1864, Wood to Lola, 21 April 1864, *Official Records of the Armies,* ser. 1, part 2, 2: 870; Scrapbook, Wood Papers; Cooke to Mallory, 23 April 1864, *Official Records of the Navies,* ser. 1, 9: 656; James Dinkins, "The Confederate Ram *Albermarle*," *Southern Historical Society Papers,* 30: 207–8; *Wilmington Daily Journal,* 22 April 1864; E. Arnold Wright, "After the Battle of Plymouth," *Confederate Veteran* 25 (1917): 16; *Battles and Leaders,* 4: 108, 147, 625–42; Freeman, *Lee's Lieutenants,* 3: 335; Still, *Iron Afloat,* pp. 156–65, 213–14; Barrett, *Civil War in North Carolina,* pp. 129–30.

Chapter 7

1. Lee to Davis, 3, 5, and 10 July 1864, in Freeman, ed., *Lee's Dis-*

patches, pp. 269–71, 275–80; Davis to Wood, 4 July 1864, Scrapbook, Wood Papers; Davis to Wood, 10 July 1864, Davis to G. W. C. Lee, 10 July 1864, Wood to Davis, 9 July 1864, Major John Tyler to General Sterling Price, 9 July 1864, Welles to S. P. Lee, 18 July 1864, S. P. Lee to Captain B. F. Sands, 19 July 1864, S. P. Lee to Captain O. S. Glisson, 19 July 1864, *Official Records of the Navies*, ser. 1, 10: 281, 287–89, 717, 721–22; Lieutenant M. S. Stuyvesant to Welles, 18 July 1864, ser. 1, 5: 467; Davis to Wood, 11 July 1864, *Official Records of the Armies*, ser. 2, 7: 458; Evans, ed., *Confederate Military History*, 2: 126.

2. *The London Illustrated News*, 2 April 1864, 29 April 1865; *Official Records of the Navies*, ser. 2, 1: 268; *Atlanta Constitution*, 19 October 1884; *Savannah Morning News*, 5 July 1903; Nellie P. Black, comp., *Richard Peters: His Ancestors and Descendants* (Atlanta: Foote and Davis, 1904), pp. 28–29; Michael P. Usina, "Blockade Running in Confederate Times," *Addresses Delivered Before the Confederate Veterans Association* (Savannah: United Confederate Veterans, 1895), p. 38.

3. *Papers Relating to the Foreign Relations of the United States: Geneva Arbitrations*, 20 vols. (Washington: U.S. Government Printing Office, 1872), part 2, 3: 144; Clary to Welles, 9 September 1864, *Official Records of the Navies*, ser. 1, 3: 183–84; Records of John T. Bourne, Confederate agent in Bermuda, cited in *Confederate Blockade Running Through Bermuda, 1861–65: Letters and Cargo Manifests*, Frank E. Vandiver (Austin: University of Texas Press, 1947), pp. 130–31, 135, 137.

4. Vessel Papers File A-168, Record Group 109, War Department Collection of Confederate Records, Military Archives Division, National Archives and Records Service, Washington; *Official Records of the Navies*, ser. 2, 1: 268; *Foreign Relations of the U.S.*, part 2, 3: 144; *Battles and Leaders*, 4: 598; Black, comp., *Peters*, p. 28; Mallory to Bullock, 22 February 1863, Mallory to John N. Maffitt, 24 February 1865, *Official Records of the Navies*, ser. 2, 2: 268–69, 804–6.

5. John Taylor Wood, "The 'Tallahassee's' Dash into New York Waters," *The Century Magazine* 56 (1898): 409; Muster Roll of the C.S.S. *Tallahassee*, August–September 1864, Record Group 45, Naval Records Collection of the Office of Naval Records and Library, National Archives; Report of Wood, 31 August 1864, *Official Records of the Navies*, ser. 1, 3: 703; *Richmond Examiner*, 18 August 1864; Wells, *Confederate Navy*, pp. 34, 119, 145.

6. Wood, "The 'Tallahassee's' Dash," pp. 409–10.

7. Ibid., p. 409.

8. Charles Lucian Jones, "The Cruise of the Confederate Steamer

Tallahassee, August, 1864," *Addresses Delivered Before the Confederate Veterans Association* (1902), pp. 109–10; "Bohemian" in *New York Times,* 29 September 1864; Wood, "The 'Tallahassee's' Dash," p. 410.

9. Mallory to Wood, 23 July 1864, Scrapbook, Wood Papers; Mallory to Bullock, 25 July 1864, *Official Records of the Navies,* ser. 2, 2: 689; Wood, "The 'Tallahassee's' Dash," pp. 410–11.

10. Scrapbook, Wood Papers; *Official Records of the Navies,* ser. 1, 1: 782; Wood, "The 'Tallahassee's' Dash," p. 411.

11. Scrapbook, Wood Papers.

12. Wood, "The 'Tallahassee's' Dash," p. 413.

13. Report of Wood, 31 August 1864, *Official Records of the Navies,* ser. 1, 3: 701–2; *New York Times,* 29 September 1864; Wood, "The 'Tallahassee's' Dash," pp. 412–14.

14. *Civil War Naval Chronology,* 1: iii.

Chapter 8

1. *New York Times,* 13 August 1864, 29 September 1864; *New York Tribune,* 15, 16 August, 1864; *Providence Journal,* 15 August 1864; Wood, "The 'Tallahassee's' Dash," p. 411.

2. *Foreign Relations of the U.S.,* part 2, 2: 339–41; *Battles and Leaders,* 4: 625; Wood, "The 'Tallahassee's' Dash," p. 417.

3. *Addresses Before the Confederate Veterans Association* (1902), p. 113; Wood, "The 'Tallahassee's' Dash," p. 415; Wells, *Confederate Navy,* p. 85.

4. *Philadelphia Public Ledger,* 15 August 1864; *London Times,* n.d., Wood Papers; *Liverpool Courier,* n.d., Wood Papers; *New York Herald* cited in *Richmond Examiner,* 18 August 1864.

5. *Official Records of the Navies,* ser. 1, 3: 137–84; 5: 474.

6. *Battles and Leaders,* 1: 706.

7. Wood, "The 'Tallahassee's' Dash," p. 414.

8. Wood to Mallory, 31 August 1864, MacDonnell to Edward Cardwell, M. P., 18 August 1864, Charles Tupper to Jackson, 18 August 1864, Jackson to William H. Seward, 20 August 1864, Series of orders from Welles to commanders of Union warships, *Official Records of the Navies,* ser. 1, 3: 159, 178, 702, 706–7; *Address Before the Confederate Veterans Association* (1902), p. 113; Wood, "The 'Tallahassee's' Dash," pp. 414–16.

9. Wood to Mallory, 31 August 1864, MacDonnell to Cardwell, 21,

23 August 1864, *Official Records of the Navies*, ser. 1, 3: 702–9; Benjamin to John Slidell, 15 September 1864, and Benjamin to Henry Hotze, a "public relations expert for the South," 15 September 1864, *Official Records of the Navies*, ser. 2, 3: 1204–6. Benjamin's suspicion concerning Richard B. Pemell, second Lord Lyons, may have been well-founded, because Lyons personally favored the Union and "wished it well in his unofficial capacity." Frank J. Merli, *Great Britain and the Confederate Navy, 1861–65* (Bloomington: Indiana University Press, 1970), pp. 26–27.

10. Wood to Davis, 26 August 1864, Mallory to Wood, 2 September 1864, Scrapbook, Wood Papers; Series of reports from commanders of blockaders off New Inlet to Welles, *Official Records of the Navies*, ser. 1, 3: 170–74; *New York Times*, 29 September 1864; Wood, "The 'Tallahassee's' Dash," p. 416.

11. Scrapbook, Wood Papers; Anna J. Sanders to Davis, 25 August 1864, *Official Records of the Armies*, ser. 2, 7: 679; *Richmond Examiner*, 17 August 1864; Shelby Foote, *The Civil War, A Narrative: Red River to Appomattox* (New York: Random House, 1974), p. 509.

12. Vance to Mallory, 3 January 1865, *Official Records of the Armies*, ser. 1, part 2, 46: 1156–58; Mallory to Vance, 28 January 1865, ser. 4, 3: 1057; Whiting to Mallory, 6 October 1864, *Official Records of the Navies*, ser. 1, 10: 774–75; *Wilmington Daily Journal*, 20, 27 September 1864; Wells, *Confederate Navy*, p. 45.

13. Wood to Mallory, 31 August 1864, *Official Records of the Navies*, ser. 1, 3: 703; Mallory to Davis, 22 October 1864, *Official Records of the Navies*, ser. 1, 10: 794–95; Series of letters from Welles to ships' commanders and Cornelius Vanderbilt, August–September 1864, *Official Records of the Navies*, ser. 1, 3: 178–85; Patrick, *Davis and his Cabinet*, p. 264.

14. Vessel Papers File T-30, Record Group 109, War Department Collection of Confederate Records, Military Archives Division, National Archives; *Foreign Relations of the U.S.*, part 2, 3: 144; *Battles and Leaders*, 4: 598–99. While in Liverpool, the former *Tallahassee* briefly had been named the *Amelia*, but there is no record that she actually sailed under that name. Although called "the ship of seven names," her appellation following that of *Amelia* is apparently unknown. In 1867 the vessel entered the Japanese merchant service as the brig *Haya Maro*, and two years later, on 17 June 1869, she struck a rock and sank while on passage from Yokohama to Hiogo-Kobe. Richard I. Lester, *Confederate Finance and Purchasing in Great Britain* (Charlottesville: University Press of Virginia, 1975), pp. 104–5.

15. James D. Horan, *Confederate Agent: A Discovery in History* (New York: Crown Publishers, 1954), pp. 113–20, 224–29.

Chapter 9

1. Mallory to Mitchell, 13 September 1864, *Official Records of the Navies*, ser. 1, 10: 69; Mallory to Mitchell, 21 January 1865, Mitchell to Pickett, 24 January 1865, Wood to Davis and Mallory, 24 January 1865, ser. 1, 2: 803, 666–67.

2. In February 1865 D. K. McRae, editor of the *Raleigh Confederate*, wrote Wood that two other newspapers of the city, the *Standard* and the *Progress*, espoused a "submissive spirit." One of the pacifists, William W. Holden, the state's most influential editor, candidate for governor in 1864, and member of a secret peace society called Order of Heroes of America, regularly advocated a separate peace in his *Raleigh Standard*. McRae wrote that this attitude would result in fewer enlistments, increased desertions, the withholding of supplies, and resignation on the part of North Carolinians at the approach of Sherman. Wood forwarded some of McRae's extracts from the *Standard* and *Progress* to Secretary of War John C. Breckinridge terming them "treasonable." Then Wood asked: "With the state of North Carolina assailed on every side, how can we hope for success when such publications are permitted?" Wood undoubtedly believed Davis should have taken advantage of the third suspension of the writ of habeas corpus, which had been passed a year earlier partly to suppress Holden's disloyal movement. McRae to Wood, 7, 14 February 1865, Wood to Breckinridge, 22 February 1865, *Official Records of the Armies*, ser. 1, part 2, 47: 1250–51; Randall and Donald, *Civil War and Reconstruction*, pp. 266, 521.

3. Scrapbook, Wood Papers; *Journal of the Confederate Congress*, 4: 537, 545; Raphael Semmes, *Service Afloat* (Baltimore: Baltimore Publishing Co., 1887), pp. 802–3.

4. Report of Mallory, 5 November 1864, Special Collections, Emory University; Still, *Iron Afloat*, p. 214.

5. Wood, Diary, Wood Papers; John B. Jones, *A Rebel War Clerk's Diary* (New York: Old Hickory Bookshop, 1961), pp. 526–31; Strode, *Davis: Tragic Hero*, 3: 166–73; Still, *Iron Afloat*, p. 222.

6. Wood, Diary, Wood Papers; Wood to Johnston, 8 April 1865, *Official Records of the Armies*, ser. 1, part 3, 47: 767–68; *Battles and Leaders*, 4: 479n.

7. Strode, *Davis: Tragic Hero*, 3: 185–89.

8. Burton N. Harrison, "Capture of Jefferson Davis," in Rowland, ed., *Davis, Constitutionalist*, 9: 232–33.

9. Wood, Diary, Wood Papers; *Battles and Leaders*, 4: 763–65; Harrison to Davis, 24 May 1877, in Rowland, ed., *Davis, Constitutionalist*, 7: 553; Albert J. Hanna, *Flight into Oblivion* (Richmond: Johnson Publishing Co., 1938), pp. 29–31, 117–18.

10. Wood, Diary, Wood Papers; Wood to Davis, 19 July 1878, in Rowland, ed., *Davis, Constitutionalist*, 8: 239; John F. Wheless [naval paymaster], "The Confederate Treasure," *Southern Historical Society Papers*, 10: 138–41; William H. Parker, "Gold and Silver in the Confederate States Treasury," *Southern Historical Society Papers*, 21: 304–12; Rowland, ed., *Davis, Constitutionalist*, 9: 252; Parker, *Recollections*, p. 367; Hanna, *Flight into Oblivion*, pp. 90–94, 114–18, 262; Patrick, *Davis and His Cabinet*, pp. 361–62; Wells, *Confederate Navy*, p. 74.

11. Wood, Diary, Wood Papers; *Battles and Leaders*, 4: 766n; Rowland, ed., *Davis, Constitutionalist*, 9: 233, 252–53; Mrs. Burton Harrison, *Recollections, Grave and Gay* (London: Smith, Elder Co., 1912), p. 225; Strode, *Davis: Tragic Hero*, 3: 216–23; Hanna, *Flight into Oblivion*, pp. 55, 78–79, 96–97, 132.

12. Wood, Diary, Wood Papers.

13. Scrapbook, Wood Papers; *Philadelphia Evening Bulletin*, 30 June 1865; *Southern Historical Society Papers*, 21: 311–12.

14. Hanna, *Flight into Oblivion*, pp. 70–81.

Chapter 10

1. Wood, Diary, Scrapbook, Wood Papers; Wood, "Escape of the Confederate Secretary of War," *The Century Magazine*, 47 (1893/94): 110; Hanna, *Flight into Oblivion*, p. 92.

2. Diary, Scrapbook, Wood Papers; Wood, "Escape," pp. 110–11; "Breckinridge Escape Diary," in Scrapbook, Wood Papers (another copy of the diary, edited by Albert J. Hanna and reprinted from the Kentucky State Historical Society *Register*, 37 [October 1939]: 323–33, is based on Breckinridge's account written while en route to England in July 1865); Hanna, *Flight into Oblivion*, pp. 125–26, 140; William C. Davis, *Breckinridge: Statesman, Soldier, Symbol* (Baton Rouge: Louisiana State University Press, 1974), pp. 528–30.

3. Wood, Diary, Scrapbook, Wood Papers; Wood, "Escape," p. 111;

Hanna, ed., *Breckinridge Escape Diary;* Hanna, *Flight into Oblivion,* pp. 136–42; Davis, *Breckinridge,* pp. 530–32.

4. Wood, Diary, Scrapbook, Wood Papers; Wood, "Escape," pp. 112–13; Hanna, ed., *Breckinridge Escape Diary;* Hanna, *Flight into Oblivion,* pp. 143–59; Davis, *Breckinridge,* pp. 533–35.

Chapter 11

1. *The Century Magazine,* 47: 114; *Philadelphia Evening Bulletin,* 22 June 1865.

2. Wood, Diary, Scrapbook, Wood Papers; Wood, "Escape," pp. 114–18; Hanna, ed., *Breckinridge Escape Diary;* Hanna, *Flight into Oblivion,* pp. 160–80; Davis, *Breckinridge,* pp. 535–37.

3. Series of letters from Wood to Lola, May–July 1858, Wood Papers.

4. Wood, "Escape," p. 121.

5. Hanna, ed., *Breckinridge Escape Diary.*

6. Wood, Diary, Scrapbook, Wood Papers; Wood, "Escape," pp. 120–23; Hanna, ed., *Breckinridge Escape Diary;* Hanna, *Flight into Oblivion,* pp. 180–88; Davis, *Breckinridge,* pp. 537–40.

Chapter 12

1. Wood, Diary, Wood Papers; Wood, "Escape," p. 123; *Battles and Leaders,* 4: 767n; Davis, *Breckinridge,* pp. 544–47.

2. Wood, Diary, Wood Papers; newspaper clipping, n.d., Trist Wood Papers; Breckinridge to Wood, 17 September 1865, Wood Papers; Hanna, ed., *Breckinridge Escape Diary; New York Times,* 29 June 1865; *Battles and Leaders,* 4: 598; Davis, *Breckinridge,* p. 548.

3. Wood, Diary, Wood Papers.

4. Scrapbook, Wood Papers; Genealogical Papers, Wood Family, Trist Wood Papers.

5. Robert C. Wood, Sr., to Wood, 25 January 1866, 24 January 1869, Scrapbook, Wood Papers; Wood to U.S. Senate and House of Representatives, 18 March 1891, Senator J. W. Daniel to Wood, 4 May 1896, Wood Papers; *United States Statutes at Large* (Washington: U.S. Government Printing Office, 1845–), 29 (1897): 801; *Battles and Leaders,* 4: 767.

6. Genealogical Papers, Wood Family, Trist Wood Papers. After the turn of the century Wood visited Washington, D.C. to negotiate with Congress for the sale of the marble bust of Zachary Taylor, which Wood inherited from his mother. A good likeness by an unknown artist, the bust was the only one in existence. The transaction was completed in 1909 between Congress and one of Wood's daughters, and in 1915 Wood's children donated to the White House a decanter and set of glasses used by President Taylor. Series of letters between J. W. Daniel and Wood, and Miss Lola M. Wood, 1903–9, Colonel Hart to Miss Wood, 26 October 1915, Scrapbook, Wood Papers.

7. Scrapbook, Family Notes, Wood Papers. The Wood children were: Anne M. (1857–59); Zach Taylor (b. 1860); Elizabeth S. (1863–64); Lola M. (b. 1865); Robert C. (1867–84); Eleanor M. (b. 1868); John Taylor, Jr. (b. 1871); George M. (b. 1872); Nina (b. 1873); Mary C. (1875–98); Charles C. (1876–99). The oldest and youngest sons, Zach and Charles, carried on the family military tradition. They graduated from the Royal Military College of Canada, Kingston, Ontario. Charles, a lieutenant in the Royal North Lancashire Regiment, served in India, then became the first graduate of the college to die in battle, and the first Canadian to fall in the Boer War. Upon request of Queen Victoria, Wood sent her a photograph of his fallen son. Zach fought Indians in Canada's Northwest Rebellion and went on to distinguish himself in the Northwest Mounted Police.

Wood died of muscular rheumatism on 19 July 1904 and was buried in Halifax. Scrapbook, Family Notes, Wood Papers; Genealogical Papers, Wood Family, Trist Wood Papers.

Bibliographic
Note

Wood dealt with secret missions, verbal instructions, and coded messages to some extent during the Civil War, yet the evidence which permits a reconstruction of his wartime career is surprisingly complete. The John Taylor Wood Papers in the Southern Historical Collection, University of North Carolina, Chapel Hill, consists of 201 items, including five volumes, and covers the period from 1858 to 1915. The family notes, which provide material for Wood's genealogy, and the scrapbook, made up of articles about Wood clipped and saved by his wife Lola between 1848 and 1893, were reproduced on microfilm in 1941 from originals in the possession of Wood's daughter, Lola M. Wood, of Maddox, Maryland. The remainder of the material is in its original form except for Wood's diary, which has been typed and is found in three volumes; the first two cover the period from 1 January 1860 to 6 September 1861 and deal with family life and public events while Wood was a professor at Annapolis, and the final volume recounts Wood's adventures from 2 April to 16 July 1865, when he accompanied Davis from Richmond and then escaped to Cuba and Canada. Wood's letters to his wife describe places he visited before the war (1858–60), such as Key West, France, Italy, and Greece, and events from March 1862 when he was serving on the *Virginia* and at Drewry's Bluff, and terminate in October of that year with the capture of the *Alleganian* during his second raid. Scattered letters received by Wood (1865–1904) at Halifax are also included in the group.

The Trist Wood Papers in the Southern Historical Collection consists of ten feet of material, including four volumes, about the Wood family and several related families from 1655 to 1949. The compilation was made by Trist Wood, son of Robert C. Wood, Jr., and nephew of Wood, in New Orleans beginning in 1915. (Robert C. Wood, Jr., compiled a small manual entitled *Confederate Hand-Book* [New Orleans: L. Graham and Son, 1900] to remove "misapprehensions" and correct "false impressions" about the war which had been "created by prejudiced and partisan writers.")

The George W. Gift Letters in the Southern Historical Collection, 188 items, include letters to his fiancée (and later wife), Ellen Shackelford of Georgia, while Gift was a member of Wood's New Bern expedition. Apparently Gift sketched the map which marks the position of the *Underwriter* at New Bern, a copy of which appears in *Official Records of the Union and Confederate Navies in the War of the Rebellion,* 30 vols. (Washington: U.S. Government Printing Office, 1894–1922), ser. 1, 9: 553. A native of Tennessee, Gift was a colorful officer with a flair for writing, and after the war he became editor of the *Napa City* (California) *Reporter.* Gift's Civil War letters are published in Harriet (Gift) Castlen, *Hope Bids Me Onward* (Savannah: Chatham Printing Co., 1945).

After the war Wood wrote three articles for *The Century Magazine* dealing with his wartime experiences. One article tells of the duel between the *Virginia* and the *Monitor* and is reprinted in Robert U. Johnson and Clarence C. Buel, eds., *Battles and Leaders of the Civil War,* 4 vols. (New York: Castle Books, n.d.), 1: 692–711. Another relates the exploits of the *Tallahassee.* The writer has also covered the subject in "Cruise of the C.S.S. Tallahassee," *Civil War Times Illustrated,* May 1976, pp. 30–40 (for an account of the earlier history of the same ship before she was converted into a raider see my article "The Atlanta: A Civil War Blockade Runner," in the *Atlanta Historical Bulletin,* 20 [Fall 1976]: 9–16). Wood's third article in *The Century Magazine* deals with the escape to Cuba, also included in *Famous Adventures and Prison Escapes of the Civil War* (New York: The Century Co., 1893), in which Wood wrote a detailed account of the encounter with the renegades and the chase by unknown pursuers. Alfred J. Hanna in *Flight into Oblivion* (Richmond: Johnson Publishing Co., 1938) wrote that the pursuers were Federals, while Wood believed they were the renegades; otherwise Hanna (who traveled the entire Florida escape route over a four-year period) accepts Wood's account of the two incidents. William C. Davis in *Breckinridge: Soldier, Statesman, Symbol* (Baton Rouge: Louisiana State University Press, 1974) accepts Wood's account, but suspects that Wood embellished his account of the two incidents in his article. Wood's diary entry reads: "Found nest of Tories and deserters from our service," and then "chased three or four hours." This is typical of Wood's sparse wartime reporting. Breckinridge's diary contains mention of "a small trading house" where they obtained supplies, and although he notes great difficulty getting across reefs, makes no mention of the chase. These minor differences, together with the fact that the dates in the Wood and Breckinridge diaries do not mesh during this period, could have resulted from Breckinridge's having apparently written his original account soon after the escape to Cuba in a letter to his son "Owen" (John W.), but in a diary format. In other words, the Breckinridge diary was probably not a diary at all.

Lieutenant Edward Hooker, the Union officer commanding the First Division of the Potomac Flotilla, was convinced that Wood, with some of his New Bern command, participated in the 5 March 1864 raid on the Union telegraph station at Cherrystone Point on the eastern shore of Virginia, where, among other things, Confederate raiders captured the army dispatch steamer *Titan*. Hooker's reports and Wood's growing reputation caused other Union officers, the northern press, and a number of secondary sources, drawing from each other, to conclude that Wood was a leader in the Cherrystone raid. Yet the writer has been unable to find southern documents that link Wood to the raid. Indeed, there is strong evidence to the contrary. Captain Thaddeus Fitzhugh of the Fifth Virginia Cavalry, the leader of the raid, named two naval acting masters who participated, but did not mention Wood, and General Robert E. Lee, while writing of Wood's activities, specifically named Fitzhugh as "the officer who destroyed the enemy steamers in Cherrystone Creek." (See Reports of Hooker, 29 February, 5 March 1864, *Official Records of the Navies*, ser. 1, 5: 397–98; Report of Fitzhugh, 5 March 1864, Lee to G. W. C. Lee, 7 April 1864, *Official Records of the Armies*, ser. 1, 33: 232, 1145.)

Wood assisted Jefferson Davis and J. Thomas Scharf in their writings. Several letters in Rowland, ed., *Davis, Constitutionalist: Letters, Papers and Speeches*, 10 vols. (Jackson, Miss.: Mississippi Department of Archives and History, 1923), vol. 9, reveal that at Davis's request, Wood wrote a brief account of the Confederate navy and answered a number of Davis's questions concerning wartime incidents. J. Thomas Scharf's *History of the Confederate States Navy* (Albany, N.Y.: Joseph McDonough, 1894), is flawed by two erroneous accounts of Wood's activities—it was William H. Parker, not Wood, who took the surrender of the *Congress* at Hampton Roads, and apparently Wood did not participate in the raid on Cherrystone Point. Scharf was a Civil War veteran (as a young midshipman he served as Gift's executive officer on the New Bern expedition) who, unlike Thucydides, could not remain objective when writing about the war in which he had participated. Historian Scharf admitted that in one chapter of his book he "rubbed it in quite hard on the United States naval authorities during the war."

Nonetheless, *Confederate States Navy* remains the best general account of the southern naval effort.

Without the newspaper articles of the mysterious "Bohemian," a member of Wood's rangers who provided valuable coverage for the Chesapeake, New Bern, and North Atlantic expeditions, the accounts of Wood's most notable raids would lack much of their color and detail. "Bohemian," as suggested by J. Cutler Andrews in *The South Reports the Civil War* (Princeton: Princeton University Press, 1970), was probably William G. Shepardson. Little is known of Shepardson's early life, but it seems likely that he had been a physician and studied in Europe. Early in 1861 he covered events in Montgomery for the *Mobile Daily Advertiser and Register* and the *Columbus* (Georgia) *Times*, and reported the battle of First Bull Run for the *Montgomery Advertiser* and *Columbus Times*. After changing to the *Richmond Dispatch* in September 1861 Shepardson began to write over the signature "Bohemian," evidently because he had to rely on sources of varying reliability while gathering news, making it difficult to sift truth from falsehood. In one instance, however, "Bohemian" was too precise; in January 1862 General Joseph E. Johnston banned all reporters from his army because Shepardson had sent a letter to the *Richmond Dispatch*, published 30 December 1861, giving the locations of various Confederate brigades in winter quarters. Next, Shepardson turned up on Roanoke Island, North Carolina, where in February 1862 a Union Force under General Ambrose E. Burnside captured the island and its Confederate defenders under General Henry A. Wise. Subsequently paroled, Shepardson returned to Richmond in May 1862 and began covering the news beat in the southern capital for the *Mobile Register*. During the latter part of the war, Shepardson served as an assistant surgeon in the Confederate navy and contributed correspondence about Wood's raids to his old employer, the *Richmond Dispatch*. His copy received wide distribution in the Confederacy, and appeared in some northern papers, making him one of the war's most notable reporters. Indeed, "Bohemian" helped make Wood famous during the war.

Wood was confident that he had removed all of President Davis's papers when Richmond was evacuated 2 April 1865, but he of course had not carried away all Confederate records, nor were all of them burned in the Richmond fire. Union General Henry W. Halleck found and shipped to Washington ninety large boxes of "Rebel archives" from the former Confederate capital. Confederate army and naval records, however, were meager compared to those of the Union. Although the situation was improved beginning in 1878 when a former

Confederate brigadier, Marcus J. Wright, became agent for the collection of Confederate records, which in turn caused southerners to become more cordial and trusting toward the project, the Confederate archives are still incomplete, especially for the last year of the war. Wood's greatest contribution to posterity was his handling of the Davis papers, because years later Davis opened his papers to government access, thereby aiding historians in piecing together the events of the great struggle. These same papers, as Wood knew, would enable his own story to be told.

Index